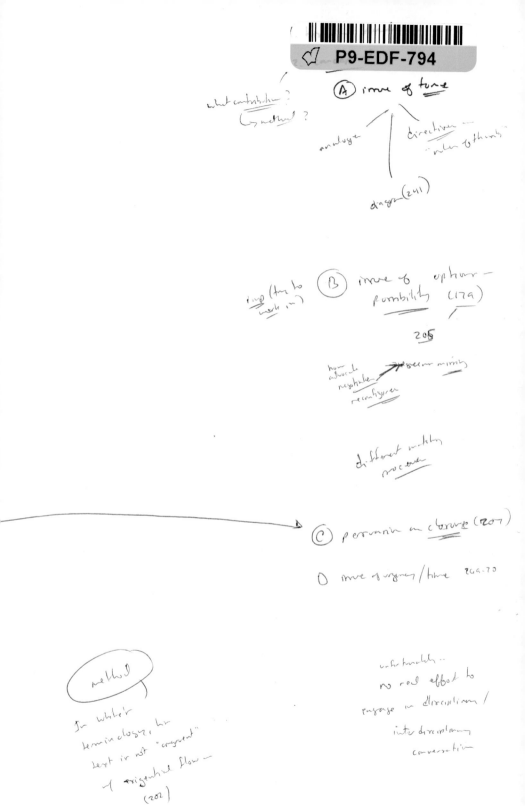

P9-EDF-794

what contribution?
(= method) ?

(A) issue of tone

analogy · directives —
rules of thumb

diagram (241)

---

esp (true to
work in)

(B) issue of options —
possibility (179)

208

too much
adversarial
negotiation reconfigured
→ seems missing

different working
processes

(C) permission in closure (207)

D issue of urgency / time 269-70

---

method

In Whitlow's
terminology, her
text is not "argument"
of trigential flow —
(202)

---

unfortunately —
no real effort to
engage in disciplinary /
interdisciplinary
conversation

The Context of Human Discourse

Studies in Rhetoric/Communication
Thomas W. Benson, *Series Editor*

Richard B. Gregg
Symbolic Inducement and Knowing:
A Study in the Foundations of Rhetoric

Richard A. Cherwitz and James W. Hikins
Communication and Knowledge:
An Investigation in Rhetorical Epistemology

Herbert W. Simons and Aram A. Aghazarian, Editors
Form, Genre, and the Study of Political Discourse

Walter R. Fisher
Human Communication as Narration:
Toward a Philosophy of Reason, Value, and Action

David Payne
Coping with Failure:
The Therapeutic Uses of Rhetoric

David Bartine
Early English Reading Theory:
Origins of Current Debates

Craig R. Smith
Freedom of Expression and Partisan Politics

Lawrence J. Prelli
A Rhetoric of Science:
Inventing Scientific Discourse

George Cheney
Rhetoric in an Organizational Society:
Managing Multiple Identities

Edward Schiappa
Protagoras and Logos:
A Study in Greek Philosophy and Rhetoric

David Bartine
Reading, Criticism and Culture:
Theory and Teaching in the United States and
England, 1820–1950

Eugene E. White
The Context of Human Discourse:
A Configurational Criticism of Rhetoric

The Context of Human Discourse:

A Configurational Criticism of Rhetoric

Eugene E. White

University of South Carolina Press

To Roberta and E. R.

Copyright © 1992 University of South Carolina

Published in Columbia, South Carolina, by the
University of South Carolina Press

Manufactured in the United States of America

Library of Congress Cataloging-in-Publication Data

White, Eugene Edmond, 1919–
    The context of human discourse : a configurational criticism of
rhetoric / Eugene E. White.
        p.   cm. — (Studies in rhetoric/communication)
    Includes bibliographical references and index.
    ISBN 0–87249–817–4 (acid-free)
    1. Rhetoric.   2. Communication.   I. Title.   II. Series.
P301.W45   1992
    808—dc20   91–39718

Contents

Foreword

In this book Eugene E. White details the rhetorical, psychological, and logical grounds for exploring rhetorical efforts with due regard for their contexts. White is an award-winning, lifetime student of political and religious discourse in the United States. Here he describes and illustrates how contexts shape rhetorical discourses and their consequences. In so doing he offers an alternative to several popular, contemporary modes of rhetorical criticism. He illustrates the implications of his position by critically analyzing historic and contemporary rhetoric in English. The centerpiece of the illustrative phase of his inquiry is a detailed analysis of John C. Calhoun's last speech, given on March 4, 1850. This complicated and perplexing rhetorical discourse demands especially close attention to configurational forces that operated prior to, at the time of, and immediately following Calhoun's effort. Elsewhere throughout his book, White also deals with numerous less complex and more contemporary rhetorical enterprises undertaken by organized groups as well as by individuals.

In some respects White's theories of rhetoric and criticism are traditional; nonetheless, his is a unique point of view. White contends that exclusive concentration on compositional forms and styles, on genres, or on allegedly direct, practical effects of rhetoric cannot uncover any rhetoric's full nature, its potentialities for influence, or its artistic merits. Formalistic analyses may suit the aims of some literary critics, and so-called neo-Aristotelian, effects-oriented analyses may satisfy some who are social-scientifically oriented, but White shows that neither approach can, alone, yield a comprehensive understanding of rhetorical processes.

A major premise of White's discussion is that all comprehensive criticism of rhetoric must be *historical* study in some degree. This is because rhetoric must already have emerged before anyone can study it. Even when rhetoric is seen or heard in progress, it is still inescapably responsive to forces of the past, comes into existence as part of an array of temporal, constantly changing, interrelated human actions, and at once reflects and seeks to influence human conceptualizations. These factors influence rhetoric's potentialities to evoke change. White's point of view further demonstrates that consequences do not flow directly from rhetorical actions. Rhetorical actions can alter people's conceptions of reality and, as a result, those people may choose to act in ways that do directly change other phenomena and events. Understanding rhetoric's potentialities therefore entails considering what its respondents were capable or incapable of accomplishing through their actions. According to this view, change *derives* from rhetorical actions, but it is *respondents'* subsequent actions that actually alter events.

In sum, White shows how and why neither historical records nor rhetorical texts, taken alone, can fully reveal the nature of rhetorical experience. Configurations of forces out of which rhetoric grows and into which rhetoric is thrust generate ever-evolving futures.

Carroll C. Arnold

Acknowledgments

What I have tried to do in this book is to present a somewhat different way of looking at communications—namely, a method that anyone can use to analyze and evaluate any kind of written or oral talk.

I have had much help in carrying out this intent. Inasmuch as the configurational approach has influenced my teaching and writing during recent years, the response of students and colleagues has helped refine my thinking. I wish to thank Thomas W. Benson, who read an early version of my study and offered many valuable suggestions. I am especially grateful to Carroll C. Arnold, who as an advisory editor for the University of South Carolina Press saw my study through its final maturing. My regret is that I did not have the benefit of Carroll's blue pencil during the early years of my career. What a difference this would have made in my subsequent writing and editing!

As I always do when I come to the final stages of preparing a manuscript, I realize how much I owe to the patience and support of my wife, Roberta Fluitt White. Because this book has taken a little longer than usual and has produced somewhat greater personal wear and tear, my indebtedness is accordingly greater. Thank you, Roberta!

The Context of Human Discourse

The Experience and
Function of Rhetoric

Chapter One

Experiencing Rhetoric

The topic of experiencing rhetoric concerns us all, because sym- *Isocrates xml* bolic inducement is the essential tool that has enabled humans to emerge from the caves and forests, to develop and spread their varie- gated cultures over the globe, and to reach feebly, yet tenaciously, into outer space. It concerns us because communication, or rhetoric, or persuasion (to me the terms are interchangeable) is constantly all around us and within us. We spend most of our waking hours talking, writing, reading, or listening, and, when we are not doing that, we are thinking—explaining and persuading to ourselves.

Communication—its analysis, interpretation, and criticism— concerns us because all of us base our lives and self-images on the symbolic inducement that is directed to us. We convince ourselves that one piece of clothing is preferable to another for today. The den- tist convinces us that we need a new crown for that broken tooth. G. B. Trudeau, in the comic strip *Doonesbury*, insinuates that we should feel more compassion for unfortunates. The dean compli- ments us for our improved student evaluations and implies that a merit raise may be forthcoming. And, of course, every time we write or speak to others we are doing the same sort of thing. We try to per- suade our children to clean up their rooms, a client to buy a piece of machinery, and the members of the school board to initiate certain changes at Central High. And so on and on.

Some attempts at persuasion work; others don't. The Levi Strauss campaign to merchandize its new line of "tailored classics" was an expensive debacle. The campaign persuasion of Ronald Rea- gan and Republican spokespersons led to a massive victory in the election of 1984, whereas that of Walter Mondale and Democratic spokespersons contributed to an embarrassing defeat. Four years later the main characters were different but the results were the same, as Republican persuaders again helped win the White House for their party. In my home town the concerted campaign by real estate developers persuaded the county planning board and the state planning commission to construct a massive bypass system, over the appeals of disorganized citizens' environmental groups.

This is a book about the comprehensive analysis of any such rhetoric. Rhetoric is any discourse someone perceives as intended to alter attitudes or beliefs. It may be a single utterance such as a particular speech or essay, or an advertisement, or a parental admonition. Or it may be an array of attempted inducements—say, a program to discourage the use of steroids by athletes, the series of inaugural addresses that have been given by American presidents since the founding of the republic, the organized campaign of a candidate for public office, the exposition and persuasion associated with some social or religious movement. The discourse may be accompanied by nonverbal phenomena, and these phenomena will also need to be considered if one can reasonably argue that they are part of the intended inducement.

In experiencing rhetoric what we generally want to try to understand are the *potentials* for inducing and what appears to have been the actual *powers* that did in fact induce. Nevertheless, there are a variety of reasons why people explore the experience of rhetoric.

We sometimes try to get a better understanding of the persons involved in communication. We do this by examining the rhetoric and associated circumstances to which they were exposed or to which they contributed. For example, we might want to learn more about what political values were most important to Americans in 1988. One avenue to acquiring that knowledge would be to study the rhetoric of Michael Dukakis and George Bush and the public's reactions to it during the presidential campaign of that year. At other times we might want to understand better the creators of rhetoric. We could look at the rhetoric those people produced and try to infer their values and motivations. A famous instance of this kind of inquiry is Kenneth Burke's essay "The Rhetoric of Hitler's Battle," now usually published as part of Burke's *The Philosophy of Literary Form*. In that essay

Burke sought to understand Hitler's motivations by making a close rhetorical analysis of the book *Mein Kampf*.

Another motivation for the study of rhetoric is to make what is essentially a *literary analysis*. Perhaps one wants to understand the *types* of rhetoric that occur and recur in society or in some particular class of situations. One would then try to discover the shared features of a collection of inaugurals, or eulogies, or farewell speeches, or editorials, or incitements to riot, or domestic arguments, or some other particular class of discourses. This kind of inquiry is commonly called generic criticism. On the other hand one might want to understand why a speech, essay, or series of rhetorical works is repeatedly admired and referred to. Nathaniel Hawthorne's *Scarlet Letter*, Lincoln's Gettysburg Address, or Martin Luther King, Jr's "I Have a Dream" speech are such rhetorical efforts. One could explore their lasting qualities by studying the texts of the works, focusing on such aesthetic features as the images constructed, the use of climaxes, metaphors, myths, or ritual symbols, or the characteristics of arguments. This and other kinds of textual analysis attempt to get at the artistic qualities of what was said, and, of course, it presupposes that certain kinds of verbal usage are especially "artistic."

Still another kind of motivation for analyzing rhetoric can be *ideological*. The ideology may be moral, political, social, or other, but the motivation for examining rhetorical events becomes the wish to discover the degree to which rhetoric fits some pre-formed system of values—values that allegedly specify moral worth, political worth, social worth, or some other kind of "worth." A rather mild formulation of an ideological approach to rhetoric is offered by Karlyn Kohrs Campbell. She favors a kind of analysis that "assumes that human division and hostility as well as human cooperation and identification depend on symbolic behavior, and because it assumes that a major function of rhetoric is to promote such cooperation and identification, the critic must be a careful student of the constructive and destructive capacities of symbolic behavior."[1] She posits that there are clearly knowable "constructive and destructive" uses of symbolic activity, and consequently she studies rhetoric to sort out the political and social worth of the rhetorical methods used. Richard M. Weaver wrote about argument from circumstance: "It has . . . power through a widely shared human weakness, which turns out . . . to be short-sightedness. . . . When all the criteria are brought to bear, then, this is an inferior source of argument, which reflects adversely upon any habitual user and generally punishes with failure."[2] This too is an ideological position that explains why Weaver could not find worth in anyone who uses this kind of argument. Indeed, this was his chief critical complaint about Edmund Burke's political rhetoric. The complaint enabled Weaver to deny Burke his usual status as a conservative politician and to brand him a liberal—in Weaver's view an inferior kind of statesman. These are fairly subtle instances of imposing ideologies in studying attempts to induce. More dramatic and dogmatic instances can be found in almost any Marxist criticism of rhetoric or literary work. The work will be studied for its conformity to Marxist political and social doctrines. There is also some Roman Catholic criticism in which consistency with papal theology is treated as a prerequisite for worth.

Still another motivation for studying rhetoric is to test and to build clearer theory of how inducing through discourse *actually works*. The fundamental question becomes, "What does this rhetoric teach us about the nature of rhetorical *influencing*?" Sometimes one simply seeks "theoretical" stimulation from looking at models, good and bad. Theodore Sorensen has written that he read all preceding presidential inaugural addresses before writing the now famous inaugural address of John F. Kennedy. Sorensen wanted to acquire better sensitivity to strong and weak stylistic formulations in inaugural settings. Several features of the Kennedy address indicate that Sorenson "soaked up" a good deal of stylistic theory. A more technical interest in enlarging theoretical knowledge is reflected in the book *Form, Genre, and the Study of Political Discourse*, edited by Herbert W. Simons and Aram A. Aghazarian. Part Two of this book contains four critical studies of Ronald Reagan's 1981 inaugural address. The scholars who made these studies were concerned to find out what judgments could be made about Reagan's speech if it were measured against typical features of the *form* called presidential inaugural. Richard A. Joslyn, a political scientist, in commenting on the four studies, stated his theoretical interest: "I have tried to keep one overriding question central. In what ways and to what extent do these analyses help us better understand political processes in general and political discourse in particular?"[3] Theoretical motivations for analysis and criticism may be of many sorts. A person who seeks to understand social movements will want, among other things, to look carefully at the rhetoric addressed to members and to "outsiders" by a number of social movements. A creator of advertisements is expected to know current advertising practices, learned in part from examining and analyzing successful and unsuccessful samples of other advertisers.

The broadest motivation for examining rhetoric critically arises when one wants to know how some rhetoric *fits into the culture* of which it becomes a part—the probable reasons for the rhetoric's coming into existence, its characteristics as rhetoric, and its probable immediate and long-range consequences. This aim is most comprehensively present in the historical-critical work done by professional rhetoricians and by some historians. The treatment of John C. Calhoun's March 4, 1850, speech that I offer as a case study in this book reflects this kind of motivation. I wanted to know everything knowable and relevant to understanding this rather strange speech. On the other hand, what I call configurational criticism is not a motivation and practice that is appropriate only for professional rhetorical scholars. Consider the following set of much less complicated examples of where learning something about the *configuration* of historical and cultural forces would be very important.

At the 1988 Democratic National Convention, Governor Bill Clinton of Arkansas nominated Michael Dukakis for President. He did so in a speech that took more than twenty minutes, although he was scheduled to use no more than fifteen minutes. Now Clinton is a strong and personable speaker, but well before he concluded his speech, there was growing noise from the convention floor and at least some delegates were drawing their fingers across their throats and waving for Clinton to sit down. How are we to understand this most unusual rhetorical event? Newspaper and broadcasting commentators made much of the overlength of the speech. Clinton's wife said in an interview, "That's the last time he'll use a manuscript speech." Governor Clinton himself later appeared on the Johnny Carson show, and he made a most revealing statement: "I thought I was to *introduce* my friend."

If we truly want to understand this event, we shall have to have information about *what happened before the address*. Was there misunderstanding or miscommunication between Clinton and those in charge of arranging the convention program? How did Clinton get the notion of "introducing" Governor Dukakis to a hall of delegates who were already set to endorse the nomination of Dukakis for President within an hour of Clinton's speaking? Did he think so much about the television audience that he forgot that the delegates before him in the hall already knew Dukakis and were ready to make him their nominee? This little rhetorical event can never be rightly understood until we get a grip on the *history* of the speech's preparation. We would not need to go further back than Clinton's speech preparation, but it would be very important to get at least that background.

On September 26, 1988, President Reagan gave his last address to the United Nations Assembly in New York. In an unusual turn for him, he praised the UN highly. His main reason for doing so was that the UN had had a good deal to do with getting a cease-fire in the Iran–Iraq war and in opening a number of other negotiations that appeared to promise peaceful settlements of internal and international conflicts. To grasp the real meaning of Reagan's speech we would need to know some details about those negotiations, what the members of the Assembly knew about them, and what the prospects for success were. With that kind of information we could estimate how Reagan's fairly general kudos to the UN would impress the delegates and the broadcast listeners and viewers. We would have to gather at least some information about the flow of earlier events and how Reagan's listeners probably understood them. We would not need to assemble the complete history of UN peace negotiations over the eight years of Reagan's tenure as President, but we would certainly need to understand the recent developments.

Consider trying to understand a coach's remarks to his team in the locker room at half time. One wouldn't need to research the coach's and the players' biographies or the full history of the game being played, but one would certainly need to gather general information about earlier relations between this coach and the team, and we would need to know clearly what had gone on in the first half of the game. We would then perhaps have enough background information to allow us to reason out why the coach spoke as he did and how significant and perhaps effective his talk was.

These examples illustrate that background information is necessary if one is to understand the probable significance and force of any body of rhetoric. But what background is to be looked at? We first must realize that when rhetoric occurs, it always occurs in *some situation* or across *some series of situations*. Governor Clinton addressed a certain convention at a certain moment. Ralph Emerson wrote an essay on "Compensation" at a particular time, gave it as a lecture in numerous cities, and published it at a particular time. Furthermore, it continues to be published for us to read at the particular times we choose to read it. Each of those moments of public encounter with Emerson's thoughts constitutes a distinct rhetorical situation that we need to understand as separate from one another if we are to explain the nature of Emerson's impact on the world at various times and under various circumstances. *Rhetorical situation* has been described as "the complex of persons, objects, events, and relations which generate rhetorical discourse." This definition is helpful, but it needs expansion. A rhetorical situation can be a continuing and changing one, as a candidate for public office campaigns over weeks. The phrase "generate rhetorical discourse" can also be too confining for a person who wants to understand how a body of rhetoric works and why. In the case of Emerson's essay the writer's aim was clearly rhetorical, and the work will still remain rhetorical if I choose to read it today, or next week. The circumstances under which I read it do not "generate" the essay as rhetorical discourse, however. The rhetoric is available, and *I* create a situation in which it can influence me rhetorically. Much the same is true of advertisements. They are rhetoric that is available to us, and we expose ourselves to them under particular sets of circumstances. We need, therefore, a broader, more flexible conception of human encounters with rhetoric, and this book addresses that need by conceptualizing rhetorical experience within a "configuration" of forces that flow through time. This conception broadens one's vision of what knowledge, beyond the discourse itself, we need or may need in order to understand the experience of rhetoric fully and accurately. For example, what lies behind my decision to expose myself to Emerson's essay later this afternoon? What readinesses do I bring to the rhetorical work—or fail to bring? These are some of the directions of the questioning that will be treated in detail in the chapters that follow.

This book is the product of my long-term attempt to improve and articulate rhetorical theory and to "fit" various significant communications into the cultures of which they are intrinsic parts. My wish is to offer a way of looking at rhetoric that is more comprehensive, more realistic, more rewarding than current views. The book explains why some persuasion works, why it makes a difference, why it changes the course of events, whereas other persuasion is merely "sound and fury, signifying nothing." It provides, furthermore, a method for estimating how well a communicator exploits the available means of persuasion, shows how the method is rooted in understandings of human symbol using, and gives a model of the method at work.

Chapter Two

The Configurational Viewpoint

Rhetoric is sometimes defined as the intended use of symbols to induce change in someone. As I have already said, there are many legitimate questions that can be asked about a piece of persuasion. The kinds of approaches used to answer these questions depend largely on the nature of the questions themselves. Students employing this definition have produced a large body of analysis and criticism, much of it very useful and some of it distinguished. Without intending to diminish the need for such studies or the contributions they have made to our understanding of communication, I suggest that the above definition of rhetoric should be modified to produce a more complete, more rounded, more useful perspective.

My definition of rhetoric as act emphasizes the social function of communication. By rhetorical act I mean *the purposive use of symbols in an attempt to induce change in some receiver(s), thereby derivatively modifying the circumstances that provoked, or made possible, the symbolic interaction between persuader(s) and receiver(s).*

This definition, it seems to me, has important consequences for rhetorical analysis and criticism. One consequence is that attention to persuasion that affects our daily lives must necessarily center on these questions: How did the piece(s) of rhetoric *function* to modify the provoking set of circumstances? How *well* did the persuader(s) use the available means of rhetoric to influence the flow of events? A second consequence is that, in order to conceptualize these questions and to provide answers for them, we must employ a configurational approach to the event(s) we study. In the following pages I lay out a scheme for explaining how communication works. If my theory is correct, anyone wanting to understand the "workings" of persuasion must necessarily begin with the conception that it occurs within and as part of a configuration.

The Configuration

There are three key concepts that must be clarified in order to grasp what will follow. They are configuration, congruency, and identification.

The Concept of Configuration

The hub of the notions I want to propose is the concept of a configuration. The term "configuration" implies that parts of a whole are set or are moving relative to the other parts of that whole. Astronomers use the term to refer to the positions of heavenly bodies relative to one another. I am using the term in a like way: to express the notion that rhetorical events occur *in relation to other events* and their developments. The psychological theory that makes most use of this notion is Gestalt psychology, a psychology that emphasizes the fact that we always perceive things in relation to other phenomena. My position is similar, for it is my contention that when someone "makes" some rhetoric in some place and time, we must inspect the totality of phenomena and forces that existed in relation to that rhetoric else we cannot fully understand what happened. We must begin with the conception that all rhetoric occurs within and as part of a configuration.

The traditional view of Gestalt, one of the earliest conceptualizations of modern psychology, is that a configuration we perceive is "a structure of physical, biological, or psychological phenomena so integrated as to constitute a functional unit with properties not derivable from its parts in summation." A few recent writers, such as Paul Meadows, in his 1945 essay "The Dialectic of the Situation: Some Notes on Situational Psychology,"[1] and Lloyd F. Bitzer, in his 1968 article "The Rhetorical Situation" and his 1980 essay "Functional Communication: A Situational Perspective,"[2] seem to have caught some of the excitement of the Gestalt notion and applied it in limited form to communicative situations. I am grateful for their perceptions, especially for the idea that a response is engendered by a provoking state of affairs, or, as Bitzer calls it, an exigence. Other writers on rhetoric have, of course, used the term "configuration" to clarify their ideas. For instance, Richard M. Weaver used the term in his *Visions of Order* to explain the "identity" of "things,"[3] and Kenneth Burke employed it on rare occasions to explain some point, as in his *Language as Symbolic Action*: "For a theology, a philosophy, a political system, or a drama are all alike in one notable respect: each involves a cycle or configuration of organically interrelated terms—and by featuring these and considering their implications we can hope to get the logic of the structure in general, and the parts in relation to the whole or to one another."[4] But neither Burke nor Weaver—nor any other major rhetorician, to my knowledge—has made configuration a prominent element in his or her formulations.

The Gestalt of communication is never static. This is the first thing we must recognize about it—hence, my use and special meaning for "configuration." Any persuasive experience is experience of a dynamic, cyclical flow of antecedents-events-consequences that, in the course of its developing, encompasses not only the particular piece(s) of persuasion that we are interested in but also all other successful and abortive attempts at modification that are relevant to experiencing that rhetoric. The second thing we must understand about the Gestalt of communication is that any persuasive experience entails certain identifiable and regularized forces that, through their configured interplay, produce the relationship of the communication(s) with the rest of the configuration, including the cause for the communication, the context and thrust of the communication as a modifying force, and the consequences of the communication. These configurational forces are discussed in chapter 3 and encountered throughout this volume.

A consequence of this concept that persuasion is an intrinsic, modifying force within a configuration is that rhetoric comes to be seen as a thoroughly practical instrument of social change and should be analyzed and evaluated as such. This emphasis on the functional and useful is consistent with the long rhetorical tradition that stretches from the teachings of Carroll C. Arnold, William Norwood Brigance, Herbert A. Wichelns, and James A. Winans, through the instruction of intervening rhetors, to the advice of Cicero, Quintilian, Aristotle, and other early Greek and Roman preceptors.

The Concept of Congruence

When we conceive of anything as configured, the question of whether phenomena are or are not congruent arises. Congruence concerns the extent to which a condition of harmony, correspondence, agreement, or consonance exists among phenomena and/or forces. Rhetoric occurs in configurational relation to other phenomena and forces. Therefore, we must ask about the consonance of those elements. For instance, is what a persuader says congruent, or compatible, with what readers/listeners are able and willing to understand, and/or accept, and/or do? How well a persuader uses rhetoric and how well a piece(s) of rhetoric functions to modify a provoking urgency depend on the degree of harmony that exists between the persuader's use of symbolic inducement and other forces in the configuration. Examining congruency is a matter of matching. The interested person matches what a persuader says and does against the constraints upon the message and thereby tries to establish the degree of congruence between the two. The greater the congruence is, the higher the degree of rhetorical merit is and the better the message functions to modify the provoking urgency.

To examine the congruence of any set of forces or phenomena is different from looking for their effects, or their literary, esthetic, logical, or ethical qualities. Are there advantages to examining congruence rather than effects or qualities that it is presumed rhetorical discourse ought to have? I think there are. Let me explain.

Congruity and Effect

Examining the congruence of rhetorical forces yields more information about what happened than looking for "effects" of communication. There are several reasons why this is so.

First, the congruence of rhetorical forces is vastly easier to estimate than their rhetorical effects. Few careful scholars still attempt the hopeless task of proving absolute causal relationships between rhetoric and effects. It is virtually impossible to show that an alleged

Collapse into effect into causality)

effect has been necessarily and exclusively produced by a particular aspect of a communication or by its total force. There is always a myriad of forces influencing individual readers or listeners before, during, and following any communication. Specific causal relationships simply cannot be isolated. On the other hand, whether configured forces are harmonious—that is, are consonant with each other— can be estimated with considerable confidence. As I hope to illustrate, the logical processes of investigating congruency are largely those of informed *comparison*, a kind of reasoning that one can use where formal causality eludes our understanding.

Second, we can perceive degrees of congruity, whereas trying to judge causes and effects involves us in an all-or-nothing enterprise. Either a causal relationship exists, and we can establish its existence, or we can say little about relationships except that they are not demonstrably causal. If we try instead to see the *extent* of congruence among related forces, we can always provide some description of the event.

② causal in either/or

some to lack from previous page

Third, whereas searching for effects involves us in looking for exclusive relationships, looking for degrees of congruence accommodates the fact that many forces influence one another when rhetoric is introduced. We are encouraged to consider such matters as persuaders' rhetorical intentions and their belief systems, for these are among the significant influential forces that are always in play when rhetoric occurs/ If they are wise, persuaders intend to create as much congruence as possible between their own strategies and the constraints of their situations; they do this in the hope that their audiences will be influenced by the "fitness" of the rhetoric as one of the interplaying forces that they as individuals need to adjust to. An interested observer of persuasion, then, needs to estimate how close the persuaders come to selecting those rhetorical options that have maximum congruity with their intentions and belief systems and the constraints within which the persuaders and the audience make their decisions.

③

How to account for effort to redefine situation?

Finally, exploring rhetorical configurations still allows one to see whatever degrees of causation are present to be discerned. If a cause does produce an effect within the configuration, that cause will be noticed as one of the forces congruent with other relevant forces.

Examining a configuration for congruences exposes causal forces if they exist, but one does not have to presuppose that particular and exclusive one-directional relations exist.

Congruity and Rhetorical Qualities

There are qualities of rhetoric that people search for in studying human communication. Observers try to see how well a communication conforms to the rules of its genre or to some other qualitative criterion. There are many such normative scales. For instance, one type of critic—Richard M. Weaver, for example—believes that a critic's aim should be to judge the "worth" or "intrinsic excellence" of communications in moving persons "from the brutish state toward the civilized ideal of the educated and the free." Weaver's way of judging intrinsic excellence was to apply a loosely designed scale of values to communications and presumably measure the persuaders' morality. On this view, the higher a persuader's morality is, the higher is the rhetorical merit of his or her communication.[5] A second example of a normative scale was provided by Karl R. Wallace, who argued that rhetoric should be "viewed as an art of advising," that the communicator should see himself or herself "as an advisor rather than, say, a salesman," and that the goal of the communicator should be to help "his audiences arrive at rational decisions."[6] The standard for measuring how well the communicator employs rhetoric, Wallace insisted, should be his or her use of "good reasons"—the more and the better the "good reasons" are, the higher the rhetorical merit.[7] Most college English teachers, journalists, public speaking teachers, and debate coaches also employ qualitative assessments. To these critics the end of communication is to communicate well, and they match the performance of students, political candidates, and the like against an arbitrary list of qualities that they believe characterize good communication.

At best, applying qualitative scales when investigating rhetoric can only yield judgments about what the scale or criteria presumably "measure." The judgment will not clarify other forces that also conspired to make the event what it was. Furthermore, qualitative norms usually reflect the values of the observer who chooses them. They

are arbitrary and therefore always arguable. A more sweeping and realistic view of rhetoric is needed if we are to understand its practical
nature and significance. Indeed, a communication can be based on
"good reasons," be eloquent in style, be expressive of high moral
principles, have sound documentation and helpful internal summaries, and still be *incongruent* with other forces that help to shape the
configuration in which the communication occurs. "A fine speech,
but before its time" is one of many commonplace evaluative analyses
of such rhetoric.

Focusing on the congruence of situational forces does not ignore
relevant rhetorical qualities. If we match what persuaders do against
the constraints on their communications, qualities that enhance the
rhetoric's *fit to the overall situation* will stand out as elements of congruence. To look at rhetoric in this way is a thoroughly practical procedure. Moreover, it comes as close as possible to the realism of the
event itself.

To explore congruency assumes that what we want to know is
how communication(s) functions to modify provoking urgencies and
that what we want to judge or estimate is how well the persuader(s)
used rhetoric *under the constraining circumstances.* These are the main
questions that anyone interested in rhetoric's social significance will
want answered. If the rhetoric had special aesthetic qualities or other
qualities that contributed or failed to contribute to modifying the urgency, exploring congruencies will expose them; but one will not be
misguided by presupposing the importance of qualities that weren't
pragmatically essential.

The Concept of Identification

Rhetoric is *action*. To observe and understand rhetoric we have to
engage in analysis and criticism. The concept of congruence implies
that there is a thrusting power in persuasion and that this thrust is a
modifying force within the configuration. But how does cognitive
and behavioral change take place in receivers? I suggest that this is
best explained by resorting to the concept of identification.

My concept of identification derives from Kenneth Burke, although Burke was not the first nor the most famous person to use the

concept. Sigmund Freud, for example, made extensive use of the idea, and Aristotle anticipated it. Burke was, however, the first to suggest that identification is "the key term for rhetoric." He insisted that identification is the *sole* avenue of persuasion, thus adding a significant new dimension to the age-old axiom: Effective communication is audience-centered.

The essence of Burke's point of view is both extraordinarily clear and provocative. In his *Rhetoric of Motives* he says, "You persuade a man only insofar as you can talk his language by speech, gesture, tonality, order, image, attitude, idea, *identifying* your ways with his." He adds that "persuasion by flattery is but a special case of persuasion in general. But flattery can safely serve as our paradigm if we systematically widen its meaning, to see behind it the conditions of identification or consubstantiality in general. And you give the 'signs' of such consubstantiality by deference to an audience's 'opinions.'" "True," he continues, "the rhetorician may have to change an audience's opinion in one respect; but he can succeed only insofar as he yields to that audience's opinions in other respects. Some of their opinions are needed to support the fulcrum by which he would move other opinions."[8]

I interpret Burke to mean that one can hope to "talk the language" of another only after one understands the other's conscious and, as far as possible, his or her unconscious motivations and needs. Only by fusing "your ways with his" will you reach him. When such identification fades, so will the willingness of the other to move toward your position.

I want to follow the essence of Burke's viewpoint to its logical conclusion. In the theory of persuasion that I shall develop, identification—in conjunction with the concepts of congruence and configuration—is the grand engine by which cognitive and behavioral change is generated.

Criteria: To Stretch Toward

The configurational model I am proposing ought to meet several standards. First, one should be able to take a configurational view of almost any kind of rhetoric. The view should enable one to examine single rhetorical acts, say, a telephone call from a university funding officer requesting a contribution; a film warning high school students about AIDS; Donald Trump's full-page advertisements ridiculing U.S. foreign policy, which ran in *The New York Times, The Washington Post,* and *The Boston Globe;* Jean R. Sasson's *The Rape of Kuwait;* John Bunyan's *Pilgrim's Progress;* or W. H. Harvey's *Coin's Financial School.* All of these represent particular forms of persuasion, and we need to be able to distinguish their particular features. We should also be able to look at, say, a series of communications by different persons such as the Senate confirmation hearings of Clarence Thomas for a position on the U.S. Supreme Court; the public communications of many persons over an extended time period such as the sermons that eventuated in the Great Awakening as Puritan ministers treated the issue of emotion in religion; communication such as the parables of Jesus or the editorials of George Will; the rhetorical strategies of a particular persuader over time such as George Bush's defense of a military response to the Persian Gulf crisis.

An ideal view of rhetoric should also embrace the private rhetoric of intimate circumstances. It ought to help us to understand, say, a domestic argument, or the interpersonal manipulations of Stephen A. Douglas and the buttonhole importunities of lobbyists for the Texas bondholders during debates over the Compromise of 1850. Without knowledge of such "inside" rhetoric, a discussion of the rhetorical input to the Compromise of 1850 would be naïvely sterile. At the same time an ideal view of rhetoric should also embrace the public rhetoric of formal situations, such as papal pronouncements or the televised Iran–Contra congressional hearings.

Further, with some modification but with its essential thrust unimpaired, an ideal approach to rhetoric should suggest ways of studying such special forms of rhetoric as Civil War music, the 'rhetoric of an antiapartheid demonstration, the rhetoric of atrocity films of the Vietnam war, the rhetoric of the Boston Tea Party, or even the rhetoric of "mat mania"—the explosion of interest in televised professional wrestling in the 1980s and 1990s.

In short, an ideal way of looking at rhetoric should allow investigation of *any* actions that we can reasonably believe were rhetorical.

Second, a satisfactory view of rhetoric should be conceptually complete and clear enough to guide an observer toward profitable questions about rhetoric and to suggest ways of finding appropriate answers to those questions. On the other hand, an ideal method of inquiry should not be so rigid or inclusive as to proscribe individual insights or prevent originality in studying communications. A sound way of understanding rhetoric ought also to enable one to do more than describe; it should yield ways of interpreting, explaining, and evaluating. At the same time, an ideal method must be receptive to a wide range of humanistic and social scientific knowledge, and conclusions to which the method of inquiry leads ought to be consonant with accepted ideas of how people behave and interact.

Third, an ideal way of looking at rhetoric ought to enable one to distinguish the component parts of a communication so as to discover their nature and functional relationships to other components. Since the approach I propose is configurational, it will fail to meet its own criteria of merit if it does not provide all the concepts and methods necessary to analyze, interpret, and interrelate whatever is knowable about the rhetorical configurations.

Finally, an ideal method of studying rhetorical events ought to yield perceptions that are significant outside and beyond the events directly studied. What one learns from an investigation should contribute to fuller understanding of human communication in general, of the nature of human interactions, and of the relation of rhetoric to those enigmas we call form, value, and belief. In short, it ought to shed light on what it is to be human.

How well the configurational mode of inquiry I propose meets these standards must be judged by readers after they have followed my arguments, claims, and illustrations that make up the rest of this book. A major kind of support that I draw from in later chapters comes from an extended case study. That case and my intentions in using it deserve preliminary explanation.

A Configurational Case Study

An important part of my attempt to explain how the communication about us works is the joining of theory to practice. I will accompany the unfolding theoretical considerations with an ongoing case study of John C. Calhoun's speech in the United States Senate, March 4, 1850. I will illustrate each theoretical concept by applying it in analysis of Calhoun's speech.

Why do I pick Calhoun's speech for my extended case study? With the record of the world's most glamorous attempts at persuasion at my disposal, why do I pick a flawed speech by a crusty, dying old slaveholder, in defense of an archaic social system, on a musty occasion remembered only by history buffs?

First, I am going to examine this configuration because it presents the ultimate challenge to analysis. Most specialists agree that the set of circumstances that necessitated the congressional debates of 1850 and eventually resulted in the Civil War is the most difficult exigence to fathom in American history. Don E. Fehrenbacher has referred to it as "that treacherous scholars' jungle," and Roy F. Nichols has been quoted as saying that "the only thing about the Civil War that historians can agree on is that there was one." By showing how configurational analysis handles this fiercely complex and frustrating urgency, I can demonstrate that the method can deal with any rhetorical urgency that may concern us.

Second, I pick this configuration because it is meaningful to us as individuals and as Americans. In shaping the way we view ourselves and the world no historic urgency has been more significant than the issue of slavery. It is not outrageous to say that Calhoun's speech represents the high-water mark of slavery in the United States and that, as Calhoun thought would be the case, the failure of his speech heralded the doom of slavery.[9] Analysis of such a significant rhetorical effort to modify a crucial urgency should have sustained interest value, especially for Americans. Furthermore, no existing estimate of Calhoun's speech begins to do justice to it.

Third, I use a single communication instead of several because a single communication can be handled more economically than can multiple speeches or essays. Nevertheless, by choosing Calhoun's address as my running example, instead of a simpler instance or series of rhetorical responses, I am able to illustrate every move a configurational analysis of rhetoric can require—including the moves and explorations of detail that only the most thorough, scholarly analysis of very complex urgencies and responses requires.

In coupling theory to practice I need a piece of rhetoric that will allow me to illustrate a configurational analysis that exploits all of the kinds of resources that are available for study. In my own analysis I have gone somewhat beyond the limits of representative libraries to find special information relative to Calhoun, but when I have done so, my specific questions and my methods of investigation still illustrate those any analyst would use in researching a simpler configuration of which rhetoric was a part. It happens that there is a special wealth of pertinent information respecting Calhoun and the issue of slavery. Certain details are to be found in fairly specialized sources. My curiosity has led me to examine collections of newspapers and private papers at half a dozen major repositories. But, inasmuch as the insights gained from these special sources merely "fleshed out," but did not significantly alter, my view of the case, the special, perhaps somewhat unrepresentative research I have done still indicates the general pattern of investigation that configurational analysis calls for. As my exposition proceeds, I shall indicate how one might comparably investigate less complicated cases about which less historical and other information is available.

I wish now to present a basic view of Calhoun's speech and the configuration of which it was a part. This is an overview such as one could gain from good general knowledge of the slavery issue in the United States in the mid-nineteenth century. For many years the flow of events had moved the North and South toward serious confrontation over slavery-related issues. This developing urgency was exacerbated by a series of happenings, including the acquisition of great tracts of potentially slave land from Mexico; the demand of California for statehood, bypassing the territorial stage; border warfare between Texas and New Mexico; and the attempt of antislavery forces in the House of Representatives to prohibit slavery in the District of Columbia. By 1850 the convergence of such forces had produced a crisis requiring congressional action. On the one hand, North and South possessed conflicting basic views of society and slavery that were not compromisable. On the other hand, there were forces making for peaceful resolution of the problem: the South, while accepting the principle of secession, was not yet ready to secede; the North, while accepting the principle of abolition, was not yet prepared to force the issue; a powerful political "instinct" to compromise still existed; major bonds of commonality still linked the sections together; most Americans still retained faith that the political process could work out accommodations between local and regional interests and national policy. Therefore, the events seemed to call for an ambiguous compromise that did not require either side to give up anything it could not yield but that enabled both sides to claim that they had won. The compromise that actually evolved hinged on the use of popular sovereignty, or the right of the inhabitants of the new territories to determine whether or not to have slavery. Ambiguity was provided by the failure of the legislators to specify when, in the existence of a particular territory, this decision would be made. This was the "tender" point in the agreement. If the settlers voted the matter soon after a territory was created, slavery would probably be excluded before it got a chance to become established; but if the settlers voted later, when they applied for statehood, slavery would have been legal from the beginning—even though most of the inhabitants might have opposed it.

Far more prescient than any other political figure of his time, Senator Calhoun realized that the huge disparity of population and economic power between the sections of the country would continue to accelerate. Unless something was done immediately to counteract this growing imbalance of political strength, the South would soon be unable to defend herself either in or out of the Union. Time was the enemy of the South. Therefore, in his speech the South Carolinian called upon the North to guarantee Southern rights and interests by constitutional revision and other means, and he called upon the South to secede if the North failed to yield.

Calhoun's speech received no endorsement from Northern senators—although Daniel Webster may have been moved by it to speak in a more conciliatory manner than was his custom. It received very little support from Southern members. Instead, by autumn, after protracted debate and after Calhoun's death, Congress adopted a series of measures that papered over the division between the sections. As the ensuing decade unfolded, Southern leaders became increasingly estranged, until they finally came to accept Calhoun's view that the political process and the intersectional relationship had failed. By then, however, as Calhoun foretold, it was too late. Slavery in the United States was destined for early extinction. The most bloody war of American history lay ahead—a monument to an inhumane cause and, in an oblique sort of way, to the failure of a crusty old man's rhetoric.

This brief review suggests the essential nature of the urgency and configurational forces that Calhoun sought to alter by means of a speech. It indicates the essential nature of the configuration: the pertinent antecedents, the rhetoric as event, and the general pattern of relevant events that followed the event. These are the three broad components of any configuration involving rhetoric. Were we trying to understand the running "debates" between George Bush and Michael Dukakis in 1988, we would need to review the same three components: antecedents, event(s), and the matrix of relevant events following the "debates." The same would be true if we were trying to understand a significant telephone conversation or an editorial. It happens that I can flesh out these components in great detail for Calhoun's speech, as I probably could not were the object of my analysis some provincial contemporary political rhetoric. In any case, however, I would still have to know the significant antecedents to the exchange, the exchange itself, and what followed in consequence—insofar as knowledge was available.

In the next chapter I will show why the flow of events, of which Calhoun's speech was a part, was a *dynamic rhetorical Gestalt* comprising regularized forces in configured interplay.

Chapter Three

Rhetoric as Historical Configuration

Any communication exists through the configured interplay of dynamic but regularized forces. Through these forces the communication achieves its reason for being, its meaning, and its consequences—its "reality." As I use "reality" here, it is not a kind of matter existing out there in timeless space, something like planets or dinosaur bones. Reality is, instead, what we ordinary, interested persons, with our natural capacities and processes, take to be "real." The point of analyzing a rhetorical configuration is to get at what any communication *is* to us and at how we can grasp its meanings.

Any communication should be understood and explored as *historical configuration*. You can't look at any rhetoric until it has happened in its context. That is why I have said that the meaning of any communication exists in the interplaying of regularized forces constituting a historical configuration—a dynamic, cyclical movement, or development—of antecedents-events-consequences.

Practical communication has its real existence in interrelated humanized forces, in interactions of persons and perceptions of events. If there is communication, someone *acts* to bond the selves and experiences of others with the communicator's. This is what Aristotle had in mind when he asserted that rhetoric is the means by which humans as social-political beings create, sustain, and alter whatever social fabric they live within.

Rhetoric, then, is at the center of our social experience. To understand how rhetoric works and with what potential and actual consequences is fundamental to understanding ourselves as social creatures. Understanding that communication is always configured supplies a needed reminder that any rhetoric gets much of its meaning from its social context. A communication is not a self-contained episode nor a sequential sound-sign system nor a "text" whose meaning ends with the last syllable. As human experience every communication *means* by virtue of the interplay of its history, its maker's creative impulses, its receivers' histories and their creative and pragmatic impulses. Consider how we ourselves perceive things.

How We Perceive Things

Before considering how we perceive communication, we need some consideration of how, in general, humans perceive.[1]

How Do We Know and Understand Our Human Functioning?

Our functioning, as we know it consciously, is basically determined by our view of the world—that is, by our sense of identity or self-system. Our self-system serves simultaneously as both consequences of our past and antecedents of our future. It is a becoming—ever evolving and changing. It is dynamic, not static. It is a constant experiencing of change. The amount and kind of change that occurs in one's self-system during any given time depends on that individual's history and nature. For all of us at all times, including when we communicate or respond to communication, our self-systems constrain the way we perceive the world and the way we respond to the world. They also constrain the way the world exerts shaping influence on us.

The self-system is one's complex of functionally interrelated anchors—or patterns—for perceiving, judging, deciding, remembering, imagining, and otherwise reacting. These functions give continuity and being to an individual. The self-system includes all the social learning and all the internal factors that influence the psychological functioning of the person at a particular moment. The self-system determines the way we size up the world and respond to it—the way we view ourselves and our relatedness to others of the present, past, and future. Our self-systems possess a psychologically necessary consistency and stability over time. If it were otherwise, our personalities, characters, goals, and behaviors would always be in flux, and we would lose our sense of identity and the ability to cope with the environment. The self-system is not so much an entity as a becoming.

Our self-systems are largely derived from three *historical* sources: our social experiences; our intrinsic method of perceiving and symbolizing what is perceived; and our formal language usage. I shall consider each of these sources briefly.

The Way We Look at the World Is Chiefly Derived from Experiences with Social Environments

We don't just have sensations. We make them "ours" by representing them to ourselves with symbols. When we have done that, we render most of experience communicable. Language is our primary social symbolic system. Language shapes the "verbal edifice" called "self." As George Herbert Mead pointed out many years ago, from our earliest moments we began to grow toward our future identities. We drew nourishment from our symbolic interactions with parents, other adults, brothers, sisters, and other children. To realize the affection of our parents, and to gain a desirable security and self-esteem, we soon learned and accepted that we had to behave in certain ways. Our socialization and enculturation proceeded so gradually and naturally that we were not aware that our selfhood was being shaped for us. We interacted with innumerable individuals, groups, and larger symbolic systems such as religious, social, cultural, and economic ones. We also drew information and ways of looking at things from the media of mass communication. In all these various interactions we were being influenced by prevailing systems of reinforcement by reward and punishment. As a result we came to identify with, have commitments for, and develop revulsions against certain symbolic "territories," "role functions," "status positions," prejudices, values, interests, and ideologies. Largely because the history of each individual's socializing experiences is somewhat different from anyone else's, our emerging self-systems are inevitably unique.

The Ways We Look at the World Are Influenced Directly by the Ways We Perceive and the Ways We Symbolize What We Perceive

We are never passive receivers of stimuli. To a considerable extent we determine what we perceive and how we shape and order streams of perceptions. Ordinarily this active, creative operation is not willed. It is accomplished spontaneously, almost instantaneously. Each nervous system rejects "irrelevant" stimuli as it elects and blends the input of "relevant" stimuli from outside and from internal states. The result is an integrated impression of "reality." But the way this reality comes into being makes it impossible for our impression of it to be an exact copy of the empirical world. Like all other aspects of cognition and behavior, every perception is influenced by the past, the present, and perhaps anticipations of the future.

We never experience the total complexity of what is "out there." At any given time we perceive only a part of the potential stimuli that impinge on us. We "make sense" of things by constructing simpler, symbolic worlds. These we call "reality." Our realities are not randomly constructed, however. What we attend to is largely the product of and the shaper of our senses of self. Other things being equal, we attend to what interests us, what seems to answer to our needs and desires, what relates to our motives, what is close to us in time and space, and what agrees with our accustomed ways of thinking, knowing, feeling, and doing. We are also apt to perceive what we anticipate and to anticipate that with which we are familiar. In short, *we* create our realities selectively and individualistically. One person's realities are not the same as another's.

When we attend to a bit of our reality, that bit has no meaning until it is joined to other pieces of reality. One cannot imagine a particle of dust all by itself—in no place, adjacent to nothing. Whatever we are aware of is in *relation* to other things. We either see these related items or we call up related items from memory. We see the speck of dust *on* something, or if the speck is only in our minds, we call up relatedness for it—it's floating, or it's blown in from the beach, and so on. As David Krech and Richard S. Crutchfield point out, "There are no impartial 'facts.' Data do not have a logic of their own that results in the same perceptions and cognitions for all people. Data are perceived and interpreted in terms of the individual perceiver's own needs, own emotions, own personality, own previously formed cognitive patterns."[2] Incoming sensations are integrated with our remembered experiences, ordinarily being altered somewhat in the process. We are probably never completely neutral toward our environments. We are given direction by our learned values and by the stabilized values and attitudes we have developed toward all personally significant relationships.

Once we become accustomed to seeing something in a particular way, we are apt to continue doing so even though the thing may have undergone substantial change. And if the datum conflicts too strongly with our firmly existing cognitive structures, we tend to prevent dissonance by doing such things as ignoring the input, disregarding the disparate aspects of it, or reassessing our estimation of the source of the information.[3] We dislike incompleteness and too much ambiguity, but incoming clues are necessarily fragmentary. Therefore we draw from our remembered past to flesh out and give meaning to these incoming bits of data. What we remember, however, is always in some symbolic form, in verbal or imagistic *presentations* of earlier experience. We do not remember experience per se. We don't remember a pin prick, we recall a symbolic construction of our experience of being pricked by a pin. Our past constantly contributes to the organization of the moment. It gives context to perceptions, "gluing" items together to produce conceptual wholes rather than leaving us with isolated bits of sensation.[4]

The last step in bringing meaning, order, and predictability to a datum of experience is to catalog it. When we catalog, we categorize. That is, we abstract from all of the perceivable qualities of an entity some set of criterial properties that serve to identify that entity and tend to explain it. A pin prick becomes a "pain" because we focus on the hurt. Such cataloging is based on selecting similarities; cataloging largely ignores the differences that distinguish one entity from other members of the same class. Once we have formed categories, they tend to have the tissue of "permanence." They establish bases for our more complex cognitive patterns, attitudes, and value systems, and they provide anchors for our sense of reality. Furthermore, their circular influence never ceases. They provide classifications for incoming perceptions, and they help us to determine what we choose to perceive, thereby perpetuating and extending our existing cognitive patterns.[5] In these ways our categories become historical, and our histories shape our future perceptions.

The Way We Look at the World Is Shaped by the Nature of Our Formal Use of Language

I have said that our social experiences, and the way we perceive and symbolize, shape our views of the world. There is a third historical influence on our world views: the way we use formal language. There is a reciprocity between perceptions and social experiences on the one hand and use of language on the other. Perceptions and experiences influence the nature and use of language, and the nature and use of language influence what we perceive and how we experience. Language supplies the categories that focus the ways we look at the world. The categories enable or force us to simplify the otherwise unbearable complexity of the perceptual world. But our categories are not immutable. As we use language, we incorporate filaments of our experience into our categories. A ghetto is technically and historically a quarter inhabited chiefly by Jews, but American concern about equal rights of residence for all persons has extended that category to apply to *any* section of a city chiefly occupied by one ethnic group. The category has been expanded as a result of experience. The expansion is a result of history. Such changes in our categories occur largely unconsciously, although we sometimes change them deliberately, as when civil rights rhetoric gave "Negro" a negative valence and "Black" a positive one. Even the categories that firmly anchor an individual's sense of identity are subject to constant, though often scarcely perceptible, change. "Willy" gradually evolves into "Bill" or perhaps even to "William."

One of the early modern writers on the subject of categories, Edward Sapir, pointed out that to a large extent our conceptions of the "real world" are "built up" on our language usage: "We see and hear and otherwise experience very largely as we do because the lan-

guage habits of our community predispose certain choices of interpretation." A succeeding scholar, Benjamin Lee Whorf, extended
this line of thought: "The categories and types that we isolate from
the world of phenomena we do not find there because they stare every observer in the face; on the contrary, the world . . . has to be
organized by our minds—and this means largely by the linguistic
systems in our minds."[6] Neither Sapir nor Whorf contended that language is *the* determiner of what and how we perceive. Language by,
or in, itself doesn't *exclusively* shape our perceptions and categoriza-
tions—we have other symbol systems that help with that, too.

Nevertheless, the subtle effects categories have on shaping our
judgments can be appreciated by examining some of the connotations
that our language, and other languages, assign to words like black,
white, God, religion, sex, parent, authority, police, and government.
Look up "black" in a thesaurus. You will find that the word almost
exclusively connotes that which we don't like, or may fear. Related
terms include: threatening, sullen, sinister, baneful, dismal, evil,
wicked, malignant, unclean, grubby, foul, murky, somber, obscure,
blotch, and degenerate. Conversely, consider the positive connotations our language gives to "white": pure, spotless, clear, honorable,
just, fair, trustworthy, and genuine. African languages, however, accord largely unpleasant connotations to "white" and pleasant ones to
"black," and the Chinese language assigns undesirable connotations
to "white" and desirable ones to "yellow." The study of the relationships between language and culture is young, but psychologists believe that the denotations and connotations of anchoring categories—
for an individual or a people—can influence how individuals react to,
not just perceive, phenomena.

Social Developments Are Historical "Continuations"

Just as we can't think of a particle of dust without relating it to
something, we can't see happenings about us except as outgrowths
or extensions or precursors of other things. If there's an accident,
we search for its antecedent "cause." George Bush is inaugurated as
President of the United States, and everyone thinks of that event as
part of a chain of presidential inaugurations and as a precursor of

inaugurations to come. Inaugurations, accidents, wars, famines, Watergate scandals, sales campaigns, and successful political candidacies are not immaculate conceptions; we see them as parts of *flows* of events. They don't "just happen." Every social occurrence has its influential antecedents, and the antecedents are historical; that is, they are past parts of *continuations.* Also, every occurrence has, or is expected to have, consequences, and consequences are developments, continuations.

The truth of this idea can be demonstrated with a little reflection. Let us imagine a domestic scene. A mature woman is sitting on a couch reading to a small boy about four years old. This is the first time she has taken care of the youngster, and the two have gotten along exceptionally well all day. The child has been responsive and happy, eating well and enjoying his games. The door opens and the mother, who has been at work all day, enters the room. Instantly the little boy bursts into tears, runs to the mother to be picked up, and begins to fumble with her dress front demanding to be breast-fed. When she delays, the boy throws a temper tantrum, continuing it until after the baby-sitter has left and the feeding has begun. The unexpected retrogression of the child from a poised, confident, normal four-year-old to a nursing infant left the baby-sitter shaken and unnecessarily worried whether she herself had done something wrong. This scene is part of a historical "continuation," consisting of antecedents and consequences. The appearance of the mother triggered a response that had been conditioned over the previous months. Very permissive in her attitude toward child care, the mother had exerted almost no control or discipline. When the child did not get what he wanted from her as soon as he wanted, he threw a tantrum—because it always worked. Furthermore, the mother satisfied personal needs for fulfillment by encouraging the child to continue nursing beyond the normal time. He had been cooperative with the baby-sitter because she was a *different* person and because he sensed from her manner that she was a no-nonsense type. The consequences of this scene can proliferate endlessly, affecting the future behavior of the child, mother, and baby-sitter—even touching a small network of other persons directly or indirectly concerned. The scene did not "begin" when the mother came home, and it did not "end" when the baby-sitter left. It was a development. This is the sense in which all social developments are historical continuations. We may "chop them up" into segments for particular purposes such as detailed analysis, but we should remember that all social events are, in fact, parts of a flow ⟩ oᴋ or stream of continuous events.

Our Basic Way of Coping with "Reality" Is Historical-Critical

Whether we build instant understandings out of the present or draw our understandings from the past, we follow very much the same procedure. All of our understandings of "reality" are the prod-ucts of acquiring and evaluating pieces of seemingly relevant informa-tion, adding to these pieces by associating them with meaningful patterns we have learned to look for, and stretching or simplifying the newly patterned data into a whole. Thus, particles of dust become, not particles, but dust to be wiped away, or to signify sloppy house-keeping, or to indicate that a machine will need to be cleaned up be-fore we use it. When we perceive, we notice, interpret the meaning of, judge, and decide what, if anything, to do about it. This way of grasping underlies all philosophical or observational-experimental cognitions.

A philosopher and an experimenter work in the same basic way. Confronted with ideas or data, they acquire them selectively, associ-ate them with other ideas or data to form comprehensible patterns, and frame these patterns into conceptual wholes that they call "pos-tulates," "hypotheses," "theories," "proofs," or something else that seems to say their information now has *comprehensive* meaning. All of our thinking models or gives form to what we take to be reality. That is how we cope with what Walter Lippmann referred to as the "blooming, buzzing world" that surrounds us.[7]

I call this way of making sense out of experiences the historical-critical method. There are several justifications for using this phrase. First, I have already shown that whatever we perceive must exist for us in the past—become history before we can interpret it. Second, all interpretations involve sorting and selecting the relevant from the irrelevant. In that process we weigh the significance of items of

weak sense of evaluation

information, and that is a critical activity that involves evaluation. Third, our basic ways of handling information involve judging in time$_1$ what happened in time$_2$. All of these moves in apprehending things are historical *and* critical.

How We Experience Rhetoric

I turn now to how we understand communications, the central subject of this book. Any communication is a becoming. We experience communication as part of a developing flow of events—communicative and other—although we take little conscious notice of that fact.

The most important characteristic of any event we would call rhetorical is that the event is fluid, involving movement of thought and action. These are what give a rhetorical event its vitality. Without exception, communications involve antecedents that envelop, mix with, and change our perceptions of communication as "an" action. As we perceive the flow of communicative actions, we progressively interpret and reinterpret the significance of antecedents and the probable consequences of the flow of communication we are experiencing.

A flow that is rhetorical may be called an *exigential* flow, for reasons that will become clear shortly. A rhetorical flow possesses certain patterns of forces in configured interplay; they identify the flow as rhetorical and provide the means for understanding and evaluating the communication. An exigential flow, including all its patterns of regularity, constitutes a configuration.

Perceptions of rhetorical acts are necessarily perceptions of ongoing actions by someone. If what we perceive/order are the data of rhetorical actions, in every instant of perception/ordering we are responding/perceiving/ordering the data of an "exigential" flow. The "reality" of any rhetoric is the flow of events—developments that we perceive as the "real" meaning of rhetorical communication. This rhetorical flow is what I call an exigential flow.

It is an exigential flow because it is at once the cause, context, and product of a communication.[8] This rhetorical flow can also provoke further rhetorical and other responding actions, generating a continuing cycle of antecedents and consequences. Insofar as we can perceive them, these cyclical movements of antecedents-events-consequences comprise (1) the situational constraints provoking and embracing communication, (2) the communication itself, and (3) the relevant consequences of the communication. This conceptualization is what persons *making* rhetoric experience as they plan and act, and it is what is there to be perceived and analyzed by informed observers of communication.

I call this experiencing an exigential flow to emphasize that developing rhetorical actions arise in response to and as part of exigences or provoking phenomena that encourage rhetorical activity. Because something(s) happens, or seems likely to happen, persons perceive that a tension-evoking juncture exists that welcomes or requires modification by means of rhetoric.[9] Whenever we speak or write, we are responding to some such perceived provocation. Unless the circumstances are sufficiently "provoking," we will not communicate at all. Every purposeful communication occurs in response to perceived changing circumstances and is intended to evoke additional changes in those circumstances. The "reality" of a communication, therefore, exists in the flow of changing circumstances of which the communication is intrinsically a part.

When we sense that a situation exists that can or should be modified by communication (that is, a rhetorical urgency exists), we may respond to it by using symbols in hope of inducing changes in readers/listeners and thereby altering the urgency in a derivative way. By our communication we seek to change *people* in order that their changes will in some way change the provoking circumstances. Our communicative response is *rhetorical* because our actions have the rhetorical objective of altering people whose responses (whether rhetorical or not) will have consequences affecting the circumstances that originally caused us to communicate. It is quite possible—even likely—that the changed state of the original urgency will, in turn, constitute new provoking urgencies that give rise to later rhetorical efforts toward modification.

Consider this example of rhetorical action. Suppose we had a transcript of a telephone conversation in which a customer agreed to buy a new life insurance policy from an agent. Where is the *meaning* of this conversation? It is only partly in the conversation itself. Part of its meaning can be found if we know about events that preceded the call. Some of its meaning hinges on what happened following the call: for example, how promptly and eagerly did the consumer send a check to cover the first premium on the policy?/This antecedent-present-future buildup of meanings is what I am calling the exigential flow that rhetoric both changes and is a part of./To put the matter differently, the meaning of a body of rhetoric is not in its provoking urgency, nor in the rhetoric's antecedents, nor in the rhetorical action itself, nor in the consequences of the rhetoric, *but in the perceived interrelationships of all of these features of the event/*To repeat, the "reality" of a communication resides in the communication's interrelationships with the other forces of the exigential flow, or configuration, of which it is a part.

How Can We Analyze and Evaluate Our Experience of Rhetoric?

If analysis and criticism of communication were a science, a technician could use the instruments of science to produce a precisely accurate measurement of the quality and effect of a particular communication or a series of communications. Taking apart and evaluating a piece of rhetoric is not a science, however. It is, instead, the art of analyzing the *interplay* among forces in a historical configuration. We have to exploit this interplay if we are to estimate how well persuaders use the available means of rhetoric to influence the flow of events.

The Idea of Constraints/Satisfactions

When I talk about interplay, I am speaking about *interrelationship*, or *interrelatedness*, or *configured relationship*. The essential idea all these terms suggest is that rhetorical configurations consist of certain forces impinging on each other/ Fully successful communication occurs only when there is basically harmonious (or congruent or compatible) agreement among these impinging forces./Hence, the master concept that will command attention throughout the remainder of this book is: *To the degree that rhetorical constraints are matched by appropriate rhetorical responses, persuasion can take place.*

Let me begin with these two definitions. *Rhetorical constraints* are forces in a configuration that influence the way a persuader chooses rhetorical responses, if he or she wants to communicate effectively. *Rhetorical responses,* or satisfactions, are those things a persuader says or does in answer to impinging constraints. We can see how constraints/satisfactions work in the way a successful college football coach talks to his team after a loss. The basic urgency to which players and coach are committed is the success of the football program— that is, to win as many games as possible and to encourage maximum development of each player as an athlete and a person. Accordingly, what happened during the game, the past history of the team, and the coach's relations with the players all constrain the coach. These constraints dictate to a major degree what ought to be said at this point. The pressures of getting ready for the game next week and for the remainder of the schedule also constrain by "suggesting" things that the coach ought to say and "screening out" things he should not say. The coach has certain rhetorical tasks to do within this framework of constraints. Knowing the constraints and knowing how to make the most of the opportunities they provide are what mark a smart coach who knows how to do the rhetorical part of his job. The coach will see that "right" talk must be talk about what can deliver the most victories (satisfactions for the players and himself). He must therefore find language and actions that encourage the players and build their confidence.

The amount of influence constraints exert on what a persuader says and does may range from absolute prescription to gentle direction. Constraints may prescribe what a persuader can and cannot say and do, leaving limited realistic choices for attempted persuasion. Such prescriptiveness is situational, of course. It is obvious that you would not show up to give the main address of Phi Beta Kappa installation ceremonies wearing hiking clothes and carrying a lantern and a knapsack. Nor would a judge mount the bench dressed in a lounging robe and smoking a cigar. Neither would a smart attorney spend time on topics the judge had declared irrelevant to the case. For successful communication, one must dress and behave in a manner appropriate to specific situations, but there are always *some*

X | rhetorical freedoms in any situation/Constraints, however rigid, pre-
scribe rhetorical necessities, but they also are the seats of rhetorical
possibilities/

In the case of the football coach, the situation clearly prescribed
his rhetorical task—he had to repair the psychological damage the
loss had done to the confidence and optimism of the players. How the
coach could go about accomplishing this depended upon his reading
of what would be most appropriate to say, what would be the best
way to say it, and how much should be said and how much left un-
said. He might point out that the reason the team lost was because of
correctable mistakes: the quarterback tried to force a pass that was
picked off and run back for a score; what would have been the winning touchdown was called back because a lineman jumped off side.
He might compliment the players for not giving up after falling behind and for almost pulling the game out. He might stress that the
remaining opponents are less strong, that if the team wins the rest of
its games, it can still go to a major bowl, and that the next opponent,
hated State U, is probably gloating over the loss and predicting that
the team will fold in the next game. He might talk about the proud,
winning tradition of their school and about the comeback spirit of
great teams in school history. He might tell them that he is proud of
them, that they had played hard and well, and that the other team
had just too much depth or had a "pro league" quarterback playing
college ball, etc., etc. Thus, the term *constraints* implies freedom
within limitations.

Constraints, then, both prescribe *limitations* and describe *possibilities* for rhetorical activities in any situation. They are always
present to influence a persuader's choices of responses or strategies.
In every rhetorical situation these six considerations will constrain—
in both positive and limiting ways:

1. The potential for modification of the urgency.
2. The capacity of the readers/ listeners to alter the urgency.
3. The readiness of the readers/listeners to be influenced.
4. The occasion—the immediate circumstances in which the
   communication takes place.
5. Relevant aspects of the persuader's self-system.

6. The persuader's real and apparent purposes in communi- (
cating.

These six "facts" about all rhetorical situations have variable importance as situations change. [It is the interrelationship—the interplay— of these factors that must be "read" by communicators and by
those who interpret and evaluate communications] For communicator
or observer, the question to be asked and answered is: What rhetorical
strategies best meet (met) the limitations and possibilities these facts
invoke(d) *when considered together?*

Constraints/Satisfactions and Rhetorical Configurations

In looking at the interplay among constraints/satisfactions in a
communicative situation, the natural question to ask first is: What is
the persuader's (persuaders') intention? Before you can evaluate *any*
human action you have to think about the purpose behind the action.
Why is that action being taken? What does the person want to accomplish by it? You can't make a realistic assessment of how well a
persuader uses rhetoric or how rhetoric functions to change a situation without making assumptions about what the persuaders are after. What do the communicators hope to achieve by their talk? Why
do they want to do this? Who is to be influenced? In what way?

The next thing one wants to know about the interplay among
constraints and satisfactions is: How well does the basic thrust, or
theme, of what is said fit the potential for modifying the urgency? In
answering this question one must focus on the *ultimate reason* for the
communication. Contrary to what may come naturally to mind, the
ultimate purpose of talk is *not* to induce change in readers or listeners.
That is an intermediate step toward the ultimate goal of applying
pressure on the urgency. [Persuaders talk in hopes of changing read-
ers/listeners, so that they will be encouraged to exert pressure on the
state of affairs that provoked communication or made it possible] The
communicator hopes to induce readers/listeners to see the urgency
somewhat differently from the way they formerly saw it and, in consequence, act differently toward whatever creates or sustains the urgency. Perhaps they will be moved to vote in a special way, buy
certain things or boycott them, contribute money or services, sell

holdings, join organizations, or in other ways produce changes in whatever exigence it is that makes the communication possible or necessary. This is always the ultimate target of rhetorical discourse. As Aristotle pointed out, communication is the principal agent of social change and the effecting of social change is the ultimate function of communication.

As an urgency changes, its potential for modification also changes. This means that both urgencies themselves and their potentials for change are dynamic. The potential for modification that an urgency has at any given moment constrains the possible rhetorical choices or satisfactions offered by a persuader. In sum, communication only works to change an urgency when (1) its basic thrust or theme (2) fits (3) the kind and amount of change that potentially could be made in the provoking urgency (4) by the readers/listeners (5) as influenced by the persuaders and their messages, under the circumstances of the occasion.

All successful communication serves to modify urgencies, even private talk that has no general social significance. Recently during a best ball of partners golf tournament, my teammate gave me some pointers as we were walking off the third green. He said I had my hands too far down the shaft of the putter and was moving slightly when striking the ball. As a result I was hitting the ball off line, pulling it to the left of the hole. I had already missed two makable putts. My partner was not engaging in frivolous banter. He wanted to modify our personal urgency of scoring as well as possible in the tournament. If his advice enabled me to make more of the putts I should make, our competitiveness as a team would correspondingly improve.

The same ideas also explain why some public rhetoric works to modify important social urgencies and why other public rhetoric does not work. An example of unsuccessful public rhetoric is President Ronald Reagan's attempts to reduce the furor over the Iran-Contra affair. During the late fall of 1986 Mr. Reagan enjoyed an affectionate relationship with the American people, and the polls said that more than 60 percent approved the way he was handling the job of President. It would require what was perceived to be a major mistake of policy to threaten his presidency. Although some observers thought the Reagan administration was "running out of gas," most persons

warmly supported the President through a series of foreign policy encounters: the Nicholas Daniloff exchange; the Libya disinformation
scheme; Reykjavik; the Nicaraguan capture and trial of American
mercenary Eugene Hasenfus.[10] Then came the bombshell of selling
arms to Iran and converting the profits into a fund for the Nicaraguan
Contras. Mr. Reagan's performance rating in the polls dropped dramatically. As the story began to emerge, a *Newsweek* poll taken on
December 4–5 found that "only 10 percent of a national sampling
believed that he was telling the truth about the Contra funding and
that only 23 percent believed he was doing all he could to uncover
the facts."

Mr. Reagan's initial reaction was to distance himself from the
crisis and wait for the storm to blow itself out. But by the end of the
first week of December he apparently concluded he must make a
more open and conciliatory statement of his position. His radio talk
of December 6 was not a full disclosure of his part in the affair, however. It was a damage-control endeavor. Mr. Reagan hoped that his
generalized assertions (essentially, his admission that "the execution
of these policies was flawed and mistakes were made" and his promise
to cooperate fully with the investigations of the affair) would match
adequately the constraints of the situation. If his communication convinced those who listened to the talk on the radio, read the text in the
papers, and/or followed accounts of it in the media, they would be
encouraged to speak up in his support, publicly and privately.
Thereby they might influence others, who in turn might influence
still others. In this way criticism of his administration would be allayed somewhat and Reagan's credibility would be repaired to some
extent. Then, later at the right times, bold rhetoric and policy initia-
tives could further improve the standing of the administration.

Like everyone else, of course, Mr. Reagan had to wait for events
to unfold before he could learn whether the basic thrust of his communication matched the potential for modification in the urgency. As
the matter dragged into 1987, it became apparent that while Mr. Reagan's rhetoric in his radio talk and in his subsequent televised speech
on March 4 may have been steps in the right direction, they did not
improve his credibility. The urgency of Mr. Reagan's administration
may have even worsened somewhat.

One of the miscalculations the President made in both his radio talk and TV speech was implicitly to expect his readers/listeners to do what they could not do. Even if the President had been able to win over substantial numbers of his readers and listeners, which he was not able to do, they could not have favorably influenced the larger public opinion by relaying Mr. Reagan's general assertions of probity and innocence. Public opinion simply was not receptive to such generalizations. Thus, the basic thrust, or theme, of Mr. Reagan's two speeches did not fit the kind and amount of change that potentially could be made in the provoking urgency by the readers/listeners. In following months there were countless other efforts by great numbers of persuaders, including Mr. Reagan, to influence the situation. Gradually the urgency wore itself out, its energies diverted into new political, social, and constitutional urgencies. However, this particular urgency was little modified by the Reagan administration's rhetorical efforts.

There is a third question that naturally occurs when one thinks about the interplay among constraints and satisfactions in a communication: How well does the persuader(s) select rhetorical options that match the readiness of readers/listeners to be influenced? Although the ultimate reason for giving a speech, writing an editorial, or issuing a policy statement is to cause desired change in a provoking urgency, any persuader's *immediate* objective is to induce change in those who read or hear the communication. There are several such potential changes. Readers and listeners can be influenced concerning the way they perceive an urgency, the person(s) attempting to persuade them, and the remedial actions being proposed. They can also be influenced concerning a persuader's relationship to the urgency and to themselves as participants in the communication. Furthermore, if communication takes place in face-to-face situations, listeners can be influenced concerning their relationship to other listeners. All of these possibilities must be borne in mind if an interested observer is to estimate what is rhetorically possible in a configuration.

How much change and what kind of change readers/listeners are willing and able to sustain depends on the nature of their self-systems and the ways they respond to the provoking urgency, the persuader(s), and the communicative occasion. What successful persuaders choose to say and how they choose to say it are conditioned by their perceptions about the readiness of the readers and listeners. These rhetorical choices are further conditioned by the persuader's own self-system and rhetorical intent. The interplay among all of these factors determines how well rhetorical satisfactions fit rhetorical constraints.

When my golfing partner told me what I was doing wrong in my putting stroke, he found me an eager listener. I knew I was not comfortable over the ball, but I couldn't figure out why. My partner had won several important tournaments, and I trusted his judgment. Going over in my mind how I had felt when hitting the errant putts, I knew instantly that what he had said was right. I also knew how to correct the putts on the next green. Thus, my partner's immediate purpose to induce change in me was achieved: what he said and the way he said it fit my readiness and ability to be influenced. Too, as I mentioned earlier, my partner's ultimate purpose was to modify the provoking urgency—that is, to make our team more competitive in the tournament. This also was achieved: the changes he induced me to make caused me to play better, and therefore we moved up in the standings.

Conversely, Mr. Reagan's communications about the Iran-Contra affair failed to accomplish either his *immediate* objective of convincing readers/listeners or his *ultimate* objective of influencing the provoking urgency. Despite their affection for him personally, most readers/listeners were negative about trading arms for hostages and skeptical concerning his professed role in the matter. Mr. Reagan's rhetoric did not give them adequate reason to change their minds. Because the readers and listeners were not won over, they would not attempt to apply the pressure on the urgency that Mr. Reagan wanted. Despite the President's record of rhetorical triumphs, in this case he did not select rhetorical options that matched the readiness of readers/listeners to be influenced.

What I have been talking about in this chapter I call the *basic assessments* of a rhetorical configuration. In the chapters that follow I shall discuss such assessments in fuller detail.

Basic Assessments of Rhetoric

Chapter Four

Importance of Rhetorical Intentions

As soon as we become aware that someone is trying to communicate, we wonder why the person is making the effort. We ask: What does he or she *want?* We know from experience that people communicate because they want someone else to change in some way. When it is not automatically clear what a persuader wants—what his or her intentions are—we make assumptions about it. Even if we assess intentions inaccurately, we will presume that practical intentions are present and that we can guess what they are. If we are forced to say we can't even guess what a communicator's intentions are, we'll be saying the communication is pointless; but even that is an assessment. Where we feel that practical objectives *ought* to be present, we either try to understand those objectives or we declare the communicator doesn't really understand what he or she is doing.

The Assumption of Intent

The thesis of this chapter is: *We can't make any qualitative judgments about any human actions, including rhetorical actions, without assuming something about why those actions were taken.* That assumption will always be a judgment about probabilities—ranging from "possibly true" to "proved beyond any reasonable doubt." We can't evaluate anything without thinking about what it is supposed to be for. Not infrequently an NFL quarterback will throw a pass well out of bounds, perhaps ten or fifteen yards from the nearest potential receiver. A terrible pass? Not at all. The voice of the color analyst informs us, "Another smart move by the quarterback. He saw that all his receivers were covered, and he threw it away. There's no point in

47

risking an interception; so he threw it out of the playing area, but not
so far that he would be called for intentional grounding." The analogy
to football is imperfect, but it makes the point that before one can
evaluate performance, one must have a notion of what the performer
wished to accomplish. Without this judgment, we can't judge how
well he or she (or they) used the available means of rhetoric to influence the flow of events. To tell ourselves anything about how well a
communication fits the configuration of influencing forces in an exigential flow, we must know or presume *what kind of fit* was being
sought. If a speaker talks about energy, we ask and have every right
to ask what, if anything, that speaker wants listeners to *do*. We can't
even listen reasonably without knowing or assuming this much. If a
comedian comments on politics, we will estimate whether he or she
is using irony/satire merely to be funny or also to offer a serious political judgment.

The following examples should make clear that the reasonableness of any analysis or evaluation of communication depends on judgments made about persuaders' intentions. I shall look at the strange
cases of Melancton Smith at the New York Constitutional Ratification
Convention and of defense attorney John Adams in the Boston Massacre trials.

Until recently students have assumed that throughout the New
York Ratification Convention, the articulate anti-Federalist leader
Melancton Smith fought a bitterly tenacious defense against ratification until, finally, his resistance was broken by situational events and/
or by the overwhelming rhetoric of Alexander Hamilton. He then
called upon his followers to vote for ratification.

Students who have accepted the idea that Smith was suddenly
won over by the accumulated impact of Hamilton's oratory have assigned high rhetorical merit to Hamilton's speaking. Smith's alleged
capitulation to Hamilton's arguments is the major supportive evidence of historians John Fiske, Esmond Wright, Louis M. Hacker,
and Broadus Mitchell, who have argued that Hamilton "won the convention to the Constitution by sheer will power," "by the sheer force
of his arguments." The conversion of the original anti-Federal majority of 46–19 to a narrow 30–27 vote for ratification was Hamilton's
"foremost political exploit." Such historians would agree with rheto-

rician Bower Aly's assessment that Hamilton's persuasive effort was "one of the most remarkable on record." They might even concur with Clarence Streit's judgment that Hamilton achieved an "oratorical miracle," the "greatest forensic feat in history."[1] *Incomplete note*

Other students, such as Jackson Turner Main, Linda De Pauw, and Clinton Rossiter, however, believe that Smith was persuaded by events happening in New York and in other states of the Confederation. To Main, Hamilton's "views were so well known in New York that his activity was perhaps more of a liability than an asset to the Federalists." To De Pauw, Hamilton tended to alienate his opponents, and his speeches did not influence the voting. To Rossiter, "While it is pleasant to think that his dazzling oratory on the floor of the convention persuaded . . . anti-Federalists to change their minds and vote for the Constitution . . . the fact is that New York ratified principally because Hamilton raised the specter of a secession by the city and southern counties . . . to convince the anti-Federalists privately that there might be no New York without the Union."[2]

A revisionist study by Robin Brooks advances an interpretation of Smith's rhetorical intent that significantly reinforces the position that Hamilton's speaking in the debates has been greatly exaggerated.[3] Brooks's study points out that Hamilton admitted his "arguments confound but they do not convince" and that Smith retained throughout the convention his disrespect for Hamilton's ideas and arguments. Smith was not converted to ratification by Hamilton's persuasiveness—public or private—but by "objective necessities." He saw distinctly that the consummation of the Union would mean the isolation of the state. During the course of the debates, the Union was effected by the ratification of the ninth state, New Hampshire, and was bolstered by the ratification of the tenth state, Virginia, the most populous and most important of all the states. Furthermore, he was informed concerning the developing separatist sentiment in New York City. As a resident of that burgeoning commercial center, he appreciated the seriousness of the threat to secede from the rest of the state should the convention reject the Constitution.

Fearing the "isolation of the state, the probable secession of New York City, and chaos in the state and party," Smith *determined to change sides*. In correspondence with major turns in the debates, he retreated in designed stages from an antiratification position through gradations of conditional ratification to unconditional acceptance. "Hamilton's speeches only gave Smith the excuse publicly to do what he had long before determined upon as necessary to preserve the peace."/By his strategy of retreat timed in conjunction with Hamilton's speeches, Smith was able to keep peace in his party and win over enough of his colleagues to produce a narrow majority for ratification. Hamilton's arguments and rhetorical strategies converted few, if any, delegates./

According to Brooks, Smith was the real hero of Poughkeepsie. His *deceptive* rhetorical intent enabled him to preserve public amity, maintain party integrity, and bring New York into the Union. If Brooks proves right about Smith's intentions, critics like Fiske, Wright, Hacker, and Mitchell will have been proved dead wrong. Their notion of how communication functioned to win the votes for the Constitution and their estimation of the merit of Hamilton's and Smith's persuasion will be obsolete, appearing even simplistic. The example also illustrates a broader point: Where communication is being judged, we must recognize that purposes can exist *explicitly* in the talk and *implicitly*, not overtly expressed in the talk./We have to study out both because often what is "really" intended is not what is announced. Instead of being "overwhelmed" by Hamilton and other pro-Constitution spokesmen, Smith—according to Brooks—used rhetoric to manipulate both pro- and anti-Constitution forces into the position he wanted.

From the alleged deceptive intent of Melancton Smith, I turn to the implicit intent that John Adams may have had in one of America's famous trials. Until Hiller B. Zobel and L. Kinvin Wroth published the three-volume *Legal Papers of John Adams* and Zobel followed up with *The Boston Massacre*,[4] most students assumed that Adams's sole purpose as defense attorney in the trials of Captain Preston and the British soldiers was to secure verdicts of innocence. Adams's speaking, according to traditionalists like Peter Shaw, "amounted to a grand gesture in defiance of the patriot side."[5] Zobel and Wroth suggest that this view is simplistic, failing to reflect either the realities of the situation or the complexities and nuances of Adams's argument. The "massacre" was "basically insignificant" as a historical event, and this was due in part to Adams's *implicit* intent to protect the reputation of Boston and the patriot cause.

The affair on Boston's King Street was more an exercise in civil disobedience than a massacre. On the night of March 5, 1770, the lone British sentry before the customhouse was threatened by a taunting mob, whose members were armed with a variety of weapons from bricks and chunks of ice to swords. In response to the sentry's call for help, Captain Preston marched a corporal's guard down from the guard house. Fearing that his small force would be overwhelmed, Preston ordered his men to load their muskets. As the crowd surged forward, one of the soldiers was knocked to the ground. The soldiers fired, and five rioters fell mortally wounded. Charged with murder, Preston and the eight soldiers were brought to trial some eight months later. All were found innocent except two soldiers who were convicted of manslaughter and, according to the custom, were branded on the thumb and released.

As a defense attorney for both Preston, whose trial was scheduled first, and for the soldiers, whose trial followed a month later, Adams's *explicit* purpose was clear: to secure acquittals. However, Zobel and Wroth found evidence in the situational data that Adams had to have had an *implicit* purpose that controlled the amount and kind of testimony he permitted as well as the direction and nuances of his defensive argument.

Zobel epitomizes the trials in this way: "No matter what went on at the court, the defendants would not have been executed." In Preston's trial the jury was packed with Crown sympathizers because of peculiarities of the venire system. Zobel argues that the composition of the jury eliminated any reasonable doubt of the outcome: "Before a single witness had been sworn, the outcome of the trial was certain." "The only doubt and excitement depended upon the slender possibility that the evidence would turn out so overwhelmingly unfavorable to Preston that not even a loyalist could avoid his oath." "Apart from that small chance, the trial, as lawyers and judges must have known, was nothing but a propaganda battle. Yet everyone acted as though a life were really at stake. That continuing charade was the most significant aspect of the entire proceedings." In the soldiers' trial the jury was also packed, in the limited sense that it did not include anyone from Boston. This trial was also a charade in that even if the soldiers had been convicted, they knew—and their lawyer, Adams, must have known—that they would receive Royal reprieves and pardons.

To defend the captain and his men, the defense had to establish that the killings were justifiable, that the soldiers feared for their lives. This meant "in effect, prosecuting the entire town of Boston for assault with intent to kill." The fact is that over the past several years, order had disappeared from Boston streets. Patriot leaders, by manipulating the notorious Boston mobs, had paralyzed the Colonial administration and had gained control of the legislature and the courts. John Adams was a solidly entrenched member of the patriot faction. After Adams had accepted the assignment of attorney for the defense and before the start of the trials, his cousin, Sam Adams, the arch-conspirator, engineered John's election to the legislature.

The situational evidence, Adams's personal urgency, and internal evidence from the trials themselves strongly indicate that Adams had an implicit purpose: to protect the reputation of the town of Boston and the patriot cause. Adams carried out his implicit intent by admitting no more testimony that was detrimental to Boston and the patriot cause than was absolutely necessary to secure a not-guilty verdict. In his argument Adams exonerated Bostonians from leading or breeding the riot by blaming it on outside agitators. Zobel and Wroth describe Adams's argument as "a clever casting of fact into a legal matrix, with a clear indication to the jurors of a way to bring in an acquittal and still retain quiet consciences, that is, by ascribing the extraordinary provocation to outside agitators, 'a motley rabble of saucy boys, negroes and molattoes, Irish teagues, and outlandish Jack tarrs.' "

If we accept any part of the interpretations by Zobel and Wroth, we will have to look further than Adams's explicit purpose. Indeed, for almost any legal plea in civil or criminal courts the contending attorneys are likely to have multiple intentions—to gain acquittal, conviction, or some other favorable but intermediate verdict. A wise attorney will calculate and target lesser goals that are possible and also palatable to his side. He or she will seldom reveal these limited intentions explicitly. Thus, in Adams's case it is not reasonable to assume that his explicit plea for acquittal of his clients encapsulated the *whole* of his intentions. Zobel claims that Adams's pleading in the Boston Massacre trials has never been "praised for what it really was, a masterpiece of political tightroping and partisan invective, wrapped inextricably in a skillful, effective jury argument." Whether Zobel is totally correct or not, if we are to evaluate Adams's defense pleas as rhetorical strategies, we need to recognize that his strategies served *both* his explicit intentions and those we suspect he held implicitly.

Can One Learn a Persuader's Intent?

If intelligently viewing communication requires that we understand a persuader's intentions, the question arises: Can a persuader's purposes be determined? The answer is both "yes" and "no." Of course, we cannot know a persuader's intent with certainty. Other people's purposes—or our own, for that matter—can never be judged infallibly. But we have to estimate them anyway. We do it in the courts, politics, religion, as well as in interpreting and evaluating other rhetoric. Virtually all of our social relations hinge on the legitimacy, though not necessarily the certainty, of careful, reasoned assessments of the intentions behind people's actions. A person who tries to interpret and evaluate rhetorical actions needs to take the terms "careful" and "reasoned" very seriously. With *careful* digging, one can usually form *reasoned* conclusions about persuaders' purposes. The firmer those conclusions are, of course, the more confidence one can have in them. And the degree of confidence one's evidence allows is something a fair and just critic ought to incorporate as part of his or her critical judgment. It is useful, therefore, to consider different levels of reasonableness that judgments about rhetorical intentions can have.

When I say that a critic should always be able to draw reasoned conclusions about a persuader's intent, I am not equating "reasoned conclusions" with "certainty" or even with "proved beyond any reasonable doubt." The amount of doubt concerning particular estimates of intent may vary considerably. In the following examples the judgments represent a spectrum of credibility or believability.

In some cases a conclusion about a persuader's intent may be reasoned, but it may have only limited credibility. For example, Robin Brooks's claim that Melancton Smith engineered a deceitful strategy in the New York Ratification Convention qualifies as a "reasoned conclusion"—that is, it is reasonable that Smith had such intentions—but the argument Brooks advances in support of his claim is not wholly persuasive.

The essential data established by Brooks are these: (1) Smith was unimpressed with Hamilton's attempted persuasion during the convention. (2) Smith believed that the Constitution was "radically defective." (3) In the second week of the convention, on June 28, Smith wrote in a letter to Nathan Dane that although New York should ratify the Constitution, the anti-Federalists should push for necessary amendments by calling for ratification with "subsequent conditions"—namely, that New York's ratification would become void unless specified amendments were adopted within one or two years. (4) On July 17 Smith introduced in the convention his proposal for ratification *with subsequent conditions*, and a week later, on July 23, he advocated that the Constitution be adopted *without* reservation.

What do these data tell us about Smith's intent? Not very much, really. It does seem more probable that he was persuaded by "objective necessities" than by Hamilton's oratory. And it is clear that he did change positions during the course of the convention. Beyond this our grasp of things becomes decidedly uncertain. The only evidence cited by Brooks about Smith's private thoughts on convention strategy was his letter to Dane. There is no indication in that letter that Smith planned to do anything except call for amendments, and there is no support for Brooks's assumption that "Smith had already resolved then to get New York into the Union at any hazard." In short, Brooks offers inadequate evidence to prove that "Hamilton's speeches only gave Smith the excuse publicly to do what he had long before determined upon as necessary to preserve the peace." Perhaps Smith deliberately sought to deceive and manipulate delegates, but this intention does not square with his distinctive reputation for candor, sincerity, and simplicity of character. It seems more likely that his actions in debate were those of a troubled, honest man trying to deal with a difficult situation and finally embracing the least troublesome alternative. Whatever his intentions may have been, the practical results of his actions were that his fellow delegates from Dutchess County and Long Island followed his leadership, and the convention ratified the Constitution by a narrow margin. However, we can still accept Brooks's claims that Smith was not a dupe of Hamilton and that he was a "hero" of Poughkeepsie for helping to bring about ratification. We can also agree that Brooks's theory of deceitful intention is provocative and should be considered in any analysis of the proceedings of the convention. Our evaluation has to be, however, that Brooks has failed to produce enough evidence of the right kind to establish a reliable estimation of rhetorical intent.

In other cases the available evidence may establish that a "reasoned conclusion" about intent is strongly believable, or probable, but falls short of proving beyond "any reasonable doubt." There is sufficient evidence to fix as "strongly believable or probable" the thesis of Zobel and Wroth that John Adams had both an explicit purpose of attempting to secure innocence verdicts for Captain Preston and the soldiers in the Boston Massacre trials and an implicit purpose of inflicting as little damage as possible to the reputation of the town and the patriot cause. This thesis does not mean that Adams designedly risked the safety of the defendants (although Preston, Governor Hutchinson, General Gage, and others believed that he did). No lives were actually at stake in the trials, and the evidence overwhelmingly demonstrated that a genuine threat to the physical safety of the soldiers existed in King Street. Minimal use of the available evidence was enough for Adams to prove the menacing nature of the mob, and there was no practical reason for him to admit damning proof that the town and the radical leaders directly contributed to the event.

Inasmuch as there is no extant statement by Adams confirming his alleged implicit intent, one must argue backward from Adams's actions to his intentions. If we assume that Adams intended the probable consequences of his actions, we can infer the state of his mind from what he said and did during the trials and elsewhere. Because

Adams admitted only a minimum of testimony about what led up to the riot, because he quarreled with junior defense attorney Josiah Quincy, Jr., about admitting testimony suggesting a plot against the soldiers, because he threatened to leave the trials unless his wishes were followed, because his argument wrongly exonerated the town from blame in the riots, and because of other evidence, it seems very probable that Adams had an implicit intent. (Specific data like these are missing from Brooks's argument.) Sufficient evidence has not been discovered, however, that would prove Zobel and Wroth's thesis beyond any reasonable doubt.

In still other cases the reasoned conclusion about the persuader's intent may be established beyond any reasonable doubt. For instance, we can be certain that John B. Anderson had a primary and a secondary intent in his speech before the Yale Independent Club, April 26, 1984. (This date was several months before Anderson announced his support for the Democratic Party presidential candidate, Walter Mondale.) Anderson principally wanted to further the cause of his National Unity Party. That is, he wished to encourage the listeners to accept that, because the existing two-party system cannot work and because the National Unity Party meets the requirements for a new party, his NUP answered the needs of the American political system. Secondarily, Anderson wanted to allay curiosity about whether he planned to run for President in 1984. He accomplished this by denying his intention to run and by explaining that he could serve the political cause best by continuing his efforts as chairman of the party. In this situation we may accept that Anderson's intentions are as firmly established as is reasonably possible—because they are confirmed by the speech text, situational data, and the explicit testimony I secured from Anderson and Dianne Taylor, then the executive director of the National Unity Party.

Occasionally one may be unable to establish that a persuader had a particular purpose—only that he or she must have had, say, one or two or three possible purposes. The judgment of how well that person used rhetoric, then, may differ according to the different possible purposes. For example, we cannot fix that Lincoln had *a* particular purpose in his First Inaugural Address. We can say, however,

that beyond any reasonable doubt he had one or more of three purposes, two of which are quite similar.

One of Lincoln's possible purposes in his First Inaugural has
been advanced by Kenneth M. Stampp and Charles W. Ramsdell.[6]
Whether or not he desired peace, Lincoln considered that war was
inevitable and that preservation of the Union could be achieved only
through recourse to arms. Because there was no alternative to war,
Lincoln designed his Inaugural to mask his hidden commitment to
conflict by simulating a posture of generous, peaceful conciliation and
defense. Because it was self-defeating to strive for peace, Lincoln
planned his rhetorical strategies in the Inaugural to coordinate with
his unfolding executive policies by which he sought to maneuver the
Confederates into initiating the conflict or to create a situation that
would eventuate in the Southerners' shooting first. The major function of the Inaugural was to develop a soothing image of benevolence
and peaceful restraint for the Union government and for Lincoln's
presidential leadership. Thus, the incubus for beginning hostilities
would more easily be placed upon the South.

A second interpretation of Lincoln's rhetorical intent in the Inaugural is advanced by Richard Current.[7] It is that although Lincoln
may not have believed that war was inevitable, he considered it very
probable. War was preferable to secession, however. The preservation
of the Union and of the Republican Party depended upon his taking
a strong position against secession. If war came, it would be short and
not very costly in lives lost and property destroyed. Therefore, Lincoln's purpose in the Inaugural was to present a firm yet conciliatory
stance that orchestrated his stated policies and subsequent actions in
such a way that if hostilities occurred, they would necessarily be initiated by the Confederates.

A third interpretation of Lincoln's intent conforms more closely
to the prevailing conception of Lincoln's inherently peaceful nature.
Essentially initiated by Lincoln himself in his explanatory Message to
Congress in Special Session, July 4, 1861, and more fully developed
by historian David M. Potter and others,[8] this theory postulates that
Lincoln not only wished peace but also, perhaps until actual hostilities began, believed that by following the proper course he might be

able to maintain the peace. Lincoln's fundamental purpose in the Inaugural was to promote a tranquilized period of "masterly inactivity." He wanted to give Unionist sentiment in the South an unharried opportunity to prevail by, on the one hand, upholding Federal authority but, on the other hand, allaying fears of the South and avoiding any suggestion of threat or coercion. Thus, unprovoked and unchallenged, the people of the South would realize that their interests could best be protected within the Union. In short, Lincoln wanted to do everything he could to ease tensions between the sections and to promote reunification.

There are several interpretations we could make about Lincoln's purposes, depending on the way we choose to look at this piece of rhetoric. We could accept all three as being credible and develop an alternative analysis for each of them. We could choose one of the purposes as being most credible, say the third purpose, because it conforms most closely to traditional views of the state of affairs and of Lincoln himself. We could assume some mix of the purposes. Or we could focus our attention on the common theme among the purposes: whichever may have been the "true" intent, all presuppose that he wanted to keep things "cool" for the time being.[9]

When judging communication we should recognize that purposes can exist explicitly, in the talk, and/or implicitly, not in the talk. Often what is "really" intended is not what is announced. The Calhoun case, which I shall pick up in the next chapter, illustrates such a circumstance. Calhoun seems to "say" that he is laying down ultimatums—not a very persuasive tack in most cases. It is when we look behind the scenes for what may have implicitly guided his behavior that we come upon possible goals that meet tests of reasonableness. In other rhetoric we might find quite the opposite case, as when a lawyer argues: "My client was elsewhere at the time, so he couldn't have committed the crime." Given the strictures of legal debate, we would have little reason for suspecting there was something else "behind" claiming the client's innocence. In other cases explicit purposes and implicit aims may be equally important. No matter which of the interpretations concerning Lincoln's First Inaugural Address is accepted, there is no question but that the address must be judged as having an explicit purpose of cooling things off if possible *and* a longer-range, implicit aim or aims about which scholars still disagree.

The points to be understood, then, are: (1) some assumptions about purposes *must* be made in order to judge rhetoric; (2) *both* explicit and implicit intentions may need to be sought as far as data will allow; and (3) by following rather simple procedures one can make reasonable, communicable judgments about intent in any communication.

Chapter Five

Determining Rhetorical Intentions

Any attempt to discover rhetorical intentions should be open-ended. If we mean to be genuinely thoughtful, we should keep those judgments about intentions open to revision wherever evidence warrants revision. For example, in studying Calhoun's March 4 speech I searched at length, but unsuccessfully, for evidence that would modify my rather unusual, final estimate of the South Carolinian's intentions. All the data I uncovered supported my preliminary findings. It is on the basis of my inability to find justifications for revision that I offer a reasoned and supported critical judgment about his intentions. That is what one aims for in criticism of rhetoric—reasoned and supported judgments. Fortunately, finding reasons and supports is usually not as complex a process as I was forced into in dealing with Calhoun. It is usually possible to estimate a persuader's intent by looking at characteristics of the communication(s) and its circumstances.

Analyzing Communication and Its Circumstances

The basic way to judge what a persuader wants to get out of talk is to look at the external constraints on the communication(s) and then at what the persuader says and does in response to these constraints.

External Constraints on a Communication

Inasmuch as what persuaders say and do are attempts to "satisfy," or answer, the demands upon their communication, a starting point in assessing their intentions is to look at the constraints they faced.

One of these external constraints is the *provoking urgency.* What is the nature of the exigence that made a rhetorical response possible or necessary? For communication to exert maximum influence on an urgency, the readers/listeners must be encouraged, either overtly or implicitly, to apply appropriate force to the state of affairs. It is a waste of effort to ask them to do what they can't do or won't do. Therefore, the nature of the urgency confronting a persuader suggests to some extent the character of his or her rhetorical intent. Let me explore this notion by returning to Calhoun's March 4 speech. A starting point in estimating Calhoun's rhetorical intentions in this speech is to study the urgencies that provoked the great senatorial debates of 1850.

Even the most hasty review of the sectional crisis of 1850 demonstrates that several slavery-related developments converged into an urgency demanding congressional action. A war had been fought with Mexico. According to many Northern Whigs it was fought for the purpose of acquiring potential slave territories for the South. More than a million square miles were added to the national domain. The Wilmot Proviso, proscribing slavery in the acquired territories, passed the House of Representatives twice, but stalled in the Senate. By 1850 the great stretches of Utah and New Mexico required territorial recognition and government. Texas troops were primed to invade New Mexico for the third time in disagreement over their joint boundary line. Texas was demanding that the federal government take over its bonded indebtedness, to compensate for having yielded control over customs duties collected within the state. A highly energetic Texas bondholders' lobby was buttonholing senators and representatives in Washington, and there was much talk of bribery in the air. Southerners were demanding the passage and enforcement of a more effective fugitive slave law. Radicals were demanding the abolition of slavery and slave trade in the District of Columbia. Under the compulsion to provide civil government for its hordes of gold-seeking immigrants, California had drawn up and ratified a constitution, elected a legislature, chosen and dispatched representatives to Congress, and had applied for statehood—bypassing the territorial stage. Each of these forces and others helped to shape the developing urgency that provoked the congressional debates on the Compromise of 1850.

To understand such an array of events and forces, we must look to see whether they had any collective *patterning* or *focusing* effects on the specific circumstances we are studying. In this case it is easy to recognize that the flow of events added up to a decisive confrontation between the dominant North and the weakening South. The slavery-related challenges and issues demanded immediate resolution, and the only agency that could provide it was the Congress. How these issues were solved would determine the fate of slavery and the future of Calhoun, his planter class, and the South in general. This was the overall urgency that speakers, especially Calhoun, faced in 1850.

Another external constraint on communication that helps to explain a persuader's probable intent is the *nature of the audience* addressed. How ready the readers and listeners are to be influenced by a message conditions the way they respond to what is said and, derivatively, the way they eventually influence the urgency. Successful persuaders accept that the potential responsiveness of audiences constrains what they can successfully do and say. Therefore, one is in a better position to judge what a persuader hoped to accomplish if one acquires knowledge about the relevant views of the audience he or she faced. Again, I illustrate with Calhoun's speech.

All Northern senators and all Southern senators, except a handful of radical Democrats, opposed Calhoun's well-known remedies for the sectional crisis.

Knowing this disposition of Calhoun's listeners helps to solve the puzzle of his rhetorical intent. The hostility of Calhoun's audience to his ideas causes me to question whether the South Carolinian actually expected others to endorse his remedies at that time. This emerging doubt alerts me to the possibility that I need to dig deeper to determine Calhoun's real purpose. Perhaps he had an implicit purpose as well as an explicit one? Perhaps he had no intent to persuade? My suspicions, thus aroused, will condition the way I unravel the remainder of the evidence.

In the case of oral talk a third external constraint that helps an observer to estimate a persuader's intent is the *speaking occasion*. A speaking occasion brings speaker and listeners together at a particular time and, in the case of face-to-face communication, a particular

place. Such an occasion is always a convergence of physical and psychological circumstances that constrain a persuader's efforts.

An occasion for oral communication is often an assemblage that
occurs in response to a provoking state of affairs—as when a university's board of trustees meets in response to the state legislature's proposed cut in appropriations. Under such circumstances the nature of
the occasion tells one a great deal about a speaker's probable intent.
Why? Because a successful persuader must respond directly to the
purpose of a meeting like this, otherwise a jarring and evident incompatibility would exist between the communication and the listeners'
expectations. At other times an occasion for oral persuasion is a regularly scheduled meeting of an established organization. Such meetings may possess only a general cohesiveness of purpose, as in the
case of a bimonthly meeting of the Economic Club of Detroit. Or the
audience may have a clear purpose for attending, as in the case with
most annual stockholders' meetings. In general, the clearer we can be
about the purpose(s) of an occasion, the clearer we can be about how
the occasion conditions, or could condition, the intentions of persuaders who appear. On the other hand, when persuasion doesn't seem to
address the immediate urgency that provoked a situation, we have
reason to suspect either (1) that the persuader was woefully inept, or
(2) that the persuader had some ulterior, implicit purpose in addressing the audience.

A look at the occasion for Calhoun's speech provides several insights into what his intentions *could* be and what they probably were.
Plainly he did not address the "adjustive" concerns of his audience
and the congressional occasion.

The occasion for Calhoun's March 4 speech was a session of the
United States Senate. The session was convened at Calhoun's request
to hear his response to the sectional crisis and to the compromise
measures proposed by Senator Henry Clay. This information tells me
that, except under the most unusual circumstances, Calhoun would
design his speech to meet these specific demands of the occasion.

Furthermore, this particular occasion focused intense public attention on Calhoun's speech. What he said would be widely reported
by the nation's press, enabling him to reach a far more extensive

audience than the assembled senators and their guests. When I add this information to what I already know about the opposition of senators to his position/I have further reason to suspect that Calhoun had little expectation of immediately converting his listeners and that he therefore may have had some other, implicit purpose./

Persuaders' Proferred Satisfactions in Relation to the Impinging Constraints

After one examines the external constraints upon a communication, the natural thing to do is to study what a persuader does in response to the constraints. In other words, if one knows what the communicator was up against, one needs to look at what he or she did about it. There are several basic kinds of rhetorical satisfactions, or strategies, that characterize any communication: (1) the basic thesis of the communication; (2) the substance of what is said; (3) the arrangement of the ideas; (4) the language with which the ideas are clothed; and (5) the paralinguistic characteristics that accompany the formal language.

Basic Thesis

The basic thesis, or basic thrust, of a communication is its apparent focus. It is what a persuader says or does to let the persuadees know what is expected from them.

Sometimes a persuader's basic thesis expressly states the nature of the influence the audience is expected to exert on the flow of events—as, "Register and vote in this election. Your vote and that of others like you can put a stop to big spending and big government." In such a case one may tentatively assume that the explicit thrust represents the explicit purpose of the persuader—albeit further research may modify this estimation.

In his speech Calhoun explicitly demanded that Northern senators and the people of the North act positively on these ultimatums:

1. accept total blame for the decline of the South relative to the strength of the North;
2. return all fugitive slaves;
3. cease agitating the slavery question;

4. provide for a constitutional amendment that would restore the South's former equilibrium of power with the North;
5. concede to the South an equal "right" in the territories acquired from Mexico;
6. reject California's admission to the Union as a state.

Calhoun also said that if the Northern senators and people of the North failed to capitulate to his demands and accepted California as a state, the Southern senators and the people of the South should embrace secession.

/I may tentatively infer that Calhoun had the explicit intent of putting a series of ultimatums to the North and of demanding that the South secede should the North fail to yield/Based on the information I have secured up to this point, however, I am confused as to whether Calhoun was satisfied to make a militant statement, whether he actually sought to persuade his hearers, or whether he had a "hidden agenda." This is the status of my investigation so far: (1) I know that it was virtually impossible that Northern senators would accept his demands. (2) Even if the senators did capitulate, they had authority to address only the last three of Calhoun's demands. (3) Even if the senators did pass legislation in response to these three demands, the House of Representatives, the President, and the people of the North would refuse to concur. (4) Southern senators, except for a few, were opposed to presenting ultimatums to the North, and they were not prepared for secession. (5) And even if Southern senators had favored secession at that time, the Southern people were not ready to leave the Union.

It looks at this point as if Calhoun pressed an unrealistic set of demands on the Senate./But, one asks, why would a knowledgeable political leader follow such an absurd course? [To try to clear up this confusion, I shall later examine the other satisfactions Calhoun offered in the speech.

Sometimes a persuader's basic thesis does not directly call for specific action. Instead, it may state, or imply, that readers/listeners should exert force on the state of affairs in a manner, time, and place of their own choosing. For example, although their works did not expressly call for readers to engage in any specific action, even casual readers would know that William H. Harvey through his fictional monologue *Coin's Financial School* sought to enlist them in the cause for free silver. They would know that Hodding Carter through his novel *The Winds of Fear* wished to arouse them against interracial hatred and violence. They would know that Thomas J. Peters and Robert H. Waterman, Jr., through their bestseller *In Search of Excellence* wanted to motivate people to improve managerial practices by applying "lessons from America's best-run companies." So whether it is stated or merely implied, the basic thesis of a communication tells a great deal about a persuader's probable intent.

Substance

By "substance" I mean the logical and psychological content of a message: the arguments, reasoning, inferences, evidence, and appeals that a persuader uses to develop his or her basic thesis. By examining what is said, one may find reason to reaffirm, question, or modify previously drawn assumptions about intent. Consider again what can be learned from studying the substance of Calhoun's speech.

Calhoun made only one substantive attempt to link his basic thesis with Northerners' interests. He tried to make Northerners fear that the Union would be destroyed if his demands were not met. However, unless the Northerners believed Calhoun spoke for a united South, they would not respond as Calhoun seemed to want them to. Further, Calhoun offered no proof that he spoke for more than a few Southerners.

I have already discovered that all but a handful of Southerners still had some faith in the political process and thought that some modus vivendi might be worked out. Although they accepted the principle of secession, most were not yet ready to apply it. They were, in short, much more optimistic than Calhoun. Therefore, except for Calhoun's censure of Northern actions, there was little substance in his speech that matched Southern senators' predispositions and beliefs.

Given these observations, the substance of Calhoun's speech further reinforces my impression that he did not have any realistic expectation of changing minds. He must have had some other reasons for speaking as he did at this time, for he was not a wholly inept politician.

Disposition

"Disposition" is the sequential arrangement, the unfolding development, of the substance of communication. One asks how persuaders structure the beginnings and endings, the major and minor contentions, the supporting evidence, the transitional statements, and so on. One may sometimes gain helpful insights by asking questions like these: To what extent does the persuader emphasize points by placing them first and last in a series, or by assigning comparatively greater coverage to them? To what extent do persuaders minimize or hide points by burying them in the middles of series, or by neglecting their development? Do the persuaders focus attention clearly on the concepts inherent in their basic theses by presenting a limited number of major contentions—ordinarily no more than a half-dozen? Are the contentions arranged into a logical progression, demonstrating that the persuader's thesis is good/bad, true/false, or desirable/undesirable?

Asking such questions should reveal whether the disposition closely furthers the basic intent of persuasion. If it doesn't, one should check whether other data suggest that this "dis-order" could be the simple result of incompetence, confusion, haste, or the like. If so, little can be inferred about intention from the dis-order. However, if other data suggest that dis-order is not typical of the persuaders' rhetorical practices, there may be reason to ask whether the persuaders may have had some hidden purposes that differ from their explicit intentions as indicated by the basic thesis.

A look at the way Calhoun put his speech together reinforces my growing doubts that he actually hoped to accomplish his basic thesis.

Calhoun devoted his first six thousand words to his claim that the South believed she could no longer remain safely in the Union because of continuing Northern aggressions. He used his next five thousand words to explain how the Union could *not* be saved. In two hundred words he asserted that the only way to save the Union was for the North to satisfy the South that "she could remain honorably and safely in the Union." Then, in about a hundred and fifty words he stated the unnegotiable conditions that the North must meet to satisfy the South and thereby prevent secession. Finally, he charged the North with complete responsibility for saving the Union and stated that the time had come to determine the fate of the Union. Thus, he gave startlingly little attention to his plans for remedial action, in contrast to the extensive coverage he assigned to the problem and to proposed remedies that would not work. This is not at all the typical proportioning of communication aimed at immediate persuasion.

Calhoun's structuring intensifies my doubt that he hoped to persuade Northerners to accept his demands. If he had seriously hoped to convince them, he should have (1) devoted far greater attention to explaining his demands and to demonstrating that they were workable and feasible and (2) offered proof that the South solidly supported his position.

I do not know whether Calhoun understood that only a handful of Southern senators accepted his views. But if he did know this, he should have perceived that, before he could change their minds, he had to build into his speech proofs that the South had *no* alternative: She must secede if the North refused to yield.

Because the structure of Calhoun's speech does not provide the focus and emphasis necessary for persuasion, I have additional reason to doubt that the explicit thesis mirrored the Senator's rhetorical intent.

Language

By "language" I mean the words persuaders use to represent their thoughts and to stir up desired meanings and feelings in their receivers. For example, what language is used and how it is used are major clues to whether a communicator is joking, being ironic, or has serious persuasive intentions. The biblical language and rhythms of Lincoln's Gettysburg Address are a major reason critics have said Lincoln offered a "prayer" of dedication. The rhythms, parallelisms, and antitheses that occurred so frequently in John F. Kennedy's speeches made it plain that he intended to persuade and exhort, and

[handwritten annotation: intention -- how do these features contribute to "reflect"]

to do so forcefully. The Mobil Oil company's restrained language in its "advertorials" is intended to convey the impression that the corporation is reflective in a "citizenly" way—that it is not exclusively concerned with sales and profits. In sum, the language used very often helps us judge what persuaders are up to.

The language Calhoun used on March 4, 1850, shows that his word choices lacked the appropriateness and the objectivity that are necessary in persuading hostile or doubting audiences. This fact gives us further reason to question whether he genuinely expected to convert others to his position *at this time.*

Calhoun's language was consistently antagonistic and coercive to Northerners. Sometimes it was even insulting. The only way that the bias of Calhoun's language could have fostered identification by Northerners was by emphasizing his threat of secession. However, inasmuch as Northern senators did not believe that the South would secede, this underscoring of an improbable threat would not encourage acceptance of his position, although it may have caused some Northerners to be more favorably inclined toward compromise.

Except for reflections of his strong pro-Southern bias, Calhoun's words had little potential to encourage Southerners to identify with *[handwritten annotation: why?]* his ultimatum to the North or with his conditional demand for secession. Also, his language was too intense for Southern senators who wished to avoid or delay a final confrontation with the North.

Because the appropriateness and objectivity of Calhoun's language was not conducive to persuading listeners to accept the thrust of his speech, it gives added reason to question whether his explicit thesis fully represented his rhetorical intent.

Paralanguage

In all communication a fifth type of rhetorical satisfaction, paralanguage, may give clues to communicators' intentions. "Paralanguage" refers to those aspects of communication that do not directly involve use of formal language. In newspapers and magazines print size, color, and form of type, allocation of space, and other features of layout can signal what substance is being emphasized or played down. This in turn can indicate the real intentions of the communicator(s).

In oral communication vocal and physical delivery and personal cha-
risma function as paralinguistic indicators of intentions./ If one is
looking at television, the features of oral paralanguage blend with (or
are discordant with) makeup, camera angles, and backgrounds, suggesting what those creating the presentation intend. A clear example
is provided by Ronald Reagan's first presidential inaugural address. It
was staged in a position from which television cameras could pan to
the crowd before him, over them down the monument-lined Mall,
and across the Potomac River to Arlington Cemetery. Reagan devoted
a considerable portion of his speech to the heroism of the entire
America citizenry, including the famous leaders whose monuments
were in view, the war dead, and ordinary citizens such as those in
the immediate audience. He specifically referred to these features
of the long vista shown by the television cameras. The paralinguistics
of the staging and camera shots subtly, almost incontrovertibly, confirmed that Reagan intended to stress his unusually inclusive version
of "heroism."

Interpreting clues from paralanguage is not always easy, however. An observer's perceptions are always subjective; in the media of
mass communication there is always a question of *who* controlled the
paralingistics, and the evidence tends to be limited and transitory.
Unless captured on tape or film, nonverbal data are ephemeral; even
when preserved, they are apt to be isolated and distorted, having
been lifted out of the total context.

An example of the hazards of deducing rhetorical intent from
characteristics of paralanguage is afforded by one of George Will's
syndicated columns. During the political campaign of 1984, Will
wrote that Vice-President George Bush looked "goofy" in posing as
"Professor Bush the semanticist," "Boy George the cheerleader," and
"the macho preppie with the tongue of a teamster." According to correspondent Will, Bush's posturing "has turned the 1984 election into
the first primary of 1988 and, though unopposed, he has lost it. That
is like losing a monologue with yourself." Examining film clips of the
campaign could possibly document Will's assessment of Bush's paralanguage. However, a conjectural jump exists from recognizing that
Bush's behavior was incompatible with his customary cool, detached,

and gentlemanly manner to accepting Will's conclusion that Bush's actions were deliberate attempts to curry favor with right-wing Republicans for the 1988 presidential nomination. Any such conclusions concerning Bush's intent would have to be verified by extensive data of other kinds.

In my illustrative study I can get some help in estimating Calhoun's intent from the paralinguistic characteristics of his speech.

Because he was suffering from the terminal stages of tuberculosis and from heart trouble (he died later that month), Calhoun remained seated while his speech was read aloud by his friend Senator James Mason of Virginia. Calhoun's original choice for a reader had been his senatorial colleague from South Carolina, Andrew P. Butler. When Butler excused himself because of poor eyesight, Calhoun's selection of Mason had highly significant paralinguistic implications: Mason was the principal author of the new, more stringent fugitive slave bill that was awaiting congressional approval. Calhoun could have found other senators who were less symbolically objectionable to Northerners. Therefore, Calhoun's selection of Mason suggests that he was not thinking of conciliation or persuasion, but of coercion and confrontation.

It is probably true that Calhoun's fragile appearance stirred some sympathy among senators. But it is very unlikely that this sympathy extended to his "radical" ideas, and I have found no evidence that he deliberately sought to exploit his appearance as an instrument of persuasion.

My study of the strategic satisfactions offered by Calhoun makes me think it even more unlikely that his explicit thesis represented his persuasive intention. He must have had something else in mind. At this point I have to recognize that I can't find out what Calhoun wanted to do by merely examining the external constraints on his speech and his rhetorical responses to them.

Exploiting a Persuader's Self-System

Fortunately, in most cases of intentionality one doesn't have to explore a persuader's self-system. One can get a good enough handle on what a person wants from his or her readers/listeners by studying the communication and its circumstances. For instance, a casual reader of William Poole's article "The First Nine Months of School" in a copy of *Hippocrates*, a magazine of health and medicine, might suspect that the author had more in mind than an intent to inform about the "humanness" of life in the womb. Such a reader would probably be satisfied to view the piece against the author's explicit intention to inform and his possible implicit desire to shape beliefs and behaviors about abortion. As another example, when Bill White, a six-time All-Star player and veteran of eighteen years as a New York Yankees' broadcaster, was selected to become the National League president, a press conference was called. Now, obviously race was a matter of consequence here, because White was the first black to head an American professional sports league and because the heat had been on baseball for its reluctance to hire black managers and top front-office administrators. Nevertheless, the head of the search committee, Peter O'Malley, owner of the Los Angeles Dodgers, and the outgoing commissioner, Peter Ueberroth, echoed the sentiments of commissioner-elect A. Bartlett Giamatti in claiming that race did not enter into the selection process. According to Giamatti, White was picked solely because he met better than any other candidate the job requirements of "judgment, integrity, intelligence, fairness, and love and knowledge of the game." White himself was diplomatic. He said that he didn't know if he had been chosen because he was black but that "in the opinion of the committee," he met the qualifications for the job. Baseball people who expressed public views praised the selection. Yankees owner George Steinbrenner said that White would "make one hell of a president of the National League." As a rhetorical action, what went on at this press conference was not very complicated. One very easily got all the meaning from it that one needed or wanted. It was clear that the intention of the participants was to say what they thought was best for baseball—that is, to emphasize White's competence (the National League was in good hands) and to minimize racial implications. For all ordinary purposes there was no need to try to refine further this estimation of rhetorical intents.

In unusual situations, however, when a really difficult case of intent occurs and when determination of intentions is sufficiently important—as in Calhoun's case—one should attempt to secure additional insights by exploring relevant aspects of the persuaders' self-systems.

In estimating rhetorical intent, it is neither necessary nor desirable to use psychoanalytical approaches. Classical Freudianists believe that one's primary identity—hence, the controlling force in later actions—is derived from early childhood experiences. Post-Freudianists like Erik H. Erikson, on the other hand, emphasize that historical and social forces—especially those of late adolescence—also have major influence in shaping one's identity.

The psychoanalytical perspective may help to unlock the deep meanings of literature or of personality, but it is unnecessary and, in most cases, unfruitful to use it to estimate persuaders' intents in particular communications. James David Barber, in his *The Presidential Character*, says that "psychoanalytical interpretations at the symbolic level" should be avoided because only trained practitioners know how to do that and because "the data will not bear it."[1] I would argue further that both classical and post-Freudianists are invariably guilty of reductionism, with post-Freudianists being only somewhat less so than their classical Freudian colleagues.

One simply cannot establish that, because of an adolescent identity crisis—or infantile experiences in the toilet, bedroom or nursery—a persuader of mature years necessarily intended to do this or that in a particular speech, newspaper editorial, or novel. In a fairly typical example psychoanalyst David Abrahamsen, in his *Nixon vs. Nixon: An Emotional Tragedy*, claims that the former President deliberately committed political suicide by the Watergate affair. His proof? Only that Nixon was an unhappy child, emotionally deformed by anger, hostility, hatred for his father, and by an unhealthy attachment for his mother. Abrahamsen draws heavily upon such items as "My Dear Master," a letter Nixon wrote to his mother when he was ten, in which he assumed the role of a dog.

My Dear Master:

> The two boys that you left me with are very bad to me. Their dog, Jim, is very old and he will never talk or play with me.
> One Saturday the boys went hunting. Jim and myself went with them. While going through the woods one of the boys triped and fell on me. I lost my temper and bit him. He kiked me in the side and we

started on. While we were walking I saw a black round thing in a tree. I hit it with my paw. A swarm of black thing came out of it. I felt a pain all over. I started to run and as both my eyes were swelled shut I fell into a pond. When I got home I was very sore. I wish you would come home right now.

Your good dog
RICHARD

Abrahamsen does not establish a direct causal linkage between the "My Dear Master" letter, or other childhood episodes, and the mature Nixon's alleged desire for self-destruction.[2] It is mere speculation that Nixon, because of an intensely unhappy childhood, sought to destroy himself by provoking Watergate. Such use of psychoanalytic evidence and inference is ordinarily too tenuous to be very helpful in estimating any persuader's intentions in a specific situation.

A further fact about modern rhetoric renders any exclusively personality-centered analysis unsatisfactory. Much public rhetoric is the product of several individuals or groups who collaborate in trying to build a focused "rhetorical selfhood" into communication. Modern legislators have staffs who produce their principals' statements. Political speakers and corporate spokespersons employ speech writers and other kinds of communication consultants. Even Calhoun consulted others, as I shall show. And how could one psychoanalyze the "personality" that produced the rhetoric of the United States National Conference of Catholic Bishops, the Chrysler Corporation, the platform of a political party, an unsigned newspaper editorial? It takes *historical and social* knowledge, rather than theories of personality, to give us insight into the purposings of those who generate such rhetoric.

If instead of using psychoanalytical or other exclusively personality-centered approaches, we exploit general historical and social information, we can frequently estimate rhetorical intentions. There are often data from which we can estimate what internalized self-system (or what collective self-system) designed the rhetoric in which one is interested.

As I have already argued, self-systems (individual or collective) condition the ways persuaders view urgencies, audiences, and occasions, and the ways persuaders conceptualize their relationships to these forces. Persuaders' self-systems determine their rhetorical choices, including their choices of purpose. Thus, to look at a situation through the perceptions of the *creators* of rhetoric helps one to judge what a persuader or set of persuaders probably wanted to gain, how they designed their rhetoric, and with what aims.

There are several kinds of explorations one can carry out when a communication and its circumstances don't fully clarify the intentionality of rhetoric being studied. One tries to determine whether the persuader(s) stated somewhere what the purpose of the communication was. If this does not produce a reliable estimation of intention(s), one needs to secure and interpret data about the persuader's or persuaders' self-systems. Then, one tries to integrate these data with other data that have been assembled and thereby arrive at a mature estimation of intentions. What are the kinds of data one would seek in these processes?

Persuaders' Testimony

Before trying to open up persuaders' self-systems, which may involve considerable effort, one should attempt to learn what the persuader(s) professed to believe the purpose was.

This use of testimony has two rather obvious limitations. If such attestations exist, they are usually secreted in private papers and correspondence and may not be available until years after the person dies—if then. A second limitation is that if persuaders intended to manipulate others, to deceive, in a communication(s), they are not likely to reveal this deception voluntarily. Such persons are much more likely to continue the charade, especially in statements deliberately left for others to see. Therefore, even when one is able to find it, such testimony may or may not be conclusive.

Here are examples of reliable testimony. Earlier I reported that an analysis of John B. Anderson's speech to a Yale University audience indicated his probable intent. By securing direct testimony from Anderson and his chief aide, Dianne Taylor, I was able to reinforce my tentative judgment, establishing it beyond reasonable doubt. If a reader had any doubt about Herman Wouk's rhetorical intent in his novel *The Winds of War*, such confusion should be dispelled by his

later statement that he had written this novel as well as the following
War and Remembrance to cause readers to embrace and somehow act on
the conclusion: "War is an old habit of thought, an old frame of mind,
an old political technique, that must now pass as human sacrifice and
human slavery have passed." There is no reason to question either
Anderson's or Wouk's statements because they are compatible with
other data about the persuaders themselves and about the messages
and the circumstances. Therefore, their testimony can be accepted as
reliable and conclusive.

    More often than not, however, as historian and former presiden-
tial adviser Arthur M. Schlesinger, Jr., warned would be the case, the
testimonial evidence that one secures about persuaders' rhetorical intent is inadequate or distorted, or both. An example of conscious, or
unconscious, distortion is supplied by John Adams. In his diary en-
try for March 5, 1773, he praised his handling of the Boston Massacre trials as "one of the most gallant, generous, manly and
disinterested Actions of my whole Life." He seems to imply that his
only intent was to secure the release of the defendants. And he wrote
this refutation in the margin of one of the pages in William Gordon's
History of Independence, opposite the charge that he had suppressed evidence against Boston: "Adams' Motive is not here perceived. His
Clients lives were hazarded by Quincy's too youthful ardour."
Adams's denial does not stick, however. The evidence I cited earlier from the trials and their circumstances strongly indicates that he
not only sought a favorable verdict for his clients but that he *also*
wanted to spare the town and the patriot cause from unnecessary
scandal.

    The problem of inadequate data is exemplified by my unsuc-
cessful attempt to find direct testimony from Calhoun about his rhetorical intent in his March 4 speech. In his private statements the
South Carolinian frequently revealed his beliefs about the immediate
situations that enveloped the March 4 speech, and about a week after
the speech he even predicted the inevitable rupture of the Union. But
nowhere can I find explicit testimony of any kind revealing what he
wanted to accomplish in the speech.

Relevant Aspects of Persuaders' Self-Systems

When a reasonable search fails to secure testimony that clarifies intentions, one has to decide whether the matter is worth spending more time and effort. If so, there is no alternative but try to open up the persuader's self-system.

Relevant Experiences and Personal Qualities

How deeply or extensively one needs to explore persuaders' relevant experiences and personal qualities depends on the particular situation. It should be kept in mind, however, that one's *only* interest in this subject is to collect data that, when combined with other data about the persuaders' self-systems, may yield a better fix on rhetorical intent.

What I have just said is as true when one explores corporate voices as when one studies an individual persuader. In his book *Rhetoric in an Organizational Society: Managing Multiple Identities*, George Cheney explores the evolution of the Peace Pastoral issued by the National Conference of Catholic Bishops in 1983.[3] He shows that a major problem for the bishops was "who they were" as issuers of a pastoral letter. They knew they were an authoritative group of high-level churchmen. They wanted to influence various opinion groups within the Catholic Church. Cheney's interviews document the fact that the bishops' individual and collective self-systems were specially marked by their primary allegiance to the historic teachings of the Church and by whatever was contained in recent papal pronouncements. However, they also had their eyes on the Reagan administration and the general public. The threat of nuclear war motivated them strongly. As they developed their document, they themselves changed: they changed from an "assemblage" of Church authorities to what they came to call a "collegial" body speaking for and to a religious community. They saw themselves as having moral authoritativeness, but they sensed that they had less authority on such secular issues as foreign and defense policies. With this divided vision of themselves they could not fully adapt to the interests of secular audiences because the teachings of the Church held their ultimate allegiance, and those teachings and doctrines were not open to adaptation. They saw themselves as speaking from within a morally authoritative institution, but addressing "outsiders" with whom their authoritativeness remained debatable at best. In a similar way, if we were interested in the persuasive messages of a political party, we would need to study the arguments and counterarguments that finally yielded that party's platform—its formal statement of its collective self-system./As with the bishops, not the platform alone but *how* it came into being and with what effects on party members would be important to discovering the self-system that evolved./

A rapid review of Calhoun's experience turns up much potentially illuminating information, such as these items, selected almost at random.

Calhoun was born into a strict Presbyterian home, with a strong work ethic. His father, a wealthy planter for the area, was the first up-country representative in the South Carolina Assembly, serving three decades until his death. As the owner of thirty-one blacks he was the fourth largest slaveholder in the South Carolina Piedmont. John received elitist training in the liberal arts and law, being educated at the prestigious Waddel School and Willington Academy, Yale College, and Judge Tapping Reeve's law school in Litchfield, Connecticut, as well as in the law offices of the distinguished Henry W. DeSaussure and George Bowie. Forgoing the practice of law, Calhoun pursued a remarkable career as planter and political figure. After one term in the state legislature, he served three terms in the United States House of Representatives, where he was a zealous supporter of extreme federal power, and for the next eight years he was a superb, nationalistic, Secretary of War in Monroe's cabinet. His nationalism during those years mirrored his intense political ambitions and the interests of the leading people of his state. His conversion to the position of extreme sectionalist began during his term as Vice-President under Adams, 1825–1829, when the opinion in his state shifted strongly to particularism and he was losing his power base. His conversion was completed during his term as Vice-President under Andrew Jackson. In the ensuing years, he practiced confrontationalism with the North as he served in the United States Senate and, briefly, as Secretary of State during Tyler's administration.

Out of such life experiences Calhoun developed distinctive qualities of personality and character. Long before 1850 he had become known for his unyielding, fixed, tenacious, systematic, logical cast of mind. A contemporary described him as being "speculative, theoretical, and philosophical." Although he had a striking ability to see great truths and principles clearly, he thought in absolute channels. He was ambitious, aggressive, "constantly agitating," intense, austere, and humorless. In the sense that he lacked compassion for, or identification with, the common and lower classes, he was insensitive to human needs. He was aristocratic in his manners and outlook. He identified political and moral virtue with himself and "castigated those opposed to himself as unprincipled." An ideologue, he was ruthless in suppressing political opposition in his own state. Tending to be overly optimistic about his influence and the success of his persuasion, he thought that the Democratic Party and the South depended on him for their survival.

From exploring persuaders' relevant experiences, self-conceptions, and attitudes in approaching persuasive tasks, one can assemble data that allow interpretation of persuaders' self-systems. Cheney did this with the bishops, and I have done it with Calhoun. To interpret such evidence we must pay attention to the persuaders' basic beliefs, their pertinent priorities, their typical strategies, and their special urgencies. Cheney could quickly see that a major, basic belief of the bishops was that the formal moral teachings of their Church were inviolable, but from his many interviews with participants he learned also that the arms race of the early 1980s had become a major concern and priority for the bishops. They adopted a pastoral letter as their medium of communication because it was a traditional, quasi-doctrinal form, but resisting what they saw as the Reagan administration's cold war strategies was a special, secular urgency for most of them.

Beliefs

Whether one is studying a group of persuaders or a single persuader, a way to discover their relevant beliefs is to become intimately acquainted with their public and private expressions. Professor

Cheney carried out a comprehensive series of interviews with people associated with the bishops' Peace Pastoral; he read their speeches, articles, and private memoranda; and he followed press commentary. In like manner, from reviewing Calhoun's experiences, past pronouncements, and personal qualities, I can assemble a list of his critically important and relevant beliefs, prior to his March 4 speech. Here is that list.

1. The safety of the South depended on his successful leadership.
2. Slavery was a moral good and social necessity. The survival of the South depended on slavery.
3. Men are not born free and equal. Liberty and equality are not natural rights. Inequality is essential to progress.
4. The Constitution is a compact. It derives its powers from the people of the separate states. Sovereignty resides in the states, not in the Congress or the territories.
5. The Congress, the Supreme Court, and the President are agents of the states.
6. The powers of the consolidated system of government are limited by the principles of strict construction, states' rights, concurrent majority, and nullification.
7. Slaves are property and cannot be excluded from any territory. As an agent of the states, the federal government holds territories in trust for the states. Its control applies only to public lands. (The Missouri Compromise violated the Constitution.)
8. Fundamental and irreconcilable differences exist between North and South concerning the morality of slavery and the relation of slavery to national progress.
9. The political parties, the normal political process, and the "politics of slavery"[4] do not provide a suitable defense of Southern interests, rights, honor, and slavery.
10. No compromise is possible between North and South because compromise can be effected only between equals and the North and South are not equal.

11. Southern safety in the Union depends on two things: Southern unity and the North's willingness to yield absolute guarantees.
12. The time for decision has come. If the North should refuse to yield, the South should secede.
13. The North might accept a patchwork accommodation, but there is no real hope that it would agree to a resolution of basic differences. On February 24, 1850, he wrote to his daughter Anna: "I see no prospect of any satisfactory adjustment."[5]
14. The North's aggressions against the South will continue and will intensify. The North is attempting to destroy slavery through ultimate emancipation or war.
15. If the South is not sufficiently unified at this time to force guarantees from the North or to secede, she will be so later.

These statements of Calhoun's beliefs seem clear and indisputable. The same thing cannot be said about his professions that the South supported his leadership and was sympathetic to secession. If his statements, such as those that follow, are accepted at face value, Calhoun believed that Southerners would follow his lead, and therefore he did not need to persuade them.

In a letter to his son-in-law Thomas G. Clemson, December 8, 1849, he wrote that "the South is more united, than I ever knew it to be, and more bold and decided. The North must give way, or there will be a rupture." On January 4, 1850, he wrote to his friend James H. Hammond: "It is becoming a common opinion, that there is little chance of saving the Union. The subject is freely talked about and discussed in private circles. It is also becoming a prevalent opinion, that the South ought not to remain in the Union, without a complete restoration of all her rights, a full recognition of our equality [in] every respect, and ample security for the future." On February 16, 1850, only two weeks before the speech, he persisted in this vein, writing again to Hammond: "There is, I think, little prospect, that the North will come to our terms or that any settlement of the questions at issue will be agreed on. That I think is the general impression. The impression is now very general, and is on the increase, that disunion is the only alternative, that is left us."[6]

There is a marked discrepancy between the above statements about Southern unity and the reality of the general Southern opposition to his leadership that existed at the time of his speech. His professions seem to be too far off the mark to be the true judgment of an astute politician, even an ailing, cloistered, and ego-driven one like Calhoun. There is no way to be sure what he actually thought on March 4, but inasmuch as his only extant statements were directed to close friends and relatives, he may have been voicing wishful thinking or hoping to bolster the spirits of his correspondents. Also, his most relevant statements were written in the weeks preceding February 16 (the date of the last such statement). This was the period when the spirit of rebellion was strongest in the South. Apparently the mood for confrontation had eased significantly by March 4.[7]

Months of reading and interviewing such as Cheney spent in finding out the intentions and ultimate self-systems of the National Conference of Catholic Bishops is not usually necessary. Nor does one usually find such inconsistencies of outlook as I have found in studying Calhoun. But the two cases illustrate that extensive research is sometimes necessary to understand "who"—what self-system—was behind rhetoric in exceptionally complex configurations. Perplexities are often eased at this point if one searches out the persuaders' priorities among goals and purposes.

Priorities of Goals and Purposes

Data concerning persuaders' beliefs, experiences, and qualities tend to reveal the hierarchies of goals that direct the persuaders' rhetorical actions. Cheney shows that exerting pressure toward slowing the arms race between the Soviet Union and the United States was the overriding secular reason the Catholic bishops were moved to prepare a pastoral letter on war and peace. He also shows that the nuclear freeze movement of the early 1980s significantly motivated the bishops during the more than two years they spent in hammering out their rhetorical document. However, the bishops were first and foremost churchmen, and the freeze idea never reached the *top* of their priorities. They showed this by treating the freeze movement as a secular, single-issue political movement, and even though they borrowed some of the language of that movement, they still tried to retain their identity as moral more than as political persuaders. This way, they felt they could claim more universal standing than the movement itself could claim.

In Calhoun's case the data I have accumulated amply document how he ordered his priorities:

1. His most important goal was to protect the interests of the slaveholding class.
2. His next most important goal was to protect the general interests of the South.
3. He wanted to preserve, extend, and justify his personal political influence. This may not have been his first goal, but it is plain that pride and intense ambition were pervasive motivating forces throughout his career, including his final weeks.
4. His least important major goal was to preserve the Union—but the Union he revered was a *confederation* of independent, sovereign states.

These were the political matters that meant most to Calhoun. The motive to do something about armaments was what motivated the Catholic bishops to explore what moral authority they could plausibly bring to bear on that problem.

Previous Strategies

For the Catholic bishops the strategy of issuing a pastoral letter was a natural one. Such letters were familiar within the Church, and these bishops had already issued such letters on economics and other matters. More importantly, the strategy fit the hierarchic arrangement of authority in the Catholic Church. A pastoral letter was recognized as something to be taken very seriously, but without the full authority of official and established teachings of the Church. A pastoral letter was therefore a natural medium for expressing the bishops' mingled religious and political ideas.

Especially when persuaders have wider ranges of acceptable
strategies than the Catholic bishops had,(it is helpful to consider how
X (those persuaders have previously advanced goals of high priority] If
some new strategy was adopted in the case we study, we will want to
ponder why the change occurred and what that suggests about persuasive intentions. If, as with the bishops, a traditional strategy was
adopted, we may judge that custom or some other established constraint had most influence in determining the shape and style of the
communication. If, as seems to be the case with Calhoun, a persuader or persuaders choose to follow the same sort of strategy in differing circumstances, we may estimate that their strategy reflects a
habit of mind and/or a theory about communication.

Calhoun's practice followed a strikingly rigid pattern over the
years that preceded 1850.(He repeatedly offered independent, hard-
nosed, confrontational communications defending the South against
alleged "aggressions" by the North.] He consistently alleged that the
only way to protect the South from the increasingly powerful North
was to extract a public recognition that the Constitution guaranteed
protection to slavery. In thousands of statements, in hundreds of skir-
mishes, Calhoun followed this basic strategy, attempting to halt the
flow of history, to dam up the forces of change behind a verbal block-
ade of resolutions and constitutional interpretations. Upon each flare-
up of regional tension Calhoun identified the North as the enemy of
the South, denounced Northern aggressions, endorsed a confedera-
tive view of the Constitution, defended the institution of slavery, demanded positive protection for Southern rights, and implicitly or
explicitly threatened the survival of the Union.

The bishops used a traditional strategy by issuing a pastoral letter. This is significant only in that it confirms that they saw themselves as both pronouncing doctrinally and seeking to persuade on
nondoctrinal matters. The meaning of Calhoun's consistent, confrontational strategy is not equally clear, however. His practice is open to
two different interpretations.

The first of these interpretation is that Calhoun persistently
used a one-track strategy of confrontation, demands, and implicit or
explicit threats because he thought that it would work, or at least that

?

it had a better chance for success than did other available strategies. But his formalistic strategies did not do the job, even though he may have thought that they could. They failed to slow the buildup of anti-slavery sentiment in the North and the continued decline in the relative strength and the security of the South. Nor did his strategies foster a unified South. Calhoun should have perceived that his hard-nosed strategy was being counterproductive, but he apparently did not do so.

(The second interpretation that can be drawn from Calhoun's previous strategies is that he was simply not interested in persuading but in "keeping the record straight.")There are communicators who by habit or choice only *proclaim*. On the basis of his previous strategies Calhoun seems to be one of these proclaimers, despite the conventional way he sometimes talked and wrote about his speeches.

Whenever one comes up with divergent interpretations about a persuader's previous strategies, or whenever a communicator's strategies seem strangely conceived for the circumstances—as in the case of Calhoun—one ought to raise this question: What kind of implicit theory of persuasion does this communication have?

Scholarly interest in implicit communication theory is fairly recent. About twenty-five years ago I found that both Solomon Stoddard and Cotton Mather had highly integrated, implicit theories of persuasion.[8] A decade later Bonnie McDaniel Johnson became probably the first to use the phrase "implicit communication theory." More recently more persons have become interested in this concept. One of these, Thomas W. Benson, suggests that "implicit communication theory refers to the collection of ideas that lay practitioners hold about the way they and others communicate. Such ideas are theoretical because they relate to one another and to generalized views of the world, though they do not necessarily exhibit internal consistency. Such ideas are implicit because, although they are often displayed in talk, they are seldom stated as generalized theoretical formulations. Human beings hold implicit 'theories' about a wide va- ? riety of matters that constrain human action in the world." Benson says further that "we use implicit theories to help us interpret, enact, and evaluate our actions and those of others. Experience does not speak to us directly. Instead we perceive and interpret experience through the filter of our theories."[9]

When it becomes necessary to determine whether a persuader has an implicit theory of communication and, if so, what its nature is, one can follow this procedure: Apply the definition of communication (see chapter 1) to the persuaders' record of relevant testimony, experiences, and previous strategies. The reason for doing this is to find out the extent to which that persuader views communication as a way of influencing change in receivers and persuasion as a matching of rhetorical satisfactions with impinging rhetorical constraints.

By putting this procedure to work in my case study, I acquired some very useful insights concerning Calhoun's intentions in his March 4 speech.

On the one hand, I learned from his personal correspondence that he considered rhetoric a persuasive tool, that he frequently was unrealistically sanguine about the effectiveness of his speeches, that he believed he could use communication to change others, and that until a few days before his death he believed he could influence national policies.[10] I was able to glean only rare additional clues from his published writings. None of these is more mystifying in its implications than the statement in his *Disquisition on Government*, published posthumously, that persuaders should not concentrate on what *ought* to move persons but on what *actually does*. "We must take human nature as it is," he wrote, "and accommodate our measures to it, instead of making the vain attempt to bend it to our measures."

On the other hand, Calhoun's consistent use of uncompromising, confrontationalist rhetoric makes it clear that he just did not understand persuasion very well or that he was a kind of habitual proclaimer/record maker. Such communication does not work very well unless the person has the ethos of a prophet or lawgiver, which Calhoun may have mistakenly thought he had. What must be considered here is that Calhoun never got straight in his thinking the difference between *offering prophetic conclusions* or *proclamations* of the truth and *inducing adherence* through providing rhetorical satisfactions in response to rhetorical constraints. To Calhoun, public communication seemed to be an instrument of coercion, of demanding—a club to beat with, not a means of winning converts through the freedom of voluntary choice.

The pattern of Calhoun's previous strategies—supplemented by my imperfect grasp of his understanding of how communication works—accurately prefigures what he would say in his March 4 speech. Consistent with his past efforts, his address was essentially a position statement—a take-it-or-leave-it document that offered almost no persuasive inducements to hostile listeners, Northerners or Southerners. However, my data also suggest that Calhoun, despite his rigid, doctrinaire stance, wanted to promote the cause that he believed in. If this is true, I have not yet put all the pieces of the puzzle together.

Cheney has shown that the Catholic bishops evolved a fairly clear conception of where and on what they could *proclaim* and of where and on what they must simply try to be *persuasive*. They even said explicitly that parts of their pastoral letter were morally certain, but other parts were open to further consideration and discussion. Given this ambiguity, it is not surprising that Cheney found that some Catholics felt the bishops' final version of their letter was not prophetic enough, while other Catholics and many non-Catholics felt the bishops had stepped beyond their moral, churchly authority in trying to persuade about secular politics. The bishops' discussions while composing their letter show clearly that they themselves were persistently concerned about just how to express the "authoritative" and the "persuasive" parts of their two-leveled communication. The inevitable result was a degree of ambiguity about their real meanings and their claims to authority—even within the Church.

Fortunately, one is rarely in such a frustrating situation as I find myself in regarding Calhoun's intentions, nor are the proclaiming/persuading roles always as troublesome as they were for the Catholic bishops. My study of Calhoun illustrates some of the problems that very tough cases can raise for critics, but this does not mean that determining intentions is always as difficult as it is with Calhoun. The bishops' self-system was clear once Cheney had collected the needed historical data. To take a still simpler case, if one were looking at Jimmy Carter's electioneering, one would soon discover that his strategies were normally tinged by moral imperatives. So one might expect that "uplift" was part of his intentions in his inaugural. In such situations Carter's persuasive strategies were "up front" and conventional, and there is little reason to doubt that his rhetorical intent was adequately revealed in his communication.

Personal Urgencies

Sometimes the internal state of a persuader or institution at the time of a communication may tell something about probable intent. Does the push of personal ambition, coercion from supporters or opponents, or problems of health and the like influence the position a persuader takes?

For instance, potential contributors to his party, as well as others, had exerted considerable pressure on John B. Anderson, before his Yale University speech, to make clear whether he was going to enter the presidential race. Ulysses S. Grant, tortured by the need to leave his family a comfortable estate and by his agonizing battle with throat cancer, not only sought to hurry his *Personal Memoirs* into print but also to tell "the unvarnished truth" from his perspective. (Within forty-eight hours after he finished writing the last page of his manuscript, Grant was dead.)

Also, Daniel Webster was beset by personal urgencies as he contemplated the remarks he was to give in the Senate on March 7, in answer to Calhoun's speech and to Clay's proposals. He had lost almost all influence in the existing power structure of the Whig Party. He had been unable to get a suitable federal appointment for his son Fletcher. In two years he would be seventy years old, and 1852 would be the last reasonable chance for him to win the presidency. If he took a strong stand against slavery and Southern interests, he could not materially improve his position with the Taylor administration or with the dominant antislavery faction of his party. Furthermore, he had been pressured by leading business interests in the Northeast and by his Cotton Whig supporters to make a conciliatory speech. Thus, Webster's urgencies—that is, his perceptions of his political interests, the interests of the business and professional groups he represented, and the national interests—converged into his rhetorical intent: to eliminate slavery as a cause for sectional conflict.

I need to ask: What were the personal urgencies that Calhoun may have had at the time of his March 4 speech? And what, if anything, can I learn from them that might help me understand better what his intentions were in that communication?

Calhoun had one major personal urgency at the time of his speech: he was terminally ill, his heart diseased and his body ravaged by advanced tuberculosis. In the weeks preceding his speech he was confined to his room most of the time, suffering from a severe attack of pneumonia and from a tenacious cold and fever. I cannot determine whether Calhoun's health had any direct connection with his rhetorical intent, however. On February 6 he wrote to his son-in-law Thomas G. Clemson: "I have been for the last week entirely free from disease. . . . I hope to be completely restored by the beginning of next week to my usual strength. The disease [pneumonia], I think, will leave no permanent ill effect behind."[11] On February 24 he wrote to his daughter Anna that he was just getting over a cold and "slight fever." "It has thrown me back a week," he said, "but there has been nothing serious about it." In the same letter, however, he admitted that he was too weak to make his planned speech in the Senate and, instead, would prepare a written copy for someone else to read for him.[12] Calhoun may not have realized at this time that he was dying (his doctor and secretary apparently did not conclude until some time after his speech that he could not recover), but he undoubtedly knew that he was gravely ill and enfeebled.

I should now exploit these data by using two approaches. The first is to recognize that sometimes a persuader's intentions may not be faithfully embodied in the text of a communication because of bad health, poor personal habits, limited ability, or faulty perception of the rhetorical situation. This leads me to ask the following questions: Could Calhoun's illness have influenced the tone of his speech, making him seem more irritable and abrasive than he would otherwise have been? Did he become so tired during the process of composing the speech that he could not give his remedial proposals the same

development that he gave to his indictment of the North and to his
explanations of what would not save the Union? Although absolute
answers to such questions are not possible, I find that, beyond reasonable doubt, neither of these questions helps to explain Calhoun's
intent.

Calhoun apparently began to dictate his speech on February 17
or 24 to Joseph A. Scoville, a reporter for the New York *Herald* who
also served as a private secretary to Calhoun, and he probably finished it by the 28th. It is of some significance to my point to pin
down the starting time. Charles M. Wiltse in his biography of Calhoun incorrectly identifies the time Calhoun began to dictate as the
evening of February 26, and he errs in stating that the speech was
completed the next day.[13] Obviously, a dying man cannot compose
and dictate a speech of almost fifteen thousand words overnight.
Moreover, Scoville told a much different story in the New York *Herald*
of May 3, 1850: In response to a request from Calhoun, "I went at
once to his room. It was Sunday evening. . . . [In 1850 February 26
fell on Tuesday. Therefore, if Scoville began to take dictation on Sunday, the date was either February 17 or 24. It could not have been the
26th.] He remarked, 'It seems odd to me I can't write a speech. I
must deliver it'; and he commenced, 'I have, Senators, believed from
the first, &c,' and *the work was continued from day to day as his strength
allowed, until it was finished*" (emphasis added). Scoville does not say
when the speech was finished. Obviously Calhoun did not begin to
dictate one evening and conclude the next day, as Wiltse says.

It was on the 28th that Senator Andrew P. Butler asked permission for Calhoun's speech to be read to the Senate on March 4.
Scoville was prepared to write further, and if Calhoun had wished to
rest for a day or longer he could have done so *before* permitting Butler
to reserve a particular date for the presentation. Furthermore, Calhoun corrected the manuscript copy before it was sent to the printer
on Sunday, March 3. He seems to have had enough time to rest and
to modify the tone or to flesh out any parts of the speech he wished.
In addition, Calhoun had carefully worked out the speech in his
mind before dictating it. The philosophy and principles of the message closely adhered to his *Disquisition on Government*, which he had

just completed, and his *Discourse on the Constitution and Government of the United States*, which he was still laboring to finish. Inasmuch as he offered no claims or warrants that he had not long pondered over and had expressed in one form or another before, and inasmuch as the skilled and solicitous Scoville took down his every word, Calhoun should have exerted minimum effort in composing the speech.

The second approach I should use to exploit the data about Calhoun's personal urgency is to assume that an old man who is seriously ill may seek to justify his ideas and behaviors to himself and to others, and may attempt to further a state of affairs that corresponds to his firmly established beliefs and values. If I add the assumption that an old advocate near death would seek to justify his values, goals, and previous actions to my findings that the coldly intense, dogmatic, doctrinaire, and even pontifical tone of the March 4 speech is consistent with the proclaiming character of his earlier rhetoric, it becomes even more probable that Calhoun *intended once more to proclaim or pronounce*. Because it has become clear that Calhoun was a habitual "proclaimer" and that he wanted to make a pronouncement on March 4, it is tempting to believe that I have wrapped up this case. But as a rhetorical detective I have a strong sense that something is missing in this assessment of intent. Could Calhoun have wanted to do something *more* than merely "keep the record straight"?

When there are unanswered suspicions like this about a communication, one should turn to the next step.

Integration of Data

The basic way to synthesize the data one collects about a persuasive effort is to follow a scheme something like this. Keeping in mind the information already gathered, one should identify and explore each purpose that reasonably could be attributed to the persuader(s). As one examines each hypothesis about intent, one should look for congruencies between a possible intent and the various pieces of evidence one has. When incongruent pieces are eliminated and the congruent pieces are fit, stretched, and glued into the most logical conceptual picture, one will have established the best possible estimation of intent that the evidence will allow. Professor Cheney found indisputable confirmation that the bishops had *both* proclaiming and persuading goals. The evidence of this appeared in correspondence among the bishops, in records of their discussions as the pastoral letter was taking form, and especially in the fact that their final draft explicitly distinguished between their claims to moral authority and their claims to offer persuasive arguments to induce several audiences to consider the possibilities of a "peace ethic" in political affairs. The issues and the data accumulated in connection with Calhoun's speech are less clearly focused, and it requires more detailed exposition to construct an integrated view of his speech in its rhetorical configuration.

Some critics have suggested that Calhoun demanded more from the North than he expected to get in order to encourage a more generous settlement for the South. Others have believed that Calhoun threatened civil war in order to frighten Northerners into accepting Clay's proposals or some similar compromise. These hypotheses are totally incompatible with my evidence. From my analysis of Calhoun's self-system, I know that he could not have had either of these implicit intents. He simply was no compromiser, as his past rhetoric and strategies plainly show. Compromise, he thought, could be made only between equals; the North and South were not equals; therefore, compromise was impossible. He truly believed that this was the time for decision. The North must meet the minimum security needs of the South, or the South must secede.

Other critics have asserted that Calhoun was attempting to work out an accommodation with the North through the cooperation of Daniel Webster and that Calhoun projected his March 4 speech as being the first in a series of public exchanges with Webster and other sympathetic Northerners. Gerald M. Capers has gone so far as to claim that "there can be no doubt that they [Calhoun and Webster] were collaborating to produce an acceptable compromise which would save the Union." Charles M. Wiltse elaborated on this theme. According to Wiltse, Webster called at Calhoun's boarding house on March 2 and "presumably" outlined what he planned to say on the 7th. Here is the main course of Wiltse's reasoning:

> Remember he [Calhoun] was not acting completely alone. Others, including Webster, knew his intentions before he spoke, and he in turn

knew what Webster was going to say on the Northern side. He was, moreover, satisfied with it. Does it not appear, then, that he had simply made in the clearest and strongest possible language the opening speech for his side in what was to be a full-scaled debate? Surely his hope was that after Webster had rejoined, the common ground might be worked out in general discussion, and possibly an agreement could be reached. He could not, therefore, commit himself in advance to specific terms. These were to be the end product of the debate.[14]

My analysis of Calhoun's use of rhetoric in his March 4 speech would be profoundly influenced if I accepted that he designed his message, in collusion with Webster, to be the opening salvo in an ongoing senatorial dialogue between the two men. I have examined the few primary sources cited by the two historians, as well as other relevant private reports, and I can find no evidence that convincingly reinforces their conclusions. Conceivably, circumstantial evidence and reasoned inferences might substantiate it as possibly, or probably, correct. Let me examine the evidence.

First, Webster's visit is not evidence that Calhoun designed his speech to be the initial probe in a widening dialogue with Webster. The visit took place on March 2, at least two days *after* Calhoun had probably finished dictating his speech.

Second, the only time that Calhoun could have altered the text of his speech to accord with a March 2 understanding with Webster was after Webster left the room and before the manuscript was sent to the printer on March 3. This would have been enough time, say, to modify the ultimatums to the North. If Calhoun made any such changes, however, they are not attested to by any witness and I did not discern any in the physical copy of the manuscript itself at the Library of Congress. Scoville does not record that Calhoun was influenced by Webster or anyone else during the writing of the manuscript or after it was completed. Furthermore, Scoville asserts that no one, except himself and the printer, ever saw the manuscript before it was set in type: "Not a soul was in the room but myself, when he was delivering this speech, and not a man living saw it, until it was in print, but myself."[15]

Third, the only "immediate" circumstantial evidence relating to Webster's visit of March 2 affirms that Webster was willing to accommodate his views to those of Calhoun—not the reverse. In the New

York *Herald*, March 7, a small notice from "our special telegraphic correspondence" appeared, dated March 6, 1850: "Some curious developments are coming out. Mr. Webster will not see any one now, though, last Saturday, he was closeted with Mr. Calhoun for about two hours, and gave the latter reason to believe that he will adopt a different course from Senators Benton and Houston, and be more favorable to the demands of the South. He would prefer to be for free soil, but yet is willing to establish some kind of compromise." Assuming that this report is reliable, Webster's conciliatory approach undoubtedly buoyed Calhoun's spirits; but I do not know what, if any, influence it had upon Calhoun's already completed manuscript.

Fourth, on Tuesday, March 5, Webster and Calhoun apparently had a long visit in the latter's quarters. The New York *Herald*, March 8, carried this account:

> Mr. Webster has spoken today [March 7] one of the most extraordinary speeches of the session. . . . If Mr. Calhoun's speech made a deep impression here, Mr. Webster's has made a deeper. But the speech of this great statesman . . . indicates less than the private movements and private interviews which have taken place between him and Mr. Calhoun, and their mutual friends. . . . On Tuesday last . . . I have been informed, from the best sources, that Mr. Webster and Mr. Calhoun had another long and very interesting conference, of six or seven hours continuance. A strong effervescence has taken place between the Southern men on the compromise, and a disposition toward a settlement has been evinced by Mr. Webster and Mr. Calhoun and their intimate friends. . . . Although the public speeches indicate some approach to compromise, the private movements and private interviews of Mr. Calhoun and Mr. Webster, with their respective friends, present a better prospect than any other manifestations.

I do not know how accurate the *Herald* account is. The question of the accuracy of the account, however, is beside the point. The datum is *post hoc;* that is, after the fact. The conversation with Webster on March 5 could not have influenced Calhoun's intent on March 4. No evidence demonstrates that a bond of rapport with Webster influenced Calhoun in preparing his manuscript of the March 4 speech.

Fifth, it seems unlikely that the enfeebled Calhoun, too weak to deliver even one speech, would seriously consider engaging in a series of debates and, in anticipation of those encounters, would modify the intent and substance of his March 4 address.

Sixth, inasmuch as Calhoun must have known that Webster lacked substantial influence within the power structure of his own party, it is improbable that he seriously believed Webster could turn Northern political opinion around.

Seventh, Wiltse is speculating when he asserts that in his March 4 speech Calhoun provided only a sketchy development of the ultimatums because he expected to develop and/or modify them in later debates. One should note that a virtue of comparing present rhetorical practice with past practice is highlighted here. Ambiguity about pragmatics and absolutism about broad doctrines was Calhounesque, and Wiltse seems to have missed that.

Eighth, in his biography of Daniel Webster, Maurice G. Baxter suggests that Webster went to see Calhoun because he felt "personal sorrow" for the dying man. Baxter adds that in a letter to Charles H. Warren, March 1, 1850, Webster predicted that Calhoun's March 4 speech would be "a kind of farewell statement of his credo: 'It will be in his usual [vein] of dogmatic assertion & violent denunciations of the North.' " There is no hint of collaboration here.[16] One should note that Webster, too, infers intent from past practices as well as present conditions. The accuracy of Webster's prediction is further illustration of my method's worth, generally.

Ninth, evidence from Calhoun's personal correspondence after the speech provides additional circumstantial evidence against the theory of Wiltse and Capers. For instance, on March 4, after Calhoun had returned to his room from the Senate, he wrote to Henry W. Conner: "You will see [in the accompanying copy of the speech] that I have made up the issue between North & South. If we flinch we are gone; but, if we stand fast on it, we shall triumph, either by compelling the North to yield to our terms, or declaring our independence of them."[17] Additionally, on March 10 he sent this observation to Thomas G. Clemson:

> Since then [the presentation of Calhoun's speech], Mr. Webster delivered his views. He took grounds more favourable to the South, than Mr. Clay, but *still far short of a permanent settlement of the*

question. . . . If he should be sustained by his constituents and N. England generally, it is not improbable, that he will take still stronger grounds; and that the question may be adjusted, or patched up for the present, *to brake out again in a few years. Nothing short of the terms I propose, can settle it finally and permanently.* [emphasis added].[18]

Neither of these statements suggests any inclination to work out a compromise with Webster. Instead, they document that, although Calhoun may have welcomed Webster's conciliatory approach, his intent in the speech was to present an uncompromisable Southern position and, if the North failed to yield acceptable guarantees, to demand that the South secede.

I have eliminated all of the traditional theories about Calhoun's intent. This leaves standing my tentative conclusion, attested to by the congruence of all the evidence: Calhoun had the explicit intent to *pronounce*. It seems that what Calhoun wanted to pronounce was this: The Northern senators and the people of the North must act positively on a series of six ultimatums; if they fail to do so but, instead, accept California as a state, the Southern senators and the people of the South should embrace secession.

Before accepting this or any other tentative conclusion about explicit intent, one should see if relevant new evidence can be drawn from the postmessage stage of the urgency, communicator, or readers/listeners. When I do this, I find it necessary to modify my tentative estimation slightly to accommodate the following piece of important new evidence drawn from after the speech.

On March 5 Calhoun returned briefly to the Senate and engaged in acrimonious debate with Henry S. Foote of Mississippi. Foote charged that Calhoun did not speak for the South, that the North was not universally hostile to slavery or to the South, and that the South could remain safely in the Union if Clay's resolutions were adopted. Constitutional revision was both unnecessary and incendiary, Foote said. In the course of the exchange, Calhoun stated "that the great object of his speech was to show that great discontent prevailed at the South, and that its cause must be removed before peace and harmony could be restored. He did not assume to name any *sine qua non* of settlement, but . . . as things now stood, the South could not remain with safety in the Union."[19]

If I may assume that Calhoun's statement to the Senate on March 5 represented his true intentions in his speech on the preceding day, (the basic thesis, or thrust, of his address did not mirror his intent) Although he spelled out in his speech what appeared to be the minimum requirements that would satisfy the South, he explicitly denied on March 5 that he had intended to set forth specific ultimatums. My final estimation of Calhoun's explicit intent, then, must reflect the greater flexibility indicated in his rejoinder to Foote: Calhoun intended to *declare* the Southern position in the most compelling manner possible and to *pronounce* that the North must provide the guarantees necessary to ensure permanently the security, rights, and equality of the South, and that if the North failed to make the necessary guarantees but instead accepted California as a state, the South should secede/I can accept this as his explicit intent without reservation.

I have no reservations that the South Carolinian's explicit purpose was to make a position statement. Nevertheless, I am not quite satisfied that this is all there is to understand about Calhoun's intentionality. Could he have had something in mind *beyond* merely proclaiming his views? I ask myself, Have I checked out all options he had at his disposal? Could he have had an *implicit* intent, perhaps? It is this "something beyond proclaiming" that I must now identify, if possible. My attempt to ferret out Calhoun's implicit intent is generally illustrative of the procedure that one might follow for any other tough case of intention.

The first thing I must do in this regard is to hunt out whether Calhoun had a *persuasive* intent in the speech. I found compelling reasons in his March 4 speech and his other similar statements to deny that he had a persuasive intent and to doubt that he had much understanding of the difference between verbal coercion and inducement to agreement. After looking at pretty much the same data, Baxter characterized the March 4 speech as an "overview and philosophical analysis."

Before I conclude that Calhoun had no intention to persuade, I should look for new evidence in statements Calhoun made after the speech. What I find, when I do this, is suggestive but not conclusive.

For instance, in his letter to Henry W. Conner on March 4, he wrote: "My speech . . . was read today in the Senate. My friends think it among my most successful efforts, and that it made a profound impression. I, trust, that our friends in Charleston will give it a wide circulation." In his letter to Thomas G. Clemson on March 10, he repeated that his speech "made a decided impression." Finally, on his deathbed he is supposed to have longed for "one hour" more "to speak in the Senate." If that wish could be granted, he lamented, "I could do more good than on any previous occasion of my life."[20] All of this evidence is ambiguous. Calhoun's statement that his speech made a strong impression is compatible with a desire to *pronounce* but not necessarily with a wish to *induce persons to change their minds*. His hope that his speech would be widely circulated in Charleston has nothing to do with persuading Northern or Southern senators or the Northern public. Even his alleged wish to have an additional hour to address the Senate does not demonstrate that he wanted to do anything other than to make another take-it-or-leave-it pronouncement.

I need to consider now two provocative final statements by Calhoun. On March 18 he wrote to Henry W. Conner:

> Mr. Webster's Speech may have produced, in the first instance, the impression you deprecate; but there is no apprehension it will be permanent. It is universally understood here that he could not sustain himself at the North with either Party; and that, to protect himself from their assaults, he has taken shelter under the Administration. Can anything more clearly evince the utter hopelessness of looking to the North for support, when their strongest man finds himself incapable of maintaining himself on the smallest amount possible of concession to the South; and on points too clear to admit of Constitutional doubts?[21]

About the time that he wrote to Conner, Calhoun confided to Senator Mason that he thought the Union would soon be dissolved.

> The Union is doomed to dissolution, there is no mistaking the signs. I am satisfied in my judgment, even were the questions which now agitate Congress settled to the satisfaction and with the concurrence of the Southern States, it would not avert, or materially delay, the catastrophe. I fix its probable occurrence within twelve years or three Presidential terms. You, and others of your age, will probably live to see it;

I shall not. The mode by which it will be done is not so clear; it may be brought about in a manner that none now foresee. But the probability is, it will explode in a Presidential election.[22]

These statements make clear that at the time they were written Calhoun had no hope that sectional differences could be adjusted. Although I have not found similar statements made on or before March 4, there is ample evidence that he had scarcely the "prayer of hope" that the North would yield as he demanded. All of the evidence points to the conclusions that (1) he disregarded what was needed to make his basic thrust persuasive, and/or that (2) he was content to issue ultimatums to the North. It is inescapable that he had no persuasive intent, in the conventional sense, in addressing Northern senators or the North generally.[23]

Did he perhaps have persuasive intentions respecting Southern senators? This too seems unlikely. What he said was not likely to induce Southern senators to change their minds. What he said could only intensify and justify the positions of the limited number of Southern senators who already agreed with him. Thus the congruence of my data supports the view that Calhoun had no explicit persuasive intent in respect to Southern senators. I conclude that he wished to pronounce what they should do if the North failed to make appropriate guarantees.

Here is why I think this judgment is correct. (1) The almost total lack of endorsement of his position after his speech proves that few Southern senators were ready to accept his leadership. Although Calhoun seems to have overestimated the radicalism of Southern political leaders and his own political influence, he should have known that he did not speak for the South and that he probably never had. (2) What Calhoun said, and how he said it, in addressing Southern senators constituted pronouncements very much like those he directed to Northern senators. There is no evidence that he was at all interested in inducing change.

Finally, it could have been that this deeply committed, calculating, powerful political manipulator was satisfied merely to make demands that he should have known would be rejected. It could have been that Calhoun implicitly intended his statement of the Southern position to prepare Southern senators and people of the South conceptually and psychologically to accept that they could not remain safely in the Union and to prepare themselves for secession. One can never know with certainty, of course. Nevertheless, much of what I have said indicates that Calhoun's deep commitment blinded him to the importance of *inducing,* that his calculations were often quite wrong—witness his assertions that the Southerners supported him—and that his manipulations were more often power plays than the fruits of inducement. Doubts about Calhoun's implicit purposes can be resolved by turning to the premise that *those who pronounce and proclaim usually try to make a record that will either be accepted immediately or recurred to as definitive when events begin to confirm the proclaimer's pronouncements, converting them to "prophecies."* Why do Luthers tack theses to walls? What motivates economists to predict a 5 percent rise or fall in bond prices? What drives "true believers" to proclaim what the future holds? One reason is that they hope/believe their pronouncements will be confirmed by future events, and so be rendered persuasive under new conditions. This can be an implicit persuasive intention of any pronouncer or proclaimer. If Calhoun had any implicit persuasive intention at all, it must have been to leave a persuasive call for the South—a call for which events were likely to create a favorable configuration of forces that would render the call persuasive.

My study of Calhoun's speech illustrates the necessity and importance of probing for intentions in interpreting discourse that occurs within an exigential flow of events. The scenario of the March 4 speech also shows how reasonable assessments of rhetorical intentions can be worked out in even the most difficult kind of case. Fortunately, in the rhetoric that goes on around us most situations are no more difficult to grasp than President Bush's repeated media defences in late 1989 and early 1990 of the Panamanian invasion to oust strongman Manuel Noriega. As circumstances changed, the emphasis of what he said varied somewhat, but Bush's intent was always the same. He clearly wanted to put the best face possible on the invasion: it was necessary; it was successful; it was worth the cost; American troops were accomplishing their mission and would be withdrawn soon; the consequences had been anticipated and would be manageable. When a persuader's motivations are more complex, as in the case of President Bush's State of the Union Address in 1990, one must study the situation more closely to make a reasoned and critical judgment of intentionality. Sometimes there is a record of how intentions were adopted or evolved. This is so with the Catholic bishops. The evidence left the bishops' multiple intentions no longer in doubt. The general point, then, is: Whether the problem is simple and clear after one assembles pertinent data or remains perplexing as in the case of Calhoun, the general methods of inquiry discussed in this chapter can yield fairly confident conclusions about the intentions of communicators. Constraints; the basic thrusts of the communications; strategies of substance, disposition, language, and paralanguage; self-systems as reflected in social responses, in testimony, in past experience and activity, in goals and priorities; and personal urgencies—these are our best sources for understanding rhetorical intentions. When pertinent data have been unearthed, the summative issues become: What does the evidence add up to? Do the data reflect a *pattern* of intentions? Even in those rare instances that are as tough to solve as that of Calhoun's in his March 4 speech, the method discussed in this chapter will help one to understand the intentions of the communicator.

Chapter Six

The Concept of Provoking Urgency

To understand communication one must understand the concept of "provoking urgency." All serious talk is practical. It serves a function. That function is to influence the circumstances that provoke people to talk. Therefore, we use symbols, ordinarily in the form of formal language, to induce others to change their perceptions of a situation and what to do about it, so that those perceptions accord more closely with our own. We hope the changes we induce in readers and listeners will lead them to exert influences we wish for on the provoking circumstances. Practical persuaders understand this if they are astute.

Early in 1986 Lee Atwater, chairman of the Fund for America's Future, gathered 180 volunteers for a special training session in Virginia. Most of them had done advance work for Ronald Reagan in 1980 and 1984. The ostensible function of the program was to encourage large crowds, favorable publicity, and smooth logistics for the campaign appearances that George Bush planned to make on behalf of Republican candidates in the off-year elections of 1986. This was actually to be a warm up for the Bush primary campaign of 1988, however. The real purpose of the program was to help Bush win the 1988 Republican nomination. Thus, the talk that Atwater directed to his volunteers in Virginia was targeted ultimately at influencing both the off-year elections of 1986 and especially the presidential sweepstakes of 1988. To some extent the Virginia training sessions contributed to the smooth handling of Bush's off-year campaigning and to his extraordinarily well-financed and well-managed push for the Republican nomination and subsequent election in 1988. The beliefs

103

and actions of the trainees did, in the long run, lead them to exert
influence on the general political situation.

At about the same time that Atwater's volunteers assembled in
Virginia, two much different attempts to persuade appeared in the
nation's press. Publicity releases and multipage ads in selected magazines introduced Acura as a new, completely separate division of the
America Honda Motor Company and its Acura Legend as a twenty-
four valve, six-cylinder car that was "breathing life into luxury."
These announcements were part of Honda's campaign to advise that
the new Acura Division would "market medium to high-priced vehicles with the emphasis on performance and luxury" and that Acura
expected soon to have a network of six hundred or more dealers. "The
Honda Division," according to the announcements, "will continue to
stress low to medium-priced vehicles; family automobiles, with the
emphasis on economy, comfort, and value for the money." The function of these announcements and the sustained campaign that followed was to help Acura compete successfully in the American
luxury, high-performance car market. The advertising program
worked. In less than two years the Acura Division was nationally established, the Legend was competing successfully with comparable
European cars, and knowledgeable people knew that a major car magazine had named the Legend "foreign car of the year." Perceptions of
the auto-market situation were indeed changed.

Morton Hunt's alarming lead article "Teaming Up against
AIDS" appeared in *The New York Times Magazine*, March 2, 1986. A
"tocsin of impending disaster," Hunt's essay pointed out that "there
isn't just one AIDS virus but a score that we know of—and *countless*
others, because it mutates at a hundred times the rate of other vi-
ruses. . . . In short, AIDS is clearly a serious threat to the entire
population." The function of the article was to alert, inform, and impress readers concerning efforts being made to find a cure for the acquired immune deficiency syndrome and concerning the dangers that
AIDS posed for society generally. By encouraging readers to learn
and to be disturbed, Hunt hoped to influence the fight against the
virus. There is no way to estimate how much good this particular article did. But as part of a continuing media blitz, it doubtless influ-

enced perceptions and contributed to the enormous task of alerting the nation.

As in the cases of these three examples, the ultimate purpose of all serious communication is to influence the state of affairs (the exigential flow) that made that communication possible or necessary. I call the part of the exigential flow that occurs prior to a particular communication, and that provokes it, the *provoking rhetorical urgency.* In this chapter I begin the study of provoking rhetorical urgencies by looking closely at the core concept: A significant provoking urgency is a developing set of perceptions. These perceptions are essentially symbolic in nature and are influenced by complex, multilevel forces that have no discrete beginnings. When they converge into stressful, cognitive states that invite or require modification by means of some sort of symbolic inducement, they constitute a provoking rhetorical urgency.

Rhetorical Urgencies Are Structured Perceptions

A rhetorical urgency is essentially symbolic in nature. Rhetorical urgencies are not really "out there" as sequences of objective events; they are patterns of thought and feeling in people's heads. Those patterns *symbolize* a version of experience by blending together the "out there" and the "in here." Virtually all urgencies *can* be seen as rhetorical. Even when natural disasters strike, the events *can* be interpreted as calling for, say, some "answer" to human suffering. If so, the disaster becomes amenable to remedy through rhetorical action. Thus, an urgency becomes rhetorical because human intelligence interprets objective data as cause for human concern. Urgencies that provoke rhetorical responses and the kinds of modifications to which they seem amenable are thus "constructed" symbolically by people who designate "raw" data as data calling for human intervention.

Participants may raise a given situation to the level of a rhetorical urgency but may differ about the nature of that urgency. This is the case with the federal deficit as an urgency. After years of bitterly denouncing runaway deficit financing, a good many people in Washington found that the Gramm-Rudman budget-balancing law forced them to rethink the nature of the budget deficit. Some politicians and theoreticians then discovered that the problem of the budget wasn't so bad after all. They said the deficit was really an aberration of the government's primitive single-budget accounting system that failed to distinguish between current spending and spending on investments. The federal government should emulate municipalities and businesses by adopting two budgets—an operating budget and a capital budget. If this were done, military expenses, student loans, research and development, and the like would be placed in the capital budget, and then the operating budget could easily be brought into the balance required by Gramm-Rudman. This view of the fiscal urgency would make it unnecessary to cut expenditures for defense or social programs or to raise taxes. Of course, many others disagreed with this analysis and continued to deplore the size of federal spending, but deficit remains an urgency that defies resolution and provokes rhetoric from several sides.

On occasion crises can exist without creating provoking rhetorical urgencies. They can exist largely unnoticed. The persons involved either don't perceive that an urgency exists when there really is one or don't adequately appreciate its severity or immediacy. For example, despite Stephen A. Douglas's persistent efforts, most persons in the late 1850s failed to comprehend fully that the underlying urgency of the times was the threat of civil war. More recently, Americans did not recognize that a cocaine problem existed among high school students until increasing use of a new form of the drug, called "crack," threatened an epidemic of abuse. Similarly, the savings and loan industry and the U.S. government's toxic waste cleanup program were in serious trouble for years before they were widely perceived to need rescue efforts, including rhetorical efforts. The world largely ignored massive destruction of the Amazon rain forest until alarmed into attention by disturbing happenings like these: The summer of 1988 in the United States was bothersomely hot and dry. Several months later the mass media devoted considerable attention to the murder of a leader of the Brazilian rubber tappers' union who was trying to save Amazon trees. About then the public learned that, in an effort to open up the area and improve its economy, Brazil had struck a tentative deal with Japan to fund a road through the Amazon to Peru and to the Pacific. During this time many Americans became aware that Brazil had burned some 300,000 square miles of its forests—an area larger than France. People who put these and other facts together awoke with explosive suddenness. The burning and loss of Amazon trees might contribute significantly to the "greenhouse effect," "a potentially dire change in the world's climate through what scientists believe will be a global warming trend!" A U.S. senator proclaimed that "the Amazon belongs to the world rather than to Brazil because of its ecological importance." Scientific expeditions and U.S. congressional investigative committees visited the area. An idea became current among Americans to exchange "debt for nature"—that is, some of Brazil's 120-billion-dollar foreign debt might be exchanged for conservation in the Amazon. This "outside" attention and advice, in turn, infuriated Brazilians who felt their sovereignty affronted. The important thing about all of this is that the ecological urgency had suddenly lost its dormancy. It has become a provoking rhetorical urgency. As Senator Dale Bumpers of Arkansas said, "So we come as thoughtful citizens of this planet to the negotiating table to decide" what can be done about the rain forests.

Conversely, perceptions can make imagined crises become actual rhetorical urgencies. Persons may believe that an urgency exists when it doesn't. Many Americans wrongly thought there was an urgency during recent scares that Gerber's baby food contained pieces of glass and during the Red scares of the McCarthy era. One of history's most famous examples of a false urgency/real rhetorical urgency was the "Popish Plot" affair, which took place in England. In the England of 1678 conditions were ripe for mass hysteria directed against Catholics. London was still recovering from the fire of 1666, which had destroyed two-thirds of the city and which allegedly had been started by Catholics. The Catholic queen and her court flaunted the country's anti-Catholic laws. On the continent Catholic Louis XIV consolidated his control over Spain, sent invading armies into the Netherlands, and threatened England's commercial and maritime hegemony. Protestants were apprehensive that on his death King

Charles would be succeeded by his Catholic brother, James. There was already a general failure of confidence in government and political leadership. There was also widespread, corrosive suspicion of Catholics. Into these predisposing circumstances a perjurer, Titus Oates, projected a complex, fabricated story that Catholics were conspiring to murder Charles, substitute his Catholic brother, and restore England to Catholicism by rebellion. This tale led much of Protestant society to believe that a provoking crisis of gravest immediacy actually existed. It was widely thought that in coordinated strikes the Catholics were going to massacre thousands of Protestants and that the queen was in league with assassination attempts on her husband's life. Largely on the basis of invented evidence supplied by Oates and testimony given by a known conspirator and confidence man, William Bedloe, seven men were executed for treason and a Disabling Act was passed excluding Roman Catholics from both houses of Parliament. Although there was no "real" substance to the conspiracy, it constituted a very "real" urgency to the alarmed Protestants, and through the rhetoric of their Parliament and their courts they modified the alleged exigency to their satisfaction.

It is important to notice that a significant exigential flow is much larger and more encompassing than any rhetorical response that becomes part of it. The Brazilian ecological urgency dwarfs any particular rhetorical response such as Senator Bumpers's. The false urgency of the Popish Plot was enormously more involved than the rhetorical machinations of Titus Oakes or any other specific response to the imagined urgency. Indeed, as the Brazilian example aptly illustrates, a significant exigential flow may have begun long before any set of speeches or editorials dealt with problems it entails. This was true of the exigential flow of which the debates about the Compromise of 1850 became a part. In fact, that exigential flow continued following the debates, up to the ending of the Civil War. To take a more personal case, when a marriage fails, the exigential flow undoubtedly encompasses far more than a final quarrel leading one of the parties to file for divorce. And lawyer-client relationships usually precede any pretrial deposition constituting a response to the urgency of resolving the marriage. The exigential flow in this kind of case will

continue at least until the divorce becomes final. In sum, exigential
flows that are significant will *precede* and will *continue after* the rhetorical responses they evoke.

The portion of an exigential flow occurring prior to a particular
communication—for example, Senator Bumpers's statement, the
Compromise of 1850 debates, or the final quarrel that breaks up a
marriage—I call the "provoking rhetorical urgency" because it provokes that rhetorical response. Because something occurs, or appears
likely to occur, the circumstances are perceived as stressful, constituting some kind of need that potentially can, or should, be changed
by rhetorical means. In the supermarket you run into an old friend
whom you haven't seen for some time. Obviously this chance meeting should provoke some sort of response—in recognition of the other's identity, the congenial rapport the two of you have shared, and
the warmth one has in seeing the other. Failure to offer an appropriate
greeting would ordinarily indicate that something is very wrong. The
point is a general one. Any time anyone communicates purposefully
to one's self or to someone else, he or she is responding to some perceived provocation. Such rhetorical provoking urgencies are large and
small. Although they usually don't constitute crises, and often not
even an unpleasant situation or problem needing to be corrected, the
circumstances seem in some degree stressful, stimulating, or "provoking." If that is not the case, no communicator will be motivated to
attempt to modify the circumstances.

All rhetorical decision making and justifying is response to urgencies that are perceived to have recognizable, temporal developments. Provoking rhetorical urgencies are perceived as having a
history, a "life span." Consider the trial of Oliver North for involvement in the Iran-Contra scandal. A huge series of events and decisions affected the character of North's trial. Consider the trial by an
anonymous court of Romanian President Nicolae Ceausescu and his
chief deputy, his wife Elena, and their summary execution by military firing squad. The upheaval in Bucharest and the more "gentle
revolutions" in Poland, Hungary, Czechoslovakia, and East Germany
were all parts of the long tumultuous flow of events chronicling
the decline of the Soviet Empire. To take still another case, those

negotiating to stabilize peace in the Middle East can't think of their efforts as unrelated to past relationships among the peoples of the area and between those peoples and interested outsiders, especially the major powers.

In appraising a provoking rhetorical urgency as a developing set of perceptions, one should observe three cautions. First, although all data are processual in character, one needs to be alert to isolatable *developments* in perceptions and to the possibilities for modifying the urgency at each state of its development.

Second, one should keep in mind that "provoking urgency" is merely a name assigned to what one can see in looking at rhetoric. Urgencies don't exist "out there" like chunks of physical material. Events and happenings don't in themselves have form or structure. For them to acquire reality perceivers have to impose structure on them. A provoking urgency, then, is a *structured perception of ongoing conditions*. It is the "reality" that someone perceives when looking at dynamic events through the lenses supplied by the definition of provoking urgency.

Third, although an observer of communication seeks to discover order and structure in the way participants perceive urgencies, one should always be very conscious that one can never capture *the* reality and immobilize it through the magic of letters and ink. The synthesizing abstractions an observer creates are not equivalents to previous fleeting moments experienced by "real" things and people. Such realities were in constant flux. When an observer finds thematic linkages among data, the linkages do no more than suggest a *perceptual* reality. Such linkages may nonetheless improve one's understanding of what happened, why it happened, and how people involved thought and felt about it. We do this when we divide people into "growth categories" like infant, child, adolescent, adult, and senior citizen. We imply that life advances by stages even though we know these "stages" are not firmly distinct from one another. Nonetheless, the idea of stages helps us to focus on clearly different aspects of living a life. These kinds of divisions and linkages often give us a better grasp—better than even the actual participants had—of the nature of rhetorical urgencies and their potential for change at the times of particular communications.

Inasmuch as I have described a rhetorical urgency as a "set of perceptions . . . influenced by complex, multilevel forces," I need to identify what these forces are. Before I do so, however, let me reject the propensity of many students to think of an exigence as a general sociological/historical backdrop on which communications can be fixed in much the same manner that an artist focuses an etching by means of mat and frame. A rhetorical urgency is not a comprehensive backdrop array of events and happenings. Furthermore, it is probably impossible to apprehend a comprehensive account of anything. According to the Pulitzer Prize–winning biographer David Donald, any comprehensive treatment will result in a "club sandwich, with layers of social, cultural, and economic history interspersed between the dry bread of . . . narrative." Instead of visualizing an urgency as a backdrop or a generalized account of events and happenings, one should conceive of it as a structured set of cognitions drawn from a *mix* of complex, multilevel forces.

Those of us who try to understand and interpret rhetoric need to discover the nature and potentialities for change in urgencies that provoke rhetoric. Both explicit and implicit patterns in an exigential flow influence participants' perceptions of urgencies. Explicit patterns are often found in immediate situations that provoke communication. When the treasury is empty, communication becomes explicitly fiscal. Influential explicit patterns can also be found in the historical development of an urgency and/or in the "structuralization of groupings" associated with an urgency.

Where readily observable patterns don't give adequate understanding of the potential for change in a situation, one should look for implicit patterns in the situation that are reflected from society. These are not relevant to any particular urgency exclusively; they pervade the belief systems of participants and exert indirect or even subconscious influence on how various states of affairs are perceived. Such patterns may exist as general social views, myths, or traditions. I call these patterns *Zeitgeist* influences. Implicit patterns also exist as social needs and pressures such as cultural, economic/technological, and ideological pressures. The role of implicit patterns is highlighted by recent debates about cultural diversity in education. Some argue that for too long an implicit pattern stressing Western history and

culture has precluded attention to the significant histories and traditions of different ethnic groups, of the Third World, of Eastern culture, and the like. On the other side it is contended that since
Western culture and traditions dominate wherever "civilization" has
reached, Westernism should continue to be the dominant, though
perhaps not the exclusive, influence in education. The provoking urgency for this debate arises from what I am calling implicit patterns
that are reflected from society./The rival communicators' perceptions, generated by *Zeitgeist* influences and by social needs and pressures, predetermine how they conceptualize the provoking rhetorical
urgencies and how they respond to them.

    In studying the explicit and largely implicit forces that influence
participants' perceptions of urgencies, we have to recognize that each
of these forces is both (a consequence of previous causes and a cause
of unending future consequences. If one could trace their progenito-
rial lines—or their unfolding consequences—they would proliferate
endlessly. Therefore, in order to make a significant provoking urgency conceptually manageable, we have to impose starting and ending points on the flow of events that interest us. We must set what
seem reasonable time frames, appropriate points at which to begin
and end study of an urgency. A general guideline for imposing beginnings and endings is to weigh the degree of relevance that data and
developments have for the communicative events we want to study.
To understand the Compromise debates of 1850 we don't need to im-
merse ourselves in David Brion Davis's majestically brilliant three-
volume work depicting the role slavery and antislavery have played in
world history.[2] But we do need a basic grasp of the divisive development of slavery in this country. To understand the Pennsylvania
ratification debates, one needs to understand political practices under
Penn's Charter. They were part of the flow of governmental experience and learning through which preindependence Pennsylvanians
lived. Since Pennsylvanians were confronted with *constructing* constitutional practices and procedures, one needs to get a handle on this.
But one knows from the outset that one doesn't have to become expert on legislation actually passed prior to 1776, because the participants in the ratification controversy spurned Colonial policies almost

entirely except where civil rights had been at issue. In short, the *relevance* of data to the particular discourses we want to study is the prime test of what to draw out of the "comprehensive bag" and what it's safe to ignore.

Perceptions Invite Modification by Rhetorical Means

An urgency becomes a provoking rhetorical urgency only when persons perceive that a stressful state of affairs welcomes or demands modification *by means of talk*. To make clear what I mean, let's visualize the following scene. A major leaguer has just stretched a long outfield hit into a triple. After his slide into the bag, he calls time for an apparent hamstring pull. As he limps around, evincing pain, the trainer comes on to the field, followed by a coach. The player seems to be resisting an order to leave the game. Finally the coach and trainer, with obvious reluctance, return to the dugout. The rival manager, watching the proceedings from his dugout, nudges the pitching coach sitting next to him. "They're overdoing things, don't you think?" "Yeah," the other responds, "I smell a big fat rat." "Well, get out there to the mound and tell our guys to expect a squeeze play," the manager says. The urgency has become a *rhetorical* urgency. In the ensuing discussion at the mound, the pitching coach, pitcher, and catcher agree that with the score tied in the bottom of the ninth and the runner a renowned base stealer, the injury was probably a fake. They were being set up for an attempt to steal home. They agree on their defensive strategy. The pitcher will restrict his windup and will throw only fast balls, low and away from the batter, making it difficult or impossible for him to bunt. The strategy works. On the first pitch the batter misses his attempted bunt, and the runner coming down the base path is easily tagged out at the plate. Words, of course, did not tag the runner. The actual physical action was by a fist holding the ball. Rhetoric served as the instrumentality for change; it controlled the means through which nonrhetorical modifying actions were set in motion and directed.

As in this imaginary urgency in a baseball game, any significant urgency represents a way people think, feel, and choose to respond, *collectively*. However, a given urgency may evoke decision making at different times for different persons. For example, according to David L. Swanson, "normally approximately one-third of the voters" in a presidential election "reach their decision before the nominating conventions, one-third decide during the conventions, and a final one-third reach decisions during the campaign period proper."[3]

Occasionally, as in the case of destruction of the Amazon rain forests, conditions come to be perceived as constituting a significant rhetorical urgency suddenly, even explosively. Another good example is the shocking public response to publication of Rachel Carson's *Silent Spring* in 1962, when her book "launched the environmentalist movement." The need to protect natural resources had been a real urgency for centuries, but it had not been widely perceived as a serious problem requiring extensive discussion and action until Carson's book came out. The clarity, vividness, and comprehensive explicitness of Carson's writing stimulated a tremendous, ongoing interest in the environment. The first of a series of Earth Days was held eight years later, and millions of Americans have taken part in antipollution demonstrations ever since.

Still another example of an explosive, then sustained, maturation of perceptions is the exigence concerning what to do about ex-president Ferdinand Marcos's hidden wealth. It was known or suspected for twenty years that Marcos, his wife, and their henchmen were amassing huge illegal fortunes. Until Marcos was deposed as president of the Philippines, however, very little could be said openly in the islands and little was done about it elsewhere. Once Corazon Aquino's revolution drove Marcos into exile, the existence of the Marcoses' wealth immediately evoked wide and enduring rhetorical responses. In the Philippines and elsewhere people were prompted to ask such questions as: How much treasure had Marcos obtained? Where was it, and in what forms? Could the Philippine government get any or all of it back? Legal investigations of the Marcoses's investments and other holdings were carried out. Indictments of Marcos and his wife were sought and secured in United States courts. Even Ferdinand Marcos's death didn't stay the rhetoric. In New York courts Imelda Marcos was declared not guilty of racketeering and other charges, but the end of the exigence was still not in sight. Once provoking rhetorical urgencies "explode," their duration may be short or long.

Significant rhetorical exigencies can arise suddenly, but more often perceptions of a significant rhetorical urgency "mature" and "decay" in a manner that sometimes seems almost predictable. For example, those of us who lived through the experience can remember the horrified fascination with which we watched the widening involvement of the United States in Vietnam, beginning with the subsidizing of the French army in the Indochina War during the early 1950s. Eventually came the slowly developing protest movement against the Vietnam war; the hesitant movement toward withdrawal of American troops from the area; and the eventual surrender of the Saigon regime in April 1975. Throughout this long exigence, perceptions of the nature of the Vietnam situation, and what to do about it, slowly and continuously changed—resulting in a succession of different urgencies. For example, the American perception of the urgency, which would not have accepted the use of U.S. combat troops in 1954, became resigned over the next decade to U.S. armed intervention. After President Dwight Eisenhower agreed to help train the South Vietnamese army, a few hundred U.S. military observers were sent to Vietnam; later the number of observers was radically increased; observers were allowed to accompany the South Vietnamese forces into combat and then ordered to engage actively in the fighting; 15,000 U.S. support troops were sent to the area and became "endangered"; and over $500 million in aid was given to the Saigon government. After the American public's perception of the urgency accepted a combative role for American forces, U.S. military involvement steadily increased. Like the perceptions of the early arms buildup, the later perceptions of "inevitable" defeat and withdrawal were gradual, almost predictable, developments.

As is implied in what was just said, the ways participants perceive provoking rhetorical urgencies alter. People sometimes become more, then less, willing to respond to proposed kinds of changes. In the Vietnam case, participants' conceptual focus may welcome a certain kind of rhetorical response at one point but not do so later on. Arguments about suppressing Viet Cong aggression could be influential in early stages of the Vietnam developments, but they were scarcely relevant in the late stages. My point is that if we are to understand communication, it is very important that we be alert to the changefulness of participants' perceptions of urgencies and of what to do about them.

In recent history we have seen attitudes toward federal spending and taxation change markedly. As attitudes toward deficit spending became increasingly negative, attitudes toward higher taxes or, as it has been euphemistically called, "revenue enhancement," became correspondingly more positive. When President Bush altered his stand on "no new taxes," deficits strengthened as a provoking urgency and taxation diminished as a provoking urgency. These urgencies were thrown into greater confusion when the Iraqi invasion of Kuwait touched off a brief war, involving large numbers of American and Allied forces. To some extent the Persian Gulf war and an extended recession encouraged rethinking of basic questions concerning the budget, the economy, taxation, and the deficit.

Rhetoric may be a source of delight at times in works of poets, composers, or dramatic wordsmiths, but even in moments of sublimity rhetoric functions in its ineluctable role as a practical instrument for effecting change. Shelley had this sense when he wrote that "He gave man speech, and speech created thought, / Which is the measure of the universe." Speech gives us the enormous advantage of flexibility in dealing with a changing environment. As conditions change we have the capacity to recognize these changes and deal with them rhetorically. More basic still to the nature of human functioning is the fact that whenever we speak or write, we do so in response to some provocation and with the intent to modify that provocation in some way.

Chapter Seven

Do human perceive
in pattern?
Do object have pattern?
that shape perception?
Do pattern when in situation?

Explicit Influences
Within an Urgency

All talk is a direct response to some provocation—which I call a provoking rhetorical urgency. The talk is intended to modify that provocation in some way. I have argued that a provoking rhetorical urgency is the way participants perceive an ongoing situation that they think can be, or should be, changed through rhetoric. These perceptions are made up of a number of components; the most important and easiest to identify are, as I have said, the relatively explicit ways of participants' thinking or perceiving about the urgency. If we know what to look for, we can see how explicit patterns of perception develop out of (1) the immediate circumstances of an urgency when a communication takes place (*situational patterns*), (2) the historical development of an urgency (*historical patterns*), and (3) the structure of the major groupings in an urgency (*group patterns*).

Situational/Historical Patterns

By far the most valuable sources of inference concerning an urgency are situational and historical patterns. In simple urgencies and even many complex ones, a search for one or both of these types of patterns can provide enough information to allow an estimate of the amount and kind of change that can be made in an urgency. A rhetorical urgency illustrating this point was the 1989 trial of sports agents Lloyd Bloom and Norby Walters. They were charged in a U.S. District Court of Chicago with racketeering, mail fraud, wire fraud, and extortion. These charges were in connection with the agents' signing some forty-three college athletes to contracts while the players still had college eligibility remaining. Signing these football and basketball players was a violation of NCAA rules and allegedly a

117

violation of law. This knowledge gives us the basic situational/historical data we need. The formal record of the trial will provide the rest of the situational/historical data—what specific laws were supposedly violated, what threats were allegedly made against the players, and the like.

What are situational/historical patterns? As in the Bloom-Walters case, a situational/historical pattern is (1) a significant way of thinking/perceiving (2) by participants (3) that is generated from the immediate circumstances or the historical development of a provoking urgency. In the Bloom-Walters case, the perceptual framework within which the entire trial must be conducted was defined by the formal charges against the defendants together with the laws under which they were charged. The charges specified what the agents allegedly did, as defined by the laws cited by the prosecution. We have a tight relationship here. The importance of consciously identifying this particular pattern is suggested by the fact that probably no other trial has been or will be conducted within exactly this situational and historical framework. Situational/historical patterns explain, or help to explain, what participants' structured perceptions of a provoking urgency are likely to have been. Let's take the simple Bloom-Walters case again. The charge together with the applicable laws tell any interested person what the trial was and was not about. It was a trial of two specific sports agents for allegedly violating some specific laws. Notice that such matters as the agents' general morality, their signees' characters and morality, whether collegiate athletics is or isn't big business, all fall *outside* the situational/historical patterns that characterize the urgency of *this trial.*

How does a person know when he or she has found a significant situational/historical pattern? You know when you can provide good reasons for the conclusion that there is a *pattern* here and that it stipulates something specific about the ways participants perceived the urgency you are studying. In the Bloom-Walters case, one can make a clear and almost unassailable argument that in this country you can't prosecute anyone without making specific charges and citing the specific laws that were allegedly violated. Thus, perceptions of what this trial was and wasn't about were defined by charge and laws. Neither alone would reveal the intrinsic character of the case.

Not even in this very clear case can an observer of rhetoric provide a conclusion that is verifiable by means of quantification or even
formal logic. "Knowing" that certain things generate ways of thinking
about a provocation is a matter of finding relevant data and being able
to give strong reasons why certain of these data would probably cause
participants to think in a particular way about *this* configuration of
rhetorical forces. Different people can look at the same evidence and
form different opinions about whether a pattern of thinking/perceiv-
ing exists and, if it does, what the nature of the pattern is and what
it says about this situation. One could, for example, claim that what
Bloom and Walters did would not constitute extortion. The legitimacy of the differing views would depend on the relative weight the
observers' arguments could carry with someone else—in the Bloom-
Walters case, with a judge.

A useful rule of thumb is that one knows one has found a significant pattern when one can make a good case that the cohering re-   ? (ルルン?)
lationships of data seem to give integration, design, or systematic or
logical shape to the way participants perceived an urgency. In the
Bloom-Walters case we know we have two significant sets of data in
the charge and the laws because we can reasonably claim that these
two items together define perceptions of what an American trial is.
Examining the rhetoric of a presidential inaugural address would
present a more complex case, but in principle as observer-critics we
would work the same way. We would try to learn about inaugural
addresses generally and about anything that seemed pertinent or
special about the immediate inauguration. Then we would try to put
this information together in a way that would help to tell us what
amount and kind of change was possible in the urgency that provoked
this particular acknowledgment that a presidential administration
was beginning.

Situational Patterns

Situational patterns are easily recognized in simple urgencies
that occur repeatedly. Clearly distinct perceptual patterns conditioning rhetorical responses exist in familiar circumstances such as those
that result in a retirement dinner, a college commencement, an election night celebration, and obituaries and funeral eulogies. Stressful

occasions arise so often and so clearly demand particular rhetorical responses that characteristic formats have evolved. Thus, stereotyped rhetorical responses have developed to produce genres or standard types of messages of introduction, presentation, acceptance, welcome, response to a welcome, and farewell. Even greater stereotypings of expectations derive from legal trial procedures: in a jury trial the distinct, inherent nature of the situation prescribes the rhetorical forms followed in the selection, examination, and cross-examination of witnesses, in presentation of evidence, in summation statements, in the judge's charge to the jury, in the official record keeping of the trial, and so on.

The Colonial New England sermon was an example of how situational stereotyping produces rhetorical genres—forms and styles—and sustains them across years or even centuries. The clarity of the situational circumstances that reoccurred on election days in New England throughout the Colonial period produced distinct, patterned perceptions in New Englanders and thereby constrained the rhetorical responses in election sermons. Beginning in Boston in the early 1630s, various settlements of Massachusetts and Connecticut arranged that a clergyman would deliver a sermon on election day, the time each year when the freeholders selected their officials. Later, when provincial governments had been instituted, an outstanding minister was regularly selected to preach an election-day sermon in one of the largest churches to a distinguished auditory, including members of the General Court, perhaps half of the clergymen of the colony, and several hundred assorted dignitaries and citizens. After the service, the legislators repaired to the capitol to select the members of the governor's council. Usually the sermon was published and distributed rather widely.

A particular sermonic form evolved to meet the solemnity of the election occasion, the elite character of the audience and speaker, and the heightened expectations of the community. Consequently, as time passed, there came to be a growing number of election sermons that served as models. Public perception conjoined the immediate circumstances to form situational patterns of anticipation that, in turn, prescribed the form of the acceptable sermon. The result was that, not unlike peas in a pod, election sermons became similar in length, form, tone, and subject matter. Year after year the speeches offered the same advice as to what legislators, officials, ministers, and the general public needed to do to make the covenant system function well and so bring glory to God and prosperity to the land. A major factor contributing to emergence of this sermonic form was, of course, the covenant theology that both reasonably and by revelation stipulated the best form of government, to which all persons in the province were presumed to adhere. This constant in the province's founding and history virtually prescribed that sermonizers pair good political practice with the obligation to glorify God.[1]

It would be a mistake to assume, however, that repeated occurrence is a prerequisite for situational patterns to exist as distinguishable responses to a rhetorical urgency. For example, some unusual types of urgencies result in eulogies in newspapers and newsmagazines and also in televised funeral eulogies in the U.S. Capitol Rotunda (as the eulogies of Presidents Kennedy and Eisenhower and of Senator Dirksen). In such cases perceptions of the situation are so clear and distinct that they produce special rhetorical responses similar in content, structure, tone, and approach. Consider some of the circumstances that evoke such patterns of thinking/perceiving.

1. An admired major personage has died, and public expectations demand that his or her passing be specially noted.

2. Inasmuch as his or her public deeds have reflected and have helped to strengthen community myths, values, and goals, such "goods" need reinforcement by praise of the deceased as the community's symbolic representative.

3. To help maintain the prestige and desirability of high office and exceptional achievement, major leaders must receive public acknowledgment and praise for their outstanding service.

4. There is an underlying pervasive realization of the transitoriness of human experience. This is symbolized by his or her death and produces a rhetorical need for reassurance of continuity.

5. The intrusion of television cameras and microphones with
   their strict time requirements, the existence of a mass audience, the preempting of commercial programs, the presence of press reporters and television commentators—all
   of these also contribute constraining influences.

These circumstances, when conjoined in the perceptions of participants, produce patterns of expectations so similar in each case that
they demand stereotypical responses, a kind of special rhetorical
genre. The situational patterns have become so clear for the Rotunda
presentations that, according to Ronald H. Carpenter and Robert V.
Seltzer, the circumstances of the urgency have produced "salient similarities in style—*regardless of their writers.*"[2]

It may be argued that the urgencies provoking Rotunda eulogies
demand rhetorical forms derived from the endlessly repeated rituals
of burying the dead, but the following examples illustrate that even
unique one-of-a-kind rhetorical urgencies may have clear and relatively uniform situational patterns.

In the fall of 1860 Democratic party leaders in the Deep South
had so stereotyped the threat posed by Northern "aggressions" and
by the Republican "conspiracy" that Lincoln's election left them with
a simplistic view of the problem and their options in response. The
actual or real urgency was very complex—so complex, in fact, that
more than a decade ago Michael L. Holt argued that all previous explanations of secession were inadequate.[3] Nonetheless, following the
election of Abraham Lincoln, the governors of five Lower South
states rhetorically turned almost immediately to secession. The governor of Alabama issued a written proclamation calling for a special
secession convention. The governors of Georgia, Mississippi, Florida, and Louisiana delivered speeches to their respective legislatures
(and, of course, to the inhabitants of their states) urging the legislatures to issue convention calls. To the governors, the situations that
provoked their rhetorical actions seemed alike.

The striking uniformity of the governors' communications is ample evidence that they shared the same perceptions of the urgency.
According to Douglas P. Starr, although the governors of Mississippi
and Florida spoke many miles apart on the same day, they "almost

echoed each other's ideas and recommendations." Each of the four governors addressed four central claims: "the supremacy of state over federal sovereignty, the refusal of the North to enforce the Fugitive Slave Law of 1850, the desirability of secession, and the need to make preparations for war." Each governor supplied as "warrants" for his claims "appeals to southern tradition, state sovereignty, patriotism, liberty, the Bible, God, equality (of states, not of the races), unjust sufferings by states in the struggle for justice, and difficulties that slaveholders had experienced in seeking legal recovery of their fugitive slaves." As backing for his warrants, each governor "cited the United States Constitution and laws and agreements among the various states for political and commercial intercourse," thereby alleging that the federal government had treated the South unjustly, illegally, and dishonorably.[4]

In presenting their almost identical cases, the governors were not acting in collusion; they were responding to what they similarly perceived to be the provoking situation. The evidence seemed so impelling, the antecedents stretched so deeply into the remembered past, and the same ground had been worked over so many times by editors, politicians, and preachers in the preceding weeks and months that Southern perception of the election crisis had formalized. Tensions, issues, causes, alternatives, and irreducible choices had resolved themselves into patterns of perception shared by a majority of the inhabitants of the Deep South. Here was formalized rhetoric that did not mirror past rhetoric but reflected common perceptions of the provoking urgency.

As a somewhat different type of example, President Richard M. Nixon brought the Republican congressional campaign of 1970 to a close with a harsh election-eve denunciation of the Democrats. He insinuated that they were soft on crime and violence. Democratic leaders drew several conclusions from the immediate situation: The situation had called for some sort of summary statement from Nixon, but the character of his speech made necessary a further summary statement from the Democrats. As Robert W. Norton has pointed out, "Like the closure phenomenon, the election process would not seem complete without the windup statements." It was clear that Mr.

Nixon had to be answered: the Democratic statement not only had to summarize but it also had to refute the president. Further, the spokesperson serving as campaign anchorperson for the Democrats had to be a major political figure who possessed a suitable image. Of the Democrats only three seemed to be strong possibilities: Edmund Muskie, Hubert Humphrey, and Edward Kennedy. Inasmuch as Humphrey was engaged in a comeback election in Minnesota and Kennedy had recently been stained by the waters of Chappaquiddick, the circumstances called for Muskie to be the spokesperson. Finally, inasmuch as President Nixon's speech had seemed jarringly partisan to many voters, the situation called for the Democratic representative to assume the role of a "magnanimous statesman," to invite "unity instead of disunity," to appear "benevolent to the opposite party," and to offer "a saneness, a sense of trust, a sense of empathy, a sense of concern." In response to these perceptions of the urgency, Muskie planned an election-eve speech that, while attempting to refute the President and help the Democratic cause, supplied the necessary healing rhetoric.[5]

In a great many communications we need to look no further than the immediate situation to find the patterns that helped to define both the appropriate rhetorical responses and the changes that were possible in the urgency.

Historical Patterns

Urgencies are sometimes more complex than those I have just cited, however. The significant forces shaping an urgency sometimes evolve over time. Analysis of immediate circumstances will not then provide enough information to support a fully reasoned rhetorical analysis. In those cases, one needs to look for patterns of thinking/perceiving in the chronology accounting for the urgency.

The Canadian government's public hearings concerning drug use in sports constituted such a situation in 1989. The government created what it called Canada's Commission of Inquiry into the Use of Drugs and Banned Practices to Increase Athletic Performance. The immediate reason the commission was created was that, after he had won the Olympic gold medal in the hundred-meter dash, Ben

Johnson had been disqualified for using drugs. The commission's rhetorical urgency was not, however, as simple as the urgency in the Bloom-Walters trial. More than Ben Johnson's disqualification was involved. The problem of drugs in Canadian sports—the broad urgency that actually provoked the hearings held by the commission—had a significant history that went back beyond Johnson's disqualification. The expressed purpose of the inquiry was to contribute to drug-free athletics generally in Canada. At the conclusion of the inquiry, Ontario judge Charles Dubin, the person in charge, would make recommendations to Canada's sports bureaucracy. New regulations and/or laws could be recommended and enacted, based on the history of performance-enhancing substances and practices. The entire recent record of sports in Canada would have to be considered, and an observer or critic who wanted to understand the rhetoric of the commission's hearings and recommendations would need to understand that past record. Just knowing about the Ben Johnson case would be insufficient.

The problem of drugs in Canadian sports had begun about twenty years before the hearings, and some questions that needed to be asked about this history were: Do patterns emerge over the two decades in perceptions of, and responses to, the urgency by (1) athletes, (2) coaches, and (3) sports officials, public leaders, and the public? When these *topoi* are applied to the historical data, distinct patterns emerge. Drug acceptance and use among highly competitive athletes increased strikingly during the late 70s and early 80s, peaked about the time of the Olympics, and apparently declined following Johnson's disqualification. Although not necessarily convinced that performance-enhancing drugs in low, controlled doses have harmful side effects, Canadian athletes by the time of the hearing seemed generally willing to abstain from future use of drugs *if* suitable regulations were enacted and enforced. A basically similar pattern seemed to characterize the perceptions of coaches. Before the Johnson scandal sports bureaucrats, government authorities, and the public had seemed largely unaware that a serious problem of drugs existed. Johnson's disgrace transformed the pattern of apathy into general dismay and eagerness to correct the situation. When we see together the historical increase in performance-enhancing practices, the evolving receptiveness among athletes and coaches for some sorts of regulations, and the public's change from general apathy to eagerness for corrections, we can see that *new* and now *intense* exigencies for investigation and change marked the provoking urgency in Canada as they never had before.

The way to discover historical patterns influencing a significant urgency is to follow these procedures, or similar ones: (1) Arbitrarily select what seems to a reasonable starting point in tracing the urgency. Careful preliminary study should suggest what this point is. (2) If the emergent patterns change by stages, divide your identification of the patterns according to what seem to be the natural and most significant time frames. (3) Analyze each time frame to identify emergent patterns of ideas or concepts that seem to epitomize or identify the essential nature or intrinsic character of that particular period. These patterns should help to explain the direction of the exigential flow during the particular time frame and to prefigure subsequent developments. What we are working toward in all of this is to discover distinctive and distinguishable patterns or shapes in the ways participants viewed the urgency at the time of the communication. In the case of the Canadian commission we come to see that the urgency for regulations evolved from a stage of relative indifference to a stage of acute concern. This tells us that a special receptivity for what the commission would do and say had grown up from forces including but not confined to Johnson's disgrace.

Before I illustrate exploration of historical patterns further, there are several general points to be made. First, in dealing with the Canadian commission's urgency or the urgency of 1850, the same discernible patterns would be significant no matter what responses to the urgency one chose to study. In studying slavery-oriented rhetoric of the 1850s, whether I chose to focus on Calhoun's treatise *Disquisition on Government*, or on Harriett Beecher Stowe's *Uncle Tom's Cabin*, the same discernible patterns of thought and perception would be relevant to my study. Those same historical, social, and psychological phenomena shaped the urgency that both pieces of rhetoric sought to address in their very different ways. Second, all responses to a given provoking urgency become components of the ongoing flow of that urgency. A communication modifies the development of the urgency. In various ways Calhoun's speech on March 4, 1850, influenced those who heard it or read it or read about it, and it thereby affected the urgency itself. A third point follows from the second: what happens to the exigential flow following a communication becomes the postmessage stage of the urgency. Developments that followed Calhoun's March 4 speech constituted the postmessage phase of the overall urgency I need to understand if I am to understand Calhoun's rhetoric fully. The same would be true if my interest were in, say, Horace Greeley's editorial attacks on Stephen A. Douglas's Kansas–Nebraska bill in 1854. The postmessage phase of Calhoun's discourse would be part of the provoking urgency for Greeley's communications. Were my interest in *Cannibals All! or, Slaves Without Masters*, published in 1857, the postmessage phases of both Calhoun's and Greeley's efforts would now be parts of the urgency that gave rise to the 1857 rhetorical document.

I reemphasize that it is fairly easy to unravel the historical developments relative to the Canadian drug-use hearings or to most other instances of rhetorical attempts to alter urgencies. I return, however, to the complicated case of Calhoun's March 4 speech.

An Issue of Freedom and Equality vs. Slavery Emerges

The exigential flow that matured into the crisis of 1850 did not really begin until the era of the American Revolution. In the Colonial period black slavery was generally accepted in North and South. When one reviews the occurrences of the Revolutionary era, one finds that it was when the ideals of freedom, equality, and the brotherhood of man pervaded the thinking of Americans and provided the rationale for the War of Independence that dramatic changes occurred in the ways many persons regarded slavery. The "central paradox of American history" was thus firmly established: the "contradictory development" in the South of liberty and equality along with slavery. The form of differing sectional responses was established.[6]

These data yield the following pattern that seems to describe the beginnings of the urgency Calhoun would address.

> *#1: Slavery became a rhetorical urgency because by the close of the Revolution, Northerners and Southerners perceived that slavery constituted a problem, or urgency. They recognized that they viewed slavery in basically different ways.*

Slavery Becomes Provocative

Although significant demographic, economic, and political changes occurred in the North and South, historians are unable to explain why it was that, by 1819, the South had somehow moved from the idealism of the War of Independence and made what Don E. Fehrenbacher has called "the most important decision in the whole history of the slavery controversy—and made it with virtual unanimity."[7] Furthermore, historians can't explain why the North suddenly moved to a militant, rigid position on slavery's expansion. Nevertheless, it is clear that the following pattern helps identify changes in the ways participants now perceived the slavery urgency.

> *#2: By the Missouri Compromise debates of 1819–1821, Southerners had come to perceive that slavery was necessary to the South and must be permanent. The Northerners, in turn, had come to perceive that they were unalterably opposed to the expansion of slavery.*

This basic split in perceptions widened, deepened, and became more sophisticated over the years and would produce the ways Northerners and Southerners responded to the urgency of 1850 and to Calhoun's speech of March 4.

Missouri Compromise Era

The Missouri Compromise debates, 1819–1821, generated many of the structured perceptions the participants had of the urgency of 1850. Glover Moore has written that the Compromise controversy "was an epitome of the entire sectional controversy before 1860, containing all of the important elements of previous and future antagonisms. . . . Its clarifying effects were not only great but appalling. . . . The westward expansion of slavery was an issue upon

which a united North could be arrayed against a united South. . . .
The events of the forties, fifties, and sixties were unmistakably fore-
shadowed in the clarification of sectional issues wrought by the Missouri Controversy. Here, clearly, was the 'knell of the Union,' the
'title page to a great tragic volume.' "[8]

From these data I conclude that several patterns of thought represented how participants now perceived the developing urgency of
slavery.

> *#3: The uncompromising stands of Northerners and Southerners in the
> Missouri Compromise debates forecast that the only kind of compro-
> mise either side could accept would be an ambiguous quasi-compromise
> that would enable them to rationalize their actions.*

This pattern of thought was to mean in 1850 that, if there was to
be a resolution of the sectional conflict, it had to contain enough ambiguity for the legislators to rationalize their actions. Thus it was that
"popular sovereignty" became the centerpiece of the Compromise
of 1850.

> *#4: Sufficient numbers of both Northerners and Southerners now felt
> so strongly about various slavery concerns that a single legislative
> package containing multiple slavery proposals could not be adopted by
> Congress; each proposal would have to be considered separately as a
> separate bill.*

No grouping of slave-related items could pass through Congress
in 1819–1821 or, later, in 1850. This was the reason why Clay's Omnibus Bill, which was designed to answer the sectional crisis, was rejected. After the measures in the defeated bill were separated into
individual bills, they successfully passed the Senate.

> *#5: Northerners and Southerners vividly perceived that parity in the
> Senate was vital to Southern interests. Therefore, they saw that the
> question of congressional authority over slavery in the territories must
> be a central issue in organizing any new territories.*

This general recognition was to make the territorial and associated question of statehood for California hotly contested in 1850. It
was the need to organize the western lands that precipitated the crisis
of 1850.

*#6: Southerners perceived they must evolve and propound a justifica-
tion for slavery that would protect their conception of themselves as
moral, competent persons.*

This was the real beginning of Southern preoccupation with the
morality of slavery and with Southern rights and honor. This preoccupation gradually became an obsession, dominating Southern response to the urgency of 1850.

*#7: Southerners perceived that, at the same time they were presenting
a solid front politically, they should exploit potential incompatibilities
among Northerners and should seek countervailing influence within
the national parties.*

Moderate Southerners in 1850 would still accept that their best
means of security lay in maintaining influence within the national political party system. They were not yet willing to abandon the political system, as Calhoun was to suggest in this speech to the Senate.

*#8: Astute Southerners perceived that the South must eventually en-
dorse the concept of secession as the ultimate strategic defense of slavery.*

Although only a few Southerners endorsed this idea at the time
of the Missouri Compromise debates, by 1850 Southerners had generally come to accept the *principle* of secession, but not the *application*
of secession.//Similarly, by 1850 Northerners had generally come to
accept the *principle*, but not the *application*, of abolition.

1830–1845:
A Period of Sporadic Urgency

Sectional tensions seemed to ease for several years immediately
following the Missouri Compromise, but over the ensuing two decades the cultural, economic/technological, and ideological differences between the sections sharpened as specific policies and events
focused attention on the differences of belief and demands that increasingly separated the sections. One of these events was the fact
that Calhoun and his radical followers in South Carolina responded to
perceived Northern antislavery pressures with the South Carolina
nullification doctrine. The doctrine was rejected by Northerners and
by nearly all Southerners, and one can see that:

#9: Most Southern leaders perceived that the slavery urgency was too sensitive and delicate to entrust to the radicals of South Carolina in general or to Calhoun's political opportunism and speculative theorizing. [9]

In 1836 there were violent congressional debates over how to handle abolitionist petitions. Past practice had been to refer such petitions to the standing Committee of the District of Columbia, where little more would be heard about them. Now this quiet practice was being challenged, showing that:

#10: Northerners and Southerners perceived that the existence of slavery and slave trade in the District was a persisting provocation of sectional strife and would have to be addressed in any comprehensive settlement of differences between North and South. [10]

Violent and abusive abolitionist propaganda made consideration of the *morality* of slavery inevitable. Northerners were becoming disturbed by the massive contradictions between inalienable natural rights and slavery and between the existence of slavery and national progress. Conversely, Southerners were upset by attacks on their morality and their competence as contributors to the nation's progress. The results were:

#11: Northerners perceived that they should do everything they could do constitutionally to eradicate slavery. Southerners began to claim that slavery was a moral good and a social and economic necessity. They began to demand, aggressively and often irrationally, that the South be accorded equality in everything concerning slavery, including its morality. [11]

Northerners' conclusion that they should do whatever they legally could to stamp out slavery was an especially important development because it rendered real compromise much more unlikely. Likewise, once Southerners took the position that slavery was morally good and a social and economic necessity, they placed themselves on an uncompromising footing. These patterns of perceptions were very much a part of the urgency of 1850. These other developments exacerbated the intensifying urgency. Of special importance were arguments about the disposition of antislavery petitions, the rise of the antislavery Liberty Party, issues about the disposition of slaves who had mutinied on ships at sea, and, most important of all, the running sectional confrontations over recovery of fugitive slaves. These factors contributed to this pattern of conflictive perceptions:

> *#12: In the view of antislavery forces in the North, the Constitution obligated them to make recapture of escaped slaves as difficult as possible. On the other hand, the South was in process of adopting the view that she had a constitutional right to demand recovery of lost slave property as a condition for remaining in the Union.*[12]

These perceptions were deeply rooted by 1850, and they meant that there could be no real compromise about slavery. Despite, or partly because of, intense Northern feeling concerning escaped slaves, Calhoun chose Senator Mason, the chief architect of the new fugitive slave bill, to read his speech to the Senate.

The Reawakening of the Territorial Dispute

After a lapse of more than twenty years, questions of territorial expansion forced slavery issues to the fore. Territories needed to be organized and California sought statehood. Both facts aggravated sectional conflict. What should be done about slavery in California became inextricably linked with what to do about it in other areas acquired through the Mexican War. Four choices were theoretically available, but three of them lacked sufficient bisectional support ever to pass in the Congress. The three options were: (1) allow slavery below an extended Missouri Compromise line but forbid it above that line; (2) allow slavery anywhere in the territories; (3) allow slavery nowhere in the territories. None of these options could succeed in the current Congress, but a fourth option had a reasonable chance of passage. It was the "popular sovereignty" option. It would let the inhabitants of a territory decide whether that territory should be free or slave. Importantly, this option as presented did not say *when* inhabitants were to make their decisions. The proposal was thus ambiguous enough to allow Northerners and Southerners to support it without giving up their original positions.

In these circumstances the following patterns of thought characterized the participants' perception of the slavery urgency.

>*#13: When California applied for statehood, the South perceived that she must resist at all costs, unless some quid pro quo benefits could be secured for the South.*

This was partly the reason Calhoun in his speech would make the admission of California the sufficient cause for the South to secede. The reason Southerners—excluding purists like Calhoun—were willing to exchange the admission of California for quid pro quo benefits was that they considered that the matter of slavery was settled there. California had bypassed the territorial stage and had applied for admission to the Union as a free state. However, Calhoun demanded in his speech of March 4 that California be remanded to territorial status or the South should withdraw from the Union. Thus:

>*#14: Extremists in both North and South perceived that popular sovereignty was unacceptable to their interests. Moderate Northerners perceived they could accept popular sovereignty, with the interpretation that inhabitants of a territory would determine the status of slavery early in the territory's existence. Conversely, moderate Southerners perceived they could accept popular sovereignty, with the interpretation that inhabitants of a territory would decide the fate of slavery at the time they applied for statehood.*

support?

If the inhabitants voted on slavery when the territories were ready for statehood, slavery would have been permitted everywhere in the territories. This was the position of Southerners, and it protected abstract Southern rights and honor. Access of slavery to the territories was not regarded so much a practical matter to Southerners as a manifestation of Southern rights under the Constitution. On the other hand, if, as Northerners chose to interpret popular sovereignty, inhabitants voted on slavery early in a territory's existence, it was clear that slavery would be excluded from the beginning. Since few people thought that the proslavery forces could muster a majority vote in any territory, this interpretation would preserve Northerners' basic position of no expansion of slavery. Of course, purists like Calhoun held rigidly to a hard-line rejection of popular sovereignty.[13]

Time Frame:
The Crisis Arrives

I have thus far found more than a dozen significant ways of thinking/perceiving that were parts of the structured perceptions comprising the urgency of 1850. As a consequence of these patterns Americans generally accepted that Congress must deal with the organization of the territories, statehood for California, fugitive slaves, and slavery and the slave trade in the District of Columbia. As the urgency moved through the summer and fall of 1849 and into early 1850, both Southern moderates and extremists had to contend with President Taylor's emerging hard-line policy of creating no new slave territories, bringing California and New Mexico (which, in Taylor's plan, included all of the Mexican Cession territory except California) directly into the Union as free states, and applying the full force of the federal government against any attempts at disunion. A complication of Taylor's plans for New Mexico's statehood was that much of New Mexico's eastern land was claimed by Texas. The military forces of Texas, which had twice invaded New Mexico, were again ready to engage United States troops defending New Mexico. A further complication was that Texas had defaulted on redeeming $11 million in notes and bonds that had been issued during the period of the Texas Republic, and Texans insisted the United States help them pay off the debt. Their argument was that part of the reason for defaulting was that upon annexation the state had lost the resources from customs duties charged at ports of entry. A final complication was that Texas's demand that the United States assume its state debt was inextricably tied to the Texas–New Mexico boundary crisis.

These data help me see additional patterns in the way participants perceived the sectional urgency in 1850.

> *#15: Astute observers perceived that the boundary conflict between Texas and New Mexico, which threatened to erupt into civil war between Texas and the United States, had to be resolved before sectional adjustments could be made. Whereas Northerners believed they must side against Texas and adopt the cause of New Mexico, which had no black slaves, Southerners saw they must side with the slave state of Texas.*

This way of thinking and the pattern of thought I identified as #4 explain why Henry Clay's Omnibus Bill was defeated. It tried to offer a *comprehensive* solution to the crisis of the summer of 1850. After defeat of the Omnibus Bill, bills were passed resolving several individual disagreements. The piecemeal path to solutions was enormously important to the ultimate resolution of the crisis. That Calhoun's pronouncements of March 4 ignored the piecemeal route to settlements is evidence that his speech was basically irrelevant to the immediate situation.

Although Southerners were extremely disturbed, their state of mind stopped short of being willing to apply the principle of secession.

> *#16: Both Northerners and Southerners perceived that the disunion crisis had become so grave by the start of the congressional debates in early 1850 that only what seemed to be a sweeping sectional adjustment could defuse the dangerous situation.*

Motivated by love of the Union, most senators searched desperately for some sort of resolution that would enable them to rationalize that they had maintained their principles on slavery.[14]

These sixteen patterns of perceiving characterized the ways Northerners and Southerners viewed the urgency of 1850. Gaining this knowledge is a major step toward understanding the potential for modifying the urgency. Many Northern and Southern senators desired so strongly to maintain the Union that they were able to support popular sovereignty on the basis of *assuming* that their sectional interpretation would prevail. In this way, the immediate crisis could be resolved. The Union would be preserved. The sections would not have forsaken their principles, and they could continue attempting to work out the problem of slavery. As I have said, the lack of clarity of this line of thought was repugnant to Calhoun, who demanded immediate, final settlement of the slavery issue.

What overall generalization can we draw from the collective meanings of the patterns of thought I have listed? It is that at the time of Calhoun's speech, most Northerners and Southerners were still willing to rely on the national party system as the forum in which to resolve the slavery urgency and protect their sectional interests. The rhetorical scene was set for quasi-compromise. Perceptions of the urgency had not yet readied participants for ultimatums such as those Calhoun propounded, although subsequent events might well bring them to the point of giving up on the political system.

Understanding the provoking rhetorical urgency for the 1850 debates is a very complex business, as my illustration shows. However, the *method* I have used is applicable to simple as well as to complex cases. Understanding the urgency of the Bloom-Walters trial required no search for background data beyond data that would be presented in the trial. Understanding the Canadian drug-use hearings required exploration of the history of the problem that constituted the urgency. We needed to go back about twenty years to locate the point at which drug use in sports was a nonissue. From that starting point the stages of attitudinal development became fairly plain: events, especially Johnson's disqualification, turned apathy into a fairly intense concern with reform in Canadian sports practices, a concern of slightly different dimensions for the several groups constituting audiences for interpretations and recommendations. This was the nature of the provoking rhetorical urgency met by the hearings. On the other hand, the crisis of 1850 had a half-century history marked by gradually changing perceptions of the slavery issue, territorial management, and political processes. Rather lengthy research was required to discern the significant stages of these developments and the differing perceptions of sectional and partisan "publics." But the critical procedures I used in this complex case were precisely the same in principle as those I would use in studying the situational and historical patterns of any provoking rhetorical urgency: (1) locate a plausible starting point that can be justified; (2) identify the stages of perceptual change that occurred between that starting point and the rhetorical occasion(s) one is studying; (3) notice what divergent "publics" or rhetorical groupings of participants one is dealing with; and (4) identify the cumulative situational and historical perceptions that shaped the specific provoking rhetorical urgency. This is the way configurational criticism works in generating understanding of the situational and historical patterns in any exigential flow of events, whether complex or simple. Fortunately for observers and critics, most rhetorical provocations are more like the Bloom-Walters trial and the Canadian drugs-in-sports hearings than the clashes about slavery that occurred between the early nineteenth century and the outbreak of the Civil War.

The Structures of Groupings

Participants in a rhetorical communication need frequently to be thought of as grouped or organized into what social scientists call "publics" but what I shall call "rhetorical groupings." Social scientists and rhetoricians use this kind of conceptualization because one simply can't get at the outlooks and attitudes of *each* person exposed to messages—advertisements, speeches, articles, or other. One can, however, usually identify *groups* of people who share distinct and identifiable outlooks, whether they are conscious of their shared perceptions or not. For example, on some subjects men, as a class, and women, as a class, tend to have different and identifiable views. So we think and talk about male attitudes and female attitudes. Makers of Cadillacs and Ferraris know that the particular public they need to address through their sales messages is made up of people who put a higher value on luxury and/or status than on money itself or the efficient use of money. Welfare recipients are not in the public or rhetorical group that these manufacturers should spend time and money trying to address. This way of conceptualizing audiences as made up of groups having shared, distinctive values and interests makes it possible to think out how to deal with mass audiences effectively. One mentally organizes the mass audience into subaudiences that share outlooks and opinions.[15]

Such rhetorical groupings can be identified in audiences of virtually any rhetorical event. How those groups or publics divide up, and why, needs to be looked at if one is to understand a complex rhetorical urgency. One wants to know who in the audience share beliefs, judgments, or interests that relate to the rhetorical urgency one is studying. For example, is it significant that people in the cattle-raising industry become upset when the topic of importing foreign beef arises? If that is relevant to understanding a rhetorical urgency, ferreting out why these people lean toward protectionism is important if we are to judge what change is possible through rhetoric on the subject of protectionist tariffs. Similarly, one might need to ask whether churchgoers constitute a significant segment of a broad audience we are concerned with. If the subject being dealt with was the legality of abortions, we would need to break this public down further, distinguishing those church groups that vehemently oppose abortions (e.g., many Catholics and some fundamentalist Protestants) from those churchgoers who do not (e.g., Conservative and Reformed Jews and most denominations represented by the National Council of Churches). In other circumstances one might need to ask whether different levels of socioeconomic groupings differ in attitudes toward, say, inflation. These are kinds of rhetorical groupings an observer of rhetoric needs to think about.

To discern significant rhetorical groupings, we need to examine what different ways of thinking we have discovered when exploring situational and historical patterns of perception/thinking. Who stood with whom in opinion, either in organized or unorganized ways? Next, we should consider the specific issue on which these groups of people divided. What did the groups agree on and what did they disagree about? Third, we need to find out what influence there may have been on group members because of their knowledge of their similarities to and differences from other opinion groups.

Simple urgencies may be responded to in substantially just one way. When the Canadian commission began its work, virtually the entire potential audience constituted a *single* opinion group. Virtually everyone expected and was ready for *some* proposals for change. But when specific proposals were made, we should expect to find several distinct rhetorical groupings developing. Athletes would probably constitute one kind of responding group. Coaches and other members of the sports bureaucracy would probably think about the proposals somewhat differently from the athletes, and the general public would probably respond still differently—probably with less attention to details of the proposals. If we knew this much, we could then ask whether awareness of such differences had any further influence on the three groups' thinking.

In some urgencies rhetorical groupings are obvious because they reflect polarization on issues. The exigential flow that produced the Great Awakening and its decline in America during the 1740s created two major groupings: the liberals, as represented by Charles Chauncy and Ebenezer Gay, and the evangelical Calvinists, as represented by Jonathan Edwards and Solomon Stoddard. Much more frequently, however, a complex urgency gives rise to several groupings. Even the most casual observer of a presidential election is aware that the urgency involves a perplexing array of groupings and subgroupings. The urgency of 1850 also produced multiple groupings.

When one has decided what groupings were significant to an urgency, the next step is to assess how these groups were structured; that is, (1) what held them together or bound them as groups; (2) what thrusts the groups made toward influencing the world outside their group; and (3) what we can reasonably expect about their responses to different kinds of attempts to alter the urgency. These are things that will tell us whether the groups simply existed as interest-sharing collections of people who may even have been unaware that they could be thought of as a group, or whether they were consciously organized groups. Where concern over inflation constitutes a provoking rhetorical urgency, we can predict that those who owe a good deal of money will be more tolerant of inflation than those who are creditors, even though debtors and creditors do not constitute organized groups or make concentrated, externalized thrusts to influence events. On the other hand, an example of a strongly, consciously organized group that makes many externalized thrusts to influence events is the National Rifle Association. For years the 2,800,000 members of this organization have opposed attempts to restrict the sales of guns or to ban permanently such weapons as semi-automatic assault-type rifles. The NRA is formally organized to foster mutual interests in firearms, hunting, and other "gun sports." What have made the NRA so effective are its externalizing thrusts—its exploitation of the media of mass communication to propound its views, its use of computer technology to stir up grass-root support, its zealous efforts to influence politicians, and so on.

It is frequently very important to notice the looseness or tightness of rhetorical groups. For example, loosely organized or unorganized debtors cannot be expected to influence financial urgencies quickly or in organized ways, whereas if gun control is an urgency, the NRA can spring into focused action at any moment it chooses.

On the whole, it is the groupings by opinion and interests that one is concerned with when estimating the effect rhetoric can have upon an urgency. Since the 1930s poll data have been available concerning national and even international opinions. Those data are of great help in discovering on what matters people had opinions and how they were or are grouped. Categories used by census takers and reporters can also suggest rhetorical groupings you may need to explore. If the rhetoric you study occurred before the days of poll taking, you may have to go to newspapers, magazines, and sometimes private reports to find out what range of relevant opinions you should expect and should explore specifically. If one were exploring American Revolutionary rhetoric, one would soon learn that there were three great political groupings in that period: people who remained loyal to England, people who resisted the British but still weren't quite ready to declare for independence, and independence-demanding, full revolutionaries. Anyone following the pattern of critical investigation set forth in this book will almost certainly have already unearthed a good deal of information of this sort, as review of my data on the crisis of 1850 will illustrate.

A second way to assay the structure of interests and opinions is to examine history more closely. A little review of the United States' position relative to the League of Nations will soon show that following World War I, American public opinion divided most sharply on the question of whether national sovereignty would be curtailed if the United States joined the League. Another tactic to use is to ask yourself who claimed to be speaking for what groups. The divisions among spokespersons can suggest what rhetorical groupings one should probably expect in the audience(s) of a particular time.

Where issues discussed have long histories, it may be necessary to trace the development of opinion groupings through a considerable period of time in order to understand their evolution and structure.

An example is how liberal and evangelical Calvinistic thought developed a schism dividing New England into hostile camps during the decline and aftermath of the Great Awakening. In my *Puritan Rhetoric: The Issue of Emotion in Religion*, I trace the development of the groupings in New England society, starting with the basic unity of the participants concerning the compartmentalization of the mind and the precarious balance between the intellect and the emotions. I show how Puritan thought evolved along bifurcated lines: one strain, customarily referred to as liberal, adhered to traditional theological and psychological concepts of God and man, morphology of conversion, and principles of sermonology. The other strain culminated in Jonathan Edwards's reaching toward a conception of unified man and pervasiveness of the emotions. Third, I examine the deepening fissure that developed between liberals and evangelicals during the Awakening when emotion triumphed over reason. So overwhelming was the victory of emotionalism that liberals were afraid to voice disagreements openly. Finally, during the decline and aftermath of the Awakening, New England society split into two opposing camps. In unraveling this development from basic social unity to hostile groupings, I show that each group differed in the cognitive/affective/behavioral way it responded to the urgency of revivalism and that each differed in the intensity with which it turned outward in attempts to influence others.

In many rhetorical situations the significant groupings of those who hold opinions about the urgency are fairly easy to discern. In the presidential campaigns of 1984 and 1988 significant differing political opinions were fairly well represented by the two major political parties. That there were other parties and some independent candidates who claimed to represent publics different from those of the major parties was not significant enough for observers of political rhetoric to consider seriously. The Socialists, the Independents, the Communists, and other splinter groups did not constitute electorally significant publics. A sufficient evaluation focus could be attained by concentrating on the rhetoric of the Republicans and the Democrats and on the prevalent attitudes of three groups: Republicans, Democrats, and self-identified Independents. Much that was in the news such as help advocacy for the homeless and environmentalism could also be ignored, except as it influenced the political positions of the three main opinion groups.

In other situations divisions of opinions are in flux, and a number of shades of opinion evolve and need direct scrutiny. This was true relative to the Vietnam war in the late 1950s and the 1960s. It was also true of the exigential flow of ideas and events influencing the 1850 debates over slavery.

From evidence I have already located, I know that non-Southerners had arrived at a stage where they were inflexibly opposed to any expansion of slavery in the territories, that they tended to favor any legislation detrimental to slavery, and that in general they opposed politics beneficial to the South. Without becoming abolitionists, a great majority of non-Southerners had committed themselves to the principle of abolitionism.

I know too that Southerners viewed Northerners as hostile to Southern interests, Southern culture, and particularly slavery and the expansion of slavery into new territories. To a growing number of Southerners, non-Southerners were to be suspected regardless of their formal political affiliations.

What these generalizations mean is that traditional party loyalties and groupings were seriously weakening, although by 1850 they had not yet ceased to be important. The main political parties in the 1840s were the Whigs and the Democrats, but, on slavery at least, Northern Whigs and Democrats had aims different from those of their colleagues in the South. Furthermore, political fissures were becoming more evident in both the North and the South. That fact is relevant to what Calhoun could expect to accomplish rhetorically.

Southern Whigs sabotaged Calhoun's attempt to unify the South in the winter of 1848–1849. They did so hoping that newly elected President Zachary Taylor would protect the South. He did not, and the Southern Whigs became dismayed by his actions and by the inability of their Washington leaders to influence him. At the end of January 1850, when Henry Clay introduced a series of compromise measures, most Southern Whigs embraced them as ways of saving the South and protecting the unity of the Whig party. However, as William J. Cooper has said, among Southern Democrats "the influence and spirit of John C. Calhoun dominated the actions of the southern Democrats," who "strove to galvanize the South into an armed ideological camp poised to strike." In sum, there were two discernible and self-identifying groupings of opinion in the South. Even so, there remained some *shared* views also. Fehrenbacher has said a "sizable" number of Southerners inclined toward disunion, but few were as yet active disunionists. Even the Democrats who followed Calhoun still hoped for sectional accommodation.[16]

In the North significant groupings of opinion also distinguished the Whigs from the Democrats. Northern Whigs assumed a stronger, more inflexible position than Democrats on questions that related to slavery. There was, however, disaffection in both parties, chiefly because neither national party took a forthright stand on extension of slavery in new territories or on the relation of slavery to national progress. Joseph G. Raybach has said that "because of its effect on party structure, because of what it revealed of the people's attitudes, and because of what it suggested concerning the future course of parties and of the nation's policies" the election of 1848 "revealed that both major parties were approaching, if they were not already in, a state of crisis." The territorial question was the crucial, crisis-raising issue for both parties in the North. Northern Democrats seemed less intransigent than Northern Whigs. The Whigs were more united on the uncompromisable goal of confining, if not abolishing, slavery. This distinction between the major political groups in the North, as well as the exodus of many thousands from these groups into the Free Soil party, bore directly on what a speech like Calhoun's could and could not accomplish in the North.[17]

The major fact acquired from this consideration of rhetorical groupings is that the system of national political groups was breaking down but still retained enough viability in 1850 to promote a quasi-compromise for the sectional crisis. Relatively few members of the various rhetorical groupings would be receptive to the finality of Calhoun's ultimatums.

My analysis of the patterns of opinion that created the sectional crisis of 1850 has necessarily been more detailed than would be required to understand rhetorical urgencies less influenced by the past and less politically complex. The analysis does, however, illustrate the general usefulness of (1) reviewing one's data to see what those materials reveal about patterns of development and change among widely held opinions, and (2) inspecting the record to see what specific significant publics or rhetorical groupings constituted the audiences to be addressed by the rhetoric. The trial of sports agents Bloom and Walters and the inquiry of the Canadian commission are more representative of the kinds of investigation usually necessary in comprehending the configurational forces that shape a significant rhetorical situation. In the Bloom-Walters case we can learn all we need to know about the provoking rhetorical urgency from the immediate and explicit facts of the case. In studying the Canadian commission, we needed to go a bit further to see how patterns of ideas about substance abuse changed over two decades of Canadian experience with sports. But because the rhetorical urgency that Calhoun tried to address raised issues of national morality that had a well-remembered national and even international history going back almost to Revolutionary times, an extensive historical tracing of evolving patterns and opinion groupings was necessary. The details of one's research method in rhetorical criticism are dictated by the nature of the urgency studied, not by rules set in concrete.

Chapter Eight

Implicit Influences Reflected from Society

Sometimes we aren't able to learn as much as we want to about participants' views of a situation from examining just the explicit influences within the urgency. We need then to explore the implicit patterns in society—patterns that pervade the belief systems of participants and exert indirect, often subconscious influences on the ways they perceive and respond to provoking urgencies. In his recent study of the French Revolution, *Prelude to Terror*, Norman Hampson found it was the influence of certain social/cultural beliefs and values upon French society in the late eighteenth century that led indirectly to the Terror, "an appalling aberration, planned and expected by nobody." Despite the extraordinary spirit of altruism, good will, and shared aspirations that characterized the French Constituent Assembly during 1789–1791, the deputies were unable to agree on a constitution and a viable political system. Like French society itself, almost all the deputies had imbibed rigid attitudes and ways of thinking from the writings of Rousseau and Montesquieu. They were "endowed with a pathological mistrust of despotism, and uncompromising commitment to popular sovereignty, a belief in an infallible general will, and a conviction that politics should be a matter of moral imperatives rather than a reconciliation of interests." Without a basis for understanding legitimacy and good faith despite disagreement and without a suitable model of representative government, the deputies were unable to build concurrence out of differences—a tragic failure that led to the Terror. This is the kind of indirect or implicit force I want now to deal with.

In American society we have been conditioned to think positively about democratic governance. Thus, whether a provoking rhetorical urgency concerns how to organize a private club or how the federal government should act toward racial minorities, virtually all Americans will be automatically inclined to prefer solutions that allow the people involved to have a continuing voice in their own affairs. Rhetoric that does not show respect for this sweeping, high value placed on democracy cannot be thoroughly attuned to constraints of urgencies in this country.

To take another example, the automobile market for middle-size and large cars grew in the 1980s. Why? For a number of economic and cultural reasons, among them a greater degree of prosperity that diminished concerns about price and fuel shortages. Further, the long-standing American delight in "performance" automobiles made people ready to consider more powerful vehicles. Producers, dealers, salespersons, and advertisers were at least subconsciously aware of these implicit influences, so they conceived and presented sales rhetoric adapted to those implicit forces. Many potential car buyers carried the same considerations within themselves and accordingly responded positively to the promotional rhetoric favoring middle-size and large cars. Influences of these sorts I have called *Zeitgeist* influences. In what follows I will discuss them in detail and then turn to social needs and pressures as other kinds of implicit influences that affect the dimensions of provoking rhetorical urgencies.

Relevant Zeitgeists

The term *Zeitgeist* means roughly "spirit of the times." Unquestionably all cultures at all times reflect and convey such influences. Therefore, to understand participants in an exigential flow of events we sometimes need to ask: Are there general social views, myths, trends, traditions, or intellectual/moral states that pervade the self-systems of the participants and thereby condition the way they perceive a particular urgency? To answer this question one looks for cultural forces that influence people's ways of thinking/feeling/doing respecting issues associated with an urgency. As I have already suggested, commitment to democratic governance is one such force in the United States. Endorsement of Greek societies is such a force among members of fraternities and sororities. Love/hate feelings about computerization influence responses to urgencies concerning business management. Ideas and myths about romantic love influence responses to issues having to do with female-male relations.

Broader, more historic examples of *Zeitgeit* influences help to explain why, in the first two decades of this century, the Progressives were able to effect reforms, nearly all of which had been unsuccessfully proposed late in the previous century by William Jennings Bryan and/or the Populists. When Theodore Roosevelt sent his famed Annual Message to Congress, December 8, 1908, the community of consciousness was vastly different from that of 1896, when Bryan pleaded for similar innovations. During the interim revolutionary changes had occurred in the ways many Americans perceived "reality." According to George E. Mowry these changes included "the rising appreciation of the principles of uncertainty and probability in the natural world," "the erosion of orthodox deterministic religious doctrines," the increasing attractiveness of "the free will principles of radical Protestantism," and "the applications of science to technology and industry." Instead of the previous deterministic formulations that made one a "cog in a universal mechanism," the new ways of thinking invited one to "make and remake his own world." "The new intellectual trends in science, philosophy, the social sciences, jurisprudence, religion, and the arts started from varied sources about the same time," Mowry says. "For a while they flowed separately. But the contours of the age brought them closer together, and somewhere around 1900 their confluence occurred. Reinforcing each other, these varying streams of thought formed a flood beating against the damlike structure of old ideas and conventions."[1]

A study of the times and the participants involved in an urgency should suggest comparable cultural continuities that helped to shape that urgency. To test out each possible *Zeitgeist* force, one simply asks the question: Could this *Zeitgeist* force realistically affect the way participants think and feel about this urgency and thereby influence the potential for modifying the urgency?

I suggest below an array of *Zeitgeist* forces that influenced the urgency that, in turn, provoked Calhoun's March 4 speech and a host of other communicative responses, such as *Uncle Tom's Cabin* (1852) by

Harriet Beecher Stowe, *The Pro-Slavery Argument* (1852) by William Harper, Thomas R. Dew, and James H. Hammond, and *Sociology for the South* (1854) by George Fitzhugh.

The Impulse of Reform

The 1840s were a decade of romanticism, emotionalism, and, according to historian David M. Potter, "pervasive humanitarianism" that "made this whole era a period of reform." The reform impulse was not unique to the United States, or course. During this decade it convulsed England and many of the countries of Europe. The impulse to reform in this country stemmed from sources such as these: "the desire to perfect human institutions"; the frontier democracy's emphasis on individual freedom and equality; the idea of progress, so intrinsic to the age; a profusion of gifted writers, such as Longfellow, Emerson, Whittier, and Hawthorne, who exalted virtue, condemned vice, and tried to perfect American society; a "basic feeling of social unrest" resulting from rapid changes in industrialization, mechanization, communication, urbanization, immigration, and the like, which frequently produced conditions sadly at variance with ideals of freedom and equality; and a pervasive evangelical religion.

The age was intensely religious, surging with revivalism. While emotionalizing the Calvinistic hatred of sin and the awful and inexorable punishment for sin, preaching stressed that people had free choice. They could save their souls if they cleansed themselves of sin. They must root out sin in their own lives and in the lives of others. Separating good from evil, virtue from vice, became terribly important.

The impulse of reform in the 1840s took different forms. The most important of these in the North was the antislavery crusade, which had become a "fierce moral attack." Slavery had become to many an anachronism impeding the current of Western civilization.

The deep humanitarian impulse was largely confined to the North, the antislavery sentiment exclusively so. To much of the Northern public slavery was sinful, a repudiation of the key republican ideals of freedom and equality. Furthermore, its presence within the Union had become a growing burden upon Christian consciences. In respect to slavery at least, the South experienced a counter humanitarian impulse. Because the South shared the North's intense religious preoccupation with sin and guilt, it was psychologically and spiritually necessary that she develop and canonize a defense of slavery as a positive good as well as a social necessity.

Thus, the humanitarian impulse influenced the North and South to move them further apart in the ways they thought about the ideals of freedom and equality and, because of this, led each section to evolve an increasingly derogative stereotype of the other.[2]

Antiblack Sentiment

Although Northerners generally condemned slavery, they subscribed as uniformly as Southerners to the myth that blacks are innately inferior. Racial prejudice did not bring North and South closer together, however. Instead, racism produced most of the opposition to the extension of slavery into the new territories. According to David Wilmot himself, his Proviso was designed to keep both slaves and free blacks out of the Southwest. Most Northerners wanted neither the competition nor the association of blacks—regardless of their state of bondage. Even Lincoln upon occasion appealed to this antiblack sentiment in his efforts to prevent the extension of slavery. As I show more fully later, antiblack sentiment paradoxically may have been a significant cause for Northern opposition to slavery itself.[3]

Nationalistic and Nascent Nationalistic Thinking

The peak of nationalist and expansionist spirit in the United States came in 1848 when the Mexican cession added the great Southwest to the nation. The North had already acquired a preponderance of population, wealth, and economic power, and it became increasingly clear that the Union "could be made the instrument" of Northern wants by legislating high tariffs, internal improvements, and the like. Centralization in government became a political "good" because centralization of power would make it easier for the government to advance the political and economic interests of the North. In consequence, nationalism and sectionalism became blended together into a new kind of "Americanism" in the North.

Southerners came to see the federal Constitution and the central government very differently than did the North. For reasons I have already discussed, intensifying regionalism in the South became an incipient Southern nationalism. This feeling would evolve into the national consciousness of the Confederacy by 1861.[4]

Sense of Implicit Contest for Control of the Central Government

We have already seen that Northerners and Southerners recognized that control over the federal government would enhance their respective sectional interests. Although people did not speak openly very much about this, it seems to have been widely assumed that the North and the South were contesting for control of the central government. These assumptions constituted part of the *Zeitgeist* affecting the kind and amount of modification that could be made in the provoking urgency of 1850.[5]

Tradition of Compromising Political Differences

According to Avery O. Craven, the American people at the time of the Compromise debates of 1850 possessed "the naive assumption that a compromise could bring peace and understanding." Whether or not Craven has overstated the matter, there is no doubt that a tradition of compromising political differences had existed in the country since its beginning and stretched back through English parliamentary experiences. The Articles of Confederation were made possible only through compromise. The Constitution was a bundle of overt compromises, as in the provisions on the status of slaves in taxation and representation, the balance between large and small states, and the slave trade. Questions that might have jeopardized its ratification were left alone or dealt with in ambiguous language, as with the nation–state relationship, power to regulate commerce, and the effect of ex post facto and contract clauses on the rights of property holders.

A major—perhaps *the* major—argument in rhetoric favoring ratification of the federal Constitution was that it accommodated the varied interests of the states and the sections while preserving a national, representative democracy.

When major confrontations had arisen, some sort of adjustment had resulted, as in the 36/30 compromise line for the Missouri crisis of 1819–1821 and the Clay Compromise Tariff for the South Carolina nullification controversy of 1832–1833. Decades later, when the Senate in 1861 set up the Committee of Thirteen to attempt to resolve differences between North and South, the motivation for setting up the committee stemmed directly from this tradition of compromising political disagreements. But then, of course, the *commitment* to compromise was gone on both sides.

Inasmuch as differences had always been accommodated in the past by compromise, it seemed realistic in 1850 to assume that some sort of compromise would be worked out. This tradition of compromising political differences strongly conditioned the expectations of the participants whose perceptions and reactions basically constituted the urgency of 1850.[6]

My case study illustrates that general cultural continuities (1) can animate considerable numbers of persons; (2) may range in character from disposition, tendency, or impulse to notion, belief, or way of thinking/feeling/doing; (3) be rooted in the experiences or mythologies of the past; and (4) exert orienting and directing influence upon the character, will, and/or behavior of the participants (5) in ways that can influence how they perceive an urgency.

Social Needs and Pressures

Zeitgeist influences tend to derive from broad past experiences and traditions, but more specific and immediate social needs and pressures also influence participants' perceptions of provoking rhetorical urgencies. For convenience, I classify these into three types of influence: *cultural*, *economic/technological*, and *ideological*. These categories are flexible and encompassing enough to guide critical inquiry toward virtually any special need or pressure that could influence perceptions of urgencies. Critics often find that one or two of these

types of influence were most important for affecting people's perceptions. For example, if we were to examine the relation of social needs
and pressures to the rhetorical urgency represented by American
Jews' increased willingness to criticize Israel, we would find cultural
and ideological influences decidedly more important than economic/
technological pressures. If we were studying the American presidential campaigns of 1980, 1984, and 1988, we would probably conclude
that economic/technological influences declined in importance because by 1988 the economy had been strong for several years and the
Soviet Union appeared to have become less threatening, so technological concerns about nuclear weapons diminished somewhat. We
would notice, however, that cultural concerns about the state of the
homeless and the legality of abortion became of increasing importance to people's perceptions of the electoral urgency of 1988, and
that economic considerations having to do with the federal deficit
were consistently important through the three elections.

Cultural Needs and Pressures

To estimate how cultural needs and pressures affect an urgency,
it is useful to take two steps: (1) Examine how organizational systems
within a society affect participants' senses of status, roles, and norms.
(2) Then gauge what, if any, influence perceived status, roles, and
norms had on the ways participants perceived and responded to
the urgency.

Students of communication ordinarily are most concerned with
these organizational systems: kinship, social class, religion, education, politics, and occupation. The relative importance of any one, or
more, of these organizational systems depends on the issues and situations involved.

A society provides the structure of role/status/norms for its
members largely through its organizational systems. Those systems
may be very broad ones, such as the democratic representational system established by the U.S. Constitution, or they may be structures
established by and for specific groups but not for others. The National Conference of Catholic Bishops to which I have alluded sup-

plies a case in point. All audiences the bishops wanted to address would adhere to the American cultural pressure for democratic, nonsectarian decision making *in secular matters*. The Catholic Church has to accept the legitimacy of that pressure whenever it deals with strictly political matters; however, the Church is itself almost rigidly hierarchic and claims to be authoritative *on moral questions*. Its bishops have a specific place in the organizational hierarchy and can claim authoritativeness when they pronounce on moral matters, provided they continue to observe the traditional teachings of the Church. Within the Church as a broad organization the bishops' moral claims would tend to be legitimized by the structure of role/status/norms established by the Church's organization. The religious system would thus be especially influential authoritatively. But audiences outside the Church would not sense the same kind of organizational pressures and would judge even the bishops' moral claims by broad nonsectarian standards—especially where educational and political issues were at stake. The point illustrated is that each basic social organization groups and grades its members and supplies norms and "beliefs and procedures by which activity can be guided and controlled." Within each system constraints of law, morality, myth, etiquette, tradition, and so on are promulgated, and each organizational member knows what constitutes "proper" and "improper" thought. For a critic, the important issue becomes: Which system or systems most significantly influenced perceptions of the various audiences *in the situation being studied?*

By examining the constraints and allowances of organizational systems pertinent to the urgency of 1850s, I should be able to estimate possible influences that perceived status/roles/norms had on the participants' perceptions of the crisis.

Considerable disagreement exists among eminent authorities concerning the essential nature of cultural needs and pressures in the North and South and the extent to which such needs and pressures contributed to the urgency of 1850. Nevertheless, there is substantial agreement that, because the South was committed to a way of life based upon slavery, it possessed a distinctive structure of role/status/

norms that "increasingly set it apart from the rest of the nation." We understand whether and how this was true if we examine role/status/ norms under several headings.

Educational Organization

Of all the types of organizational systems, the school exerted the least relevant impact on the status/role/norms of the participants— and, hence, upon the urgency. Although by 1850 the basic principles of American education had been formulated and to some extent established in the North, formal education did not directly touch most Northerners, and there was very little enthusiasm in the South for free public education.[7] Therefore, I can eliminate this type of organizational system from my examination.

Kinship

The kinship organizational system offers a more promising avenue to understanding the life styles of the participants involved in the urgency of 1850. When I talk about kinship, I am primarily concerned with matters like methods and results of socializing and acculturating the young, basic family living patterns, and the values and attitudes transmitted through family nurturing. These manifested themselves especially in the South as a distinctive folk culture.

The kinship system throughout the country had important similarities. In Potter's view,

> The vast majority of Americans still lived by the cultivation of the soil, and their lives were patterned by the rhythms and rigors of nature. Pitting their muscle against the elements, these men were independent, aggressively individualistic, and fiercely hostile to external controls. Prizing the opportunity to become unequal in personal achievement and hating the inequality of pretension to status, they cherished an unsleeping distrust of public authority and glorified the virtues of simplicity, frugality, liberty, and self-reliance. Despite the nuances of regional difference, Americans conformed to this basic pattern from one end of the Union to the other.

Some aspects of personal relationships and relationships of persons to land set the South apart from the North. In his "The Enigma of the South," Potter suggested that "the relation between the land

and the people remained more direct and more primal in the South than in other parts of the country." Inheritance of land and slaves had incalculable importance not only for the planter class but also for all slaveholders and, through the kinship system, for Southerners generally. To a greater extent than in the more industrialized and commercialized North, the South "retained a personalism in the relations of man to man" and "offered a relationship of man to nature in which there was a certain fulfillment of personality." "In the folk culture of the South," Potter theorized, "it may be that the relation of people to one another imparted a distinctive texture as well as a distinctive tempo to their lives."

Most accounts emphasize that Southerners also inherited and passed along a distinctive sense of personal honor and of community. William J. Cooper has emphasized that "a particular code of personal and communal honor" played a critical role in the kinship system of the South. With Charles Sydnor and Bertram Wyatt-Brown, Cooper argued that, significantly different from the North, in the South the ideals of individual and community dignity, virtue, courage, independence, responsibility, and unsullied reputation coalesced into a powerful sociopsychological code, permeating society. Most important for my purposes, this code became inextricably identified with the defense of slavery and the South. As transmitted through kinship ties, any reflection upon the Southern life style or the institution of slavery became an intolerable insult not only to community honor but also to personal honor. "Individual southerners defending slavery," according to Cooper, "wove the fabric of societal unity."

Students likewise agree that Southerners were characteristically more violent than Yankees. Possibly perpetuated from the contentious Celtic ancestors, Southerners hated pacifism and enjoyed feuding, dueling, and general combativeness. Inasmuch as the plantation system was based on violence, actual or threatened, and inasmuch as the entire community shared the policing and disciplining of slaves, "violence tended to be more personal and more socially acceptable than elsewhere."

Emory M. Thomas concludes, "Planters and plain folks formed an essentially solid Southern society. Southern folk culture was an adhesive factor that bound people together and offered them identity with each other and with geographical location in the Old South." Thus, the status/role/norms transmitted in the kinship system throughout the country reinforced the recognition by persons everywhere that they were Americans. But the life style that was continued in the kinship system of the South was a reflection and reinforcement of both the Southern commitment to slavery and the peculiarly Southern factors of geography, social class, economics, technology, politics, and ideology. Therefore, the Southern kinship system necessarily promoted the self-conscious recognition that Southerners were an endangered minority under moral attack, with critically distinctive needs and problems.[8]

Social Class

The organizational system of social class possessed great significance for the urgency of 1850. Economic developments were tending to divide Northerners into classes with differing social, economic, and political interests, but the North may still be considered essentially a middle-class society. The communication flow may have been dominated by the opinion leaders, but the common people were much less ready to follow these leaders in social and economic matters than was true in the South. Thus, the social class system in the North promoted a much more democratic system of status/role/norms than existed in the South.

Professor Thomas believes that Southern society comprised a "fairly broad-based status pyramid." At the peak of the pyramid was the planter class. The planters were heads of families who owned land and twenty or more slaves—approximately 46,000 out of the 1.5 million heads of families in the South. Below the planters was the large middle class of small slaveholders, yeoman farmers, and a small group of merchants, factors, craftspeople, and the like. Just above the base of the pyramid, which consisted of slaves, was a "mudsill" composed of "landless hunters and 'squatters.' " Although "class distinctions were ambiguous," even among the "mudsill" classes an "un-American aristocratic tradition" prevailed. "The planters exercised hegemony in Southern society because nonplanter whites deferred to their social 'betters' and because Southern plain folks in the main accepted planter values and ideology." Although "class consciousness existed among some nonplanters," it "was slow to develop among the masses." In part because "plain people and planters were bound by ties of self-interest and racial solidarity," Thomas believes that Southerners "blended the traits of aristocracy and democracy within the same social structure."

Hence, the relevant status/role/norms embraced and transmitted by the Southern class system contained "an aristocratic, anti-bourgeois spirit with values and mores emphasizing family and status, a strong code of honor," political and social leadership of the planters, and paternalism or neopaternalism as "the standard of human relationships."[9] The social class system helped condition Northerners to reject Calhoun as a persuader and Southerners to accept him as a spokesman, but not necessarily as *the* spokesman, for the South.

Religion

The marvelously adaptable nature of Christianity enabled both Northern social reformers and Southern defenders of the social status quo to exploit Christianity as a divine reinforcement for the status/role/norms they endorsed. Sharing Christianity probably contributed to what American nationalism there was during the urgency of 1850; but the regions' different interpretations of Christian "truths" tended also to push the sections further apart.[10] Religious pressures for separation could ultimately be used to justify secession if the urgency of 1850 could not be fully resolved.

Occupational System

I have pointed out that "the vast majority of Americans still lived by the cultivation of the soil." Nevertheless, whereas the South was virtually as agricultural and rural as it had been during the time of Jefferson, the North had begun to respond to the dynamic forces of modernization and a different way of life. Already the Northern values of "enterprise, adaptability, and capacity to excel in competition" differed from the Southern emphasis on status, "loyalty, courtesy and physical courage." The small slaveholders, yeoman farmers, and

townspeople of the South drew upon and contributed to the more re-
laxed, leisurely, and personalized life style of the cotton, sugar, and
tobacco plantations. The South used some of the tools and objectives
of commercialism and capitalism, but it did not embrace the status/
role/norms of capitalism. In such ways, the occupational system reflected and reinforced both the national cultural patterns and the
differing status/role/norms of the North and South.[11]

Political System

All Americans belonged to the same political system. People everywhere revered the Union as a democratic republic in which the
citizens were sovereign. They treasured a common political heritage
of military heroes, presidents and statesmen, battles, warships,
shrines, national holidays, patriotic songs, and international friends
and enemies. They venerated the same Constitution, exalted the
same political values—the most important of which were liberty and
equality. At least for public consumption, they accepted the same
status and role for all citizens—that is, that all adult white males
shared ultimate authority and responsibility for political action. In
this way the operation of the political system encouraged a strong national sentiment.

Conversely, however, the sectional manifestations of the political
system contributed to divergent responses of Northerners and Southerners to the urgency. Middle-class Northerners apparently exercised
a greater role in initiating and determining political action than did
their Southern counterparts. They had no trouble equating the Constitution and Union with their own regional interests; they seemed to
be the same. Also, although they discriminated against blacks, in
their own way they valued the ideals of liberty and equality.

In their participation in the political process, Southerners could
not value the Union or the Constitution with the same undivided loyalty evinced by Northerners. Inasmuch as they placed a higher value
on the survival of their civilization than on survival of the Union, it
seemed apparent by 1850 that if push came to shove, Southerners
would reluctantly choose their region over the nation.

In sum, especially in the Lower South, the operation of the Southern political system encouraged critically different status/role/ norms from those of the North. This divergence meant the inhabitants of the North and South would necessarily view the urgency of 1850 from radically different perspectives.

Studying the cultural needs and pressures under which Americans lived in 1850 adds something to the understanding gained from other lines of inquiry, and it confirms much of what I learned earlier. What is added is the important fact that marked cultural differences separated North and South and that these differences undoubtedly contributed to the participants' perceptions of the urgency of 1850. A similar inquiry concerning another urgency would also be likely to add new knowledge and confirmations. A similar inquiry concerning the Bloom-Walters case would remind a critic that while kinship, social class, and religious systems had little to do with how the issues in the case would be perceived, presuppositions about collegiate education, about amateurism, about athletes' rights and needs for professionalism, and about the appropriateness of the legal rules involved would all influence the judgments of those who heard the pleas in the case. Concerning the case of the Catholic bishops, the politico-religious doctrine of separation of church and state appears as a major and fully recognized constraint on what and how the bishops could plausibly argue about war, peace, and national defense.

Economic/Technological Needs and Pressures

I have now shown how one may comb through the organizational systems of society to discover how cultural needs and pressures may influence the way participants perceive an urgency. One can learn still more about some urgencies by asking how economic/technological patterns in society help shape belief systems. In this connection, I use "economic" to refer to the production, distribution, and consumption of commodities, and "technological" to refer to the means used by a society to provide itself with the objects of material culture.

Although examination of economic/technological patterns may sometimes be very helpful in understanding communication, I don't want to exaggerate its potential usefulness. Economic/technological influences in society may not tell much about the potential for modifying some urgencies, such as pornography, excessive torts legislation, tax reform, illegal drugs on college campuses, or driving under the influence.

One would also be guilty of reductionism to claim that economic and technological influences provide the single necessary explanation of the potential for modification in an urgency. It was much too simplistic for Charles A. Beard and Mary R. Beard in *The Rise of American Civilization* to assert that the Civil War resulted from economic differences that separated Southern planters from Northern capitalists and Western farmers. It is also reductionism for social commentators to isolate economics as *the* cause of racial disorders in Miami and elsewhere. That the rioters in Miami did not believe their violence stemmed exclusively from economic/technological needs and pressures was attested to by numerous blacks interviewed by the media. Improved housing, training programs, and job opportunities would not remedy the dissatisfaction of blacks, they argued, without basic changes in the attitudes of others toward them as persons.

On the other hand, economic/technological patterns often do influence the way participants view urgencies. This influence is decisive at times, when such forces provide a necessary contributing explanation. For instance, the Civil War was not fought solely because the economic system of the South was based on the forced labor of millions of blacks. There were other causes. In themselves, however, the other causes were not sufficiently divisive to produce war. Without slavery there would have been no war. Therefore, although slavery was not *the* cause, we must recognize it as a *necessary* contributing cause of the Civil War.

What does one look for when estimating how economic/technological forces impinged on perceptions of a rhetorical urgency? One looks for two general kinds of things. (1) One asks whether there were any especially relevant needs and pressures relating to the objects of material culture; and (2) one asks *whose* perceptions and responses would be especially influenced by matters relating to production, distribution, and consumption of material things.

Thus, if you wished to study Michael Dukakis's rhetoric during the 1988 presidential campaign, you would assume initially that economic causes helped shape the provoking urgency. I can very easily come up with a list of several dozen items that could be relevant to an inquiry into the economic/technological conditions of a situation. But not all of these would be relevant to a study of Dukakis's rhetoric in 1988. Inflation would be scarcely worth exploring in 1988. The same thing would be true of interest rates. The balance of payments didn't loom very large by November 1988. Energy costs were not critical. And so on. Fortunately, for almost a half-century, we've had regular surveys about what people see as "troubles" or "issues" of the day. Therefore, to get a line on what's worth studying relative to modern rhetoric, you probably ought to go to the public opinion polls first. Find out which economic/technological things people were sensitive to in 1988 and center your exploration on how those forces might have influenced the way participants viewed the election urgency.

When I apply the concept of economic/technological pressures to the urgency of 1850, I find few ideas that are genuinely new. Much of the evidence simply amplifies and clarifies what I learned earlier while studying cultural needs and pressures. Redundancy like this doesn't represent failure or pointlessness, however. On the contrary, it is a very positive sign that one is getting a handle on implicit forces. A simple rule of thumb is that when your application of basic critical categories begins to tell substantially the same things about an urgency, you are getting close to a full understanding of how implicit influences actually helped structure perceptions. Turning to the 1850s, this is what I have found in the present topics.

Economic/Technological Differences Between North and South

As I knew, the South's economy was based on a static, decentralized agricultural system of staple crops and primitive technology. Its energy source was substantially supplied by slave labor. Its produce was shipped by rivers and seas for sale in a world market.

The North's economy was significantly different from that of the South. Nascent modernism had brought industrial and urban capitalism, manufacturing, commercial agriculture, diversified farming, grain production, mass transportation, and an improving communication system to the region. Produce was shipped by a rudimentary network of roads and canals to domestic markets.

Divisive Quality of Economic/Technological Differences

Economic/technological differences caused Northerners and Southerners to perceive differently the crisis of 1850. Holman Hamilton believes that such differences may have been "a more fundamental cause of sectional friction than the annexation of Texas, the Mexican War, or the ardor of reformers and seers."

According to Eric Foner, Northerners in general believed that "the southern economy was backward and stagnant, and slavery was to blame." Some prescient Northerners, like William H. Seward, recognized that "aside from all moral consideration, slavery would have to be abolished as an intolerable obstacle to regional and national development."

The economic system of the South discouraged industrialization and economic diversification. The South was "destined" to remain almost exclusively a producer of raw materials. The slaveholders reinvested much of their profits in slaves and land—that is, in precisely the same means of production as the original investment. In contrast, Northern capitalists invested the bulk of their profits not in labor but in the expansion and modernization of plant and equipment, thereby acquiring "qualitative" progress. The North was evolving toward a processing society. Lack of industry was the major reason the South was rapidly falling further behind the North in economic strength. The slaveholders possessed the surplus capital to establish industry, but they refused to do so. Why? Because growing cotton was more profitable than almost any other kind of investment, because planters feared the establishment of a sizable urban white working force that might thwart the existing system of autocratic social control, and because planters hesitated to set the precedent of giving special incentives to slaves in return for the more demanding factory work.

Furthermore, unlike the economic system of the North, in which the employer was responsible only for paying the stipulated wage to his workers, slaves were considered property and were bound to their masters twenty-four hours every day. To protect his investment the master had to assume responsibility for the physical and emotional well-being of his slaves. This paternalism pervaded the entire society, reinforcing the economic status quo and, of course, the social and political hegemony of the planters.

Because the Southern economic system contributed to soil depletion, Southern leaders were convinced that, in order for the South to survive, slavery must expand into new territories. Therefore, the claim to equal rights in the territories was an uncompromisable interest of Southerners.

The fact that the Southern economy was less expansive, productive, and diversified than the Northern economy led people in the two sections to view the urgency of 1850 very differently. As I have shown in several ways, equality of rights in new territories was the specific point of controversy, and a major reason the issue was so incendiary was economic. Some Southerners saw "salvation" in the expansion of slavery into the territories. Enthusiastic about diversification and wage labor, Northerners opposed helping the "stagnating slaveocracy" and supported legislation favorable to diversified, protected, domestic development.[12]

Specifically exploring economic/technological needs and pressures does not produce much new information about the urgency of 1850, but in other cases perceptions of economic/technological developments crucially affect reasons for and perceptions of persuasion. The Peace Pastoral of the Catholic bishops is a clear case. Professor Cheney made a careful examination of differing perceptions of nuclear power, weaponry, and the nuclear threat in the early 1980s. This enabled him to see what motivated the bishops to consider a pastoral letter in the first place. It also explained the diverse reactions that the Pastoral stimulated within the Catholic Church and outside of it. Again, if we investigated rhetoric having to do with the worth of multinational corporations, economic and technological pressures would prove to be very important influences.

Ideological Needs and Pressures

In the view of historian Gordon Leff, economic/technological needs and pressures must be studied in conjunction with ideological forces. "Together," Leff says, "they form the starting-point for knowledge of men's ideals and interests, which makes their actions and modes of thought intelligible."[13] We can't fully understand the urgency of 1850 or urgencies in an Islamic republic without noting the role of ideology in those situations. This is not to say that ideological needs and pressures are critically significant in all communication. Such forces would probably not be of primary importance in discussions of such questions as: Which computer system should be installed in the office? Was a city ordinance violated? Was the deceased murdered and, if so, who committed the deed?

In other cases, such as the urgency of 1850 and rhetoric in an Islamic republic, one must take the role of ideology seriously. In both cases specific beliefs had been organized into overarching creeds. In an Islamic republic the theological teachings—the theology of the Koran—would undergird all public and private decisions. In the urgency of 1850 virtually all differentiating forces in these regions culminated in the ideological patterns expressed in the world views of Southerners and of non-Southerners, and these world views severely constricted the amount of modification that was possible in the sectional crisis. Likewise, ideological considerations are extremely important if one considers rhetorical attempts by political figures to reduce terrorism emanating from the Middle East or the attempted persuasion of editor Richard A. Viguerie in his *Conservative Digest*.

To estimate the potential influence of ideological needs and pressures on a rhetorical urgency, I like the definition by Milton Rokeach, a professor of sociology and psychology: "An *ideology* is an organization of beliefs and attitudes—religious, political or philosophical in nature—that is more or less institutionalized or shared with others, deriving from external authority."[14]

Several concepts in this definition call for clarification and expansion. First, some general observations.

1. Ideology is by no means restricted to doctrinaire or dogmatic formulations, as the Marxist ideology or the ideology of the National Socialistic Party.

2. Nor is ideology limited to the total content of thinking of a society or subgroup. An observer of rhetoric is potentially interested in any ideological idea that may help explain how participants perceive and respond to a particular rhetorical urgency.

3. The composition of an ideology is not confined to explicit patterns that the participants recognize, understand, and can express in language. An ideology may range from explicitly self-conscious ideations to implicit—that is, learned but largely unconscious—modes of thought and feeling. An example of an implicit kind of ideological position is the disdain for manual labor that was pronounced in the antebellum South.

4. Ideologies tend to be generally held views that exist independently of the thinking of any particular individual. Ideologies evolve out of historical experiences and existing social conditions. For example, our American bias in favor of representative-democratic governance has grown out of the nation's past, and that ideological bias is present regardless of the fact that some individual citizens may believe that a managed society is preferable to a democratic one.

5. Ideologies are not monolithic. This is so because there may be considerable variation in the ways individuals respond to a group's overall views. Those variations in the ways ideologies are held and shared depend on people's needs, their sense of identification with belief groups, and their satisfaction or frustration with elements of a given ideology. For example, a great many Northerners who opposed slavery prior to the Civil War thought immediate emancipation of slaves was not a good idea. The social upheaval caused by immediately freeing all slaves would be too high a cost to pay for the principle of freedom. Therefore, they preferred more gradual solutions to the problem.

6. Their position illustrates that ideologies possess intrinsically what Eric Foner calls "the social consciousness—of a social group, be it a class, a party, or a section." This

social consciousness, or sense of relationships, "involves the way in which a group perceives itself and its values in relation to the society as a whole," as well as its conception of what the society's future should be.[15]

The way one discovers ideological frameworks is to ask which beliefs, values, and attitudes cohere to form more or less institutionalized inferences about things, events, ideas, and persons. Sometimes one can perceive structures of ideas that are highly organized and go together tightly for a society or subgroup of persons. The value of collective bargaining is a readily discerned ideological element in most labor unions' activities. Occasionally other ideologies are clearly articulated, as in the *Communist Manifesto*, in religious creeds, in pledges of allegiance, and the like. More often ideologies, even if systematic, have to be extracted from one's data.

In my *Puritan Rhetoric: The Issue of Emotion in Religion*, I found that the Puritan ideology consisted of a structured system of explicit premises and implicit interrelationships concerning the nature of God, the nature of man and his faculties, homiletics, duties of the preacher, ends of the listener, and the morphology of conversion.[16] What we call the Puritan ideology is actually the *linkage* of the shared ways in which these various facts and values were put together to form an encompassing religious outlook.

Sometimes one may find that a relevent ideology is neither highly organized nor explicitly stated; it is basically an implicit consensus. For example, our Revolutionary fathers were not given to political theorizing. They were clearly influenced in their perceptions and responses by the directives of the European and British Enlightenment, however. The concepts of natural rights and natural law inspired the Declaration of Independence and provided the popular creed—the myths and symbols that fueled the Revolution itself. Perhaps because the thrusting power of the Revolution came from earnest faith rather than from ordained theory, the patriots never codified their political ideology. Nevertheless, Clinton Rossiter, in his *Political Thought of the American Revolution*, found that the following, variously derived, beliefs implicitly constituted the "Revolutionary faith":

The political and social world is governed by laws as certain and universal as those which govern the physical world. . . . The higher law, or law of nature, is . . . a set of moral standards governing private conduct . . . a system of abstract justice to which the laws of men should conform . . . a line of demarcation around the proper sphere of political authority . . . the source of natural rights . . . to life, liberty, property, conscience, and happiness. . . .

If the natural character of man is an alloy of virtue and vice, his natural state is pure freedom and equality. . . . No man has any natural right of domination over any other; every man is free in the sight of God and plan of nature. . . .

All men have certain fundamental rights. These rights are natural, traceable directly to the great plan of nature, if not indeed to God . . . absolute . . . eternal . . . essential . . . and unalienable. . . .

In addition to those rights believed to be natural and unalienable, these derivative rights are the possession or aspiration of all men living under free government: the freedoms of speech, press, assembly, and petition; civil supremacy; representation and free elections; jury trial and attendant judicial safeguards. . . .

Good government . . . is a free association of free and equal men for certain well-defined purposes. . . . Good government is based on the consent of the governed.

The purpose of society is to extend to each man in it, in return for his talents and exertions, the benefits of the strength, skills, and benevolence of the other men with whom he is associated. . . .

Representation and jury trial form the last and firmest line of defense against arbitrary power. . . . Government is divine, an ordinance of God, but governors are human, deriving all power from the consent of the governed. . . .

Government must be plain, simple, and intelligible . . . representative and non-hereditary . . . as near to the people as possible . . . constitutional, an empire of laws and not of men. . . . The one organ essential to free government is a representative legislature. . . . [However,] the most successful and trustworthy governments are those in which the totality of political power is divided among three separate branches: a legislature, preferably bicameral; an executive, preferably single; and a judiciary, preferably independent. In turn, these branches should be held in position by a system of checks and balances. . . .

That form of government is best which produces the greatest number of good, free, and happy men. The best of all possible governments will be popular, limited, divided, balanced, representative, republican, responsible, constitutional—and virtuous.[17]

Sometimes ideological pressures grow out of broad historical experience, as Rossiter shows was the case in the American Revolutionary experience. Sometimes these pressures are more clearly the products of economic and cultural commitments. They were in the sectional crisis of 1850, and they were in Eastern European countries and in the Soviet Union as the communist systems broke down in 1989 and later. On the other hand, there are times when ideologies *create* specific economic and cultural features of a situation. Ideology works this way wherever the recent notion of an Islamic republic is accepted. By what relationships and in what directions these forces worked—if they worked at all—is important to comprehending the exigential flow of events that give rise to provoking rhetorical urgencies. We must keep in mind also that ideological and economic/technical pressures often interact in highly influential ways.

My data relative to the urgency of 1850 show that the Revolutionary ideology influenced Northern perceptions somewhat more strongly and specifically than Southern perceptions. Although neither Northern nor Southern preconceptions were monolithic or held with uniform intensity, the ideologies I sketch below fairly represent the views of substantial numbers of people in the two sections. The ideological positions I assign to the South were most uniformly and intensely held by inhabitants of the Lower South, were somewhat less strong in the Middle South, and were much less strong in the Upper South. Such facts support two general points about studying ideological influences anywhere: (1) Special attention needs to be given to *degrees of uniformity* with which ideologies were shared, and (2) the *intensity of allegiance* to an ideology needs to be gauged.

Relevant National Ideology

Substantial agreement existed concerning the purpose and nature of government, the privileges and responsibilities of citizens, and the political process in general. There was even more agreement than disagreement concerning the powers and limitations of the national government and the proper relationship between the federal and state governments. The ideology that bound the American people together remained a unifying force in 1850, pervasive and enduring. Despite regional differences, no intrinsic tragic flaw existed that was so basic and instrumental that it would generate seriously differing regional ideologies—none, that is, except the institution of slavery.

Northern Ideology

For reasons I have already noted, Northerners wanted the national government to be strong and vigorous enough to assist in transforming the country's agriculture, transportation, industry, and domestic commerce. Roy F. Nichols could therefore say that the basic ideological political effort of Northerners was "to break the 'almost complete' dominance which the Southerners exercised over the national offices and policies."

In 1850 very few Northerners wished to interfere with the existence of slavery in states where it was already established. They rationalized the discrepancy between their concepts of themselves as moral persons loyal to the Revolutionary faith and their reluctance to oppose existing slavery in the following ways. They reasoned that if slavery were confined to states where it already existed, it would eventually disappear. More importantly, they felt the national government had no constitutional power to interfere. Most felt that the only way to abolish slavery in the South was to amend the Constitution, but such amendment was not possible in the foreseeable furture. So by abolishing slavery in their own states and by refusing to support any national legislation that favored slavery, most Northerners could feel they were doing all that was constitutionally allowable for the time being.

The catalytic introduction of the Wilmot Proviso forced Northerners to take a resolute stand—one that they could back up morally without threat to their own racism, and one that would at the same time favor their general economic and political interests. The general principle that there should be no extension of slavery thus acquired a clearly ideological and aggressively doctrinaire quality, despite the prospect that holding rigidly to this position might threaten the Union.

This ideological construction of beliefs, values, and attitudes strongly conditioned the way most non-Southerners perceived the urgency of 1850.

Southern Ideology

"The Confederate experience began in the Old South . . . as the cause," Thomas wrote. "The Southern cause was the transcendent extension of the Southern life style; the cause was ideology." Thomas explained that "Southern ideology was a belief system, a value system, a world view, or *Weltanshauung*." This system grew firmer and more complete as threats to the slave system developed nationally and internationally. As early as 1833 Southerners could see actual abolition of slavery in the British West Indies. From the North and abroad the Southerners' morality and competence were severely challenged, but Southerners defended their "peculiar institution." Avery Craven has said that the "real tragedy" of the "southern story" was that Southerners "remained socially and intellectually *comfortable* where they were, while the whole Western world, of which cotton made them a part, rushed headlong into the modern world of nationalism, industrial capitalism, democratic advancement, and a new respect for human rights." In response, Southerners evolved a systematic ideology that alleviated tensions between their self-conceptions and their actual morality and competence.

The ideology the South developed declared blacks inferior beings and asserted that slavery was a divinely ordained condition for persons designed to be hewers of wood and drawers of water. Hence, instead of being a sin, slavery was a moral and social good. Accordingly, it was said, Southerners were obeying biblical teachings and examples in caring for blacks, who did not know how to care for themselves. Of course, not all Southerners bought this moral argument; however, virtually all white Southerners were committed to the perpetuation of slavery.

Probably as a product of the above creed, Southerners asserted a political ideology that derived from selected aspects of American

constitutional history: Congress and the Supreme Court were agents
of the states and could not constitutionally transgress the powers re-
served to the states, which included power to protect institutions peculiar to a state.

Three implications of the overall Southern ideology significantly
influenced Southerners' perceptions of public affairs in 1850. Since
the Southern system was the epitome of righteousness, any criticism
of the system was morally reprehensible, and any compromise implied a despoiling of honor and morality. This assumption implied,
further, that conformity of thought and expression should be demanded. The Southerners believed that they were under political as
well as moral attack. They assumed that the North sought to capture
the federal government and reduce the South to a politically inferior
position; furthermore, many Southerners believed that if the North
became sufficiently strong, it would attempt to free the slaves.

What is perhaps most important about the ideological positions
of North and South in 1850 is that each section's position was
grounded in *moral* absolutism. This absolutism was more intensely
held in the South than in the North, but wherever it occurred
it meant that "real" political compromise was now *morally*
unacceptable. [18]

I have now completed my study of the implicit influences reflected from society that pervaded the belief systems of participants
in the urgency of 1850, exerting indirect and perhaps subconscious
influences on the way participants perceived and responded to that
urgency. It is fair to ask at this point how my analysis of implicit
forces has advanced my thinking about the urgency of 1850. Where
am I now respecting the urgency that I would not be had I failed to
look for implicit influences?

My study of implicit influences reinforces my impression that
inexorable forces in American society were grinding toward an ultimate showdown between North and South. These inexorable forces
were the beliefs, values, and attitudes stemming in large measure
from the reliance of the South on slavery and of the North on free
labor. In addition, the biggest payoff from studying implicit influences is that I have been able to identify the *moral* dimensions of the

sectional positions. When a position is declared moral, modification and compromise are no longer possible. I am now in a position to estimate how these moral dimensions influenced the way participants perceived compromise efforts and Calhoun's ultimatums.

As I have emphasized, we can find out all we need to know about most provoking rhetorical urgencies by looking for the relatively explicit influences within the urgencies. On the other hand, when issues are highly complex, when they evolve from subtle social and cultural changes, it becomes necessary to look beneath the surface and to explore implicit influences that may have conditioned participants' perceptions. For example, we would never fully understand the overall reception of Martin Luther King, Jr.'s "I Have a Dream" speech unless we realize that within the civil rights movement there was a serious, but not generally articulated or obvious, competition among civil rights leaders over whether or not to continue King's nonviolent policies. For my study of the urgency of 1850, inquiry into implicit influences was essential because of the complicated, evolving nature of national and regional experiences, economic pressures, and ideologies. Few urgencies require such extensive study of implicit influences, and even fewer will constitute situations in which all of the implicit forces come so neatly together in ideological influences. As always in criticism of rhetoric, the natures of the provoking rhetorical urgencies we explore, not formal rules, determine what data we must uncover and interpret.

When one has explored implicit influences—if need be—one is ready to draw all of one's background and critical knowledge together in the hope of forming an explicable, convincing critical judgment of the rhetorical effort(s) under study. This is the subject of my next chapter.

Chapter Nine

Potentialities for
Change in an Urgency:
Converting Explicit/Implicit
Patterns into Givens

Assessing the potential for change in urgencies comes naturally to us. We do this routinely in the course of daily living. Parents anticipate economic conditions and employment practices in helping their children make career choices. Financial planners assess changing market conditions when giving advice to clients about investments. Executives of motel chains evaluate evolving circumstances—such as interest rates, available money supply, traffic patterns, cost of gasoline, development of better fuel-efficient cars, and general economic conditions—in deciding whether to expand by constructing new installations at certain sites or begin a program of retrenchment. University presidents forecast student enrollment when making decisions to cut some programs and enlarge others. Naturally, parents, financial planners, motel executives, and university presidents often make mistakes in reading exigential flows. Nevertheless, all of us interpret impinging urgencies because this is the only way we can respond to the changing world around us and because—with perceptive care—we can sometimes make insightful judgments.

Of course, I have posed an imperfect analogy, but the analogy closes if we consider the activities of a dentist who tries to get a patient to floss her teeth daily, a businessperson who wishes to change a zoning ordinance, a public relations agent who seeks to improve the image of a client, a teacher who wants to reduce drug use in the high school, or anyone who attempts to alter the course of events. This includes all of us. We all use communication to influence others in order, derivatively, to modify urgencies. The ultimate success of our efforts depends partly on how well our messages match the potential for change in the urgencies. We consciously or subconsciously estimate this potential for change all of the time, often with considerable success. Further, we certainly can't understand or evaluate a communication in its fullest sense without being aware of its relation to the urgency that provoked it. The need for such awareness is so much a part of the way we look at communication that we are not really conscious that we size up situations that provoke talk.

In the spring of 1989 many of us watched the unfolding drama of John Tower's confirmation hearings as a nominee for Secretary of Defense. The proceedings seemed almost programmed. Like a Shakespearean tragedy, the exigential flow unraveled as a tale of conflict, duplicity, tragic flaws, bile, mendacity, and an inexorable grinding of fate. Even before the nomination was announced, explicit patterns were in place. For example, the Constitution requires that the Senate offer consultation and advice concerning such high-level presidential appointments. Once President Bush nominated Tower for Defense Secretary, a pattern called for the FBI to check his background and for the Senate Armed Services Committee to screen his suitability for the position and make a recommendation to the full Senate which, after debate, would vote on the nomination.

Several patterns involved Tower himself. His principal qualification was his record of distinguished experience and competency in defense matters. His candidacy had several liabilities, however. His FBI report contained allegations that he had an alcohol problem and a history of "excessive womanizing." Another charge against him was that he had received "exorbitant" consulting fees from defense contractors following his retirement from the Senate. According to rumor, he wanted the position badly and had campaigned to get the nomination. On the basis of his career as senator from Texas, Tower was expected to hang tough, fighting tenaciously for his candidacy, his reputation, and his political security.

The basic pattern concerning the issue of ratification was that inasmuch as Tower was recognized as an expert in defense matters, the only ostensible reason he would be denied ratification was that a majority of senators believed personal weaknesses seriously impaired his ability to do the job.

A number of patterns involved President Bush. Although all Presidents need to support their nominees in order to protect the office of the President and the viability of their own presidencies, this need was especially important to Bush. He could not withdraw the nomination under fire. He had to fight for his man to the end. He had to appear strong, tough, and consistent in his support, because he was fighting the "wimp factor," alleging that his administration had gotten off to a slow, indecisive start. He was also under obligation to Tower for past political favors, and he had to consider back-home support in Texas for the nominee. On the other hand, it was clear that Bush must not press the nomination too hard, because he could not afford to alienate the Democrats who controlled both houses of Congress.

Various patterns also involved the political system. Confirmation became a party issue when the chairman of the Armed Services Committee, Sam Nunn, a highly respected Democrat from Georgia, announced he would vote against confirmation. The President countered by denying there "was a shred of documented evidence" in the FBI report and reaffirming his support for Tower. Assuming no new significant evidence surfaced for or against Tower, the pattern of influences called for the committee to vote along strict party lines to send a negative recommendation to the Senate. The Senate was also likely to split according to party affiliations. This meant that, after much justificatory oratory, the Democratic majority would "end" the urgency by rejecting the nomination but that energies engendered by the confrontation eventually would find expression in subsequent urgencies, as in the later ethics investigation of Speaker of the House Jim Wright, Democrat from Texas.

The influences I have identified are ill organized as enumerated, and their *collective* meanings remain unclear. One cannot yet make a sharp estimate of what modification was possible in the Tower nomination urgency. Yet that is precisely the kind of prediction we need in order to judge how well the various rhetors' rhetoric adapted to this particular urgency. As I have mentioned, what we do in such ordinary cases is to consider whether the details will add up to broader conclusions that stipulate what would be the general consequences of the patterns of influence we have isolated. I offer the following as intermediate generalizations to help us understand the potentialities for modifying the Tower nomination urgency. (1) Both political necessity and personal choice would impel the President to support his nominee during the entire proceedings, but he would do it with tact and restraint. There was little prospect that any rhetoric would change his pattern of response in this situation. (2) Tower's personal nature and his sensitivity to the situation would cause him to defend himself with tenacity and decorum as the hearings developed. There was little likelihood of modifying this dimension of the situation. (3) Chairman Nunn's public announcement against Tower's confirmation and President Bush's continued support of Tower reflected the fact that the confirmation had become a partisan issue, and this partisanship was unlikely to be altered by further rhetoric. (4) The FBI background report on Tower was sufficiently ambiguous to allow Democrats and Republicans to rationalize their contradictory views of what the report proved. (5) In consequence of these things, without some new and startling evidence, the parties' opposed interpretations were not likely to change.

These are basic interpretations of what the raw data about John Tower's confirmation proceedings add up to. They are propositions or conclusions "given" by the data. Collectively, they invite the broad conclusion that at least after Nunn's announcement, there was very little possibility of modifying the nominating urgency through discourse. The issue having been made partisan, Democrats and Republicans in the full Senate would spend their time *justifying* the positions their parties had already taken. Given these circumstances, it becomes clear that almost *no* rhetoric could modify the urgency once Senator Nunn had announced his position. The nomination would be rejected no matter what any individual senator said. Nothing rhetorical was likely to stop the now predetermined rejection.

To make such predictions, we have to draw inferences from the patterns we see in raw data and use those inferences as bases for gen-

eralizations about what can and cannot be influenced by rhetoric at
any of the several stages in the flow of events. Put in different words,
we extract kernel concepts about the potentials for modifying the urgency, and those kernel statements in turn enable us to make general
forecasts concerning the rhetorically probable course of events. I call
these kernel concepts "givens" because they are "given" to us from
inferences about situational facts.

What Givens Are

Like all other aspects of a rhetorical configuration, givens are not
entities; they are becomings. Givens are kernel concepts that we
evolve inferentially from the explicit/implicit patterns of influence we
have seen in our data. Givens, therefore, will change as the patterns
of influence change. Because givens are conclusions, they give focus
to our thoughts about the potential for modifying an exigential flow
at a particular time. What they give us is an estimate of the amount
and kind of change that can be made in participants' structured perceptions of a rhetorical urgency. In the Tower case the givens tell us
that after Nunn's announcement, participants' perceptions would be
that this was an entirely partisan battle which the Democrats would
almost surely win.

Extracting givens is a culminating attempt to give structure to
one's understanding of a provoking urgency. Givens are mental con-
structs. They are our basic conclusions about how patterns of influence shape perceptions of an urgency. Because they are subjective
interpretations, different people examining the same set of explicit/
implicit influences may discern somewhat different givens. This does
not invalidate the process. It merely reaffirms a fact of life: sometimes
observers don't agree on what the same data mean. For example, in
political campaigns the same data lead competing political parties to
markedly different broad interpretations, and there is likely to be at
least some justification for each party's conclusions.

It's extremely important to think of givens as evolving. They are
not frozen, unchanging. Patterns of influence change, and the inferences they allow change. Givens therefore *become*. Franklin L.
Baumer says in his *Modern European Thought* that the concept of

becoming involves "a mode of thinking that contemplates everything . . . as not merely changing, but as forever evolving into
something new and different."[1] Each given is thus constantly changing and evolving, becoming either stronger or weaker as a conclusion.
Its relationship to the provoking urgency is also changing, causing it
to exert greater or less influence on the potential that the urgency has
for modification.

The amount and kind of change that can be made in an urgency
at a particular time depends on (1) the influence that givens collectively show is exerted on the urgency, and (2) the amount and kind of
change that each given shows is possible. As change occurs in one or
more givens over time, the possibilities for modifying the urgency
also change. We can illustrate how this happens by imagining that the
American people reversed the way they felt about the urgencies of
fiscal policy in the early 1980s. As David A. Stockman said, in the
early 1980s Americans liked and wanted to keep their "welfare state."
Therefore, no massive changes in fiscal policy were possible. But
suppose instead that while the budget was being considered they had
sent unmistakable protests to Washington in 1981 and 1982 demanding cuts in federal expenditures for domestic programs. If they had
demonstrated that they were fed up with paying for welfare programs
and had threatened to vote out those politicians who supported them,
the change in their attitudes would have dramatically increased the
possibilities for the Reagan Revolution and its rhetoric to modify the
provoking urgency of designing a budget.[2]

In other words, givens identify specific possibilities (or impos-
sibilities) for change in an urgency at a particular time. When most,
or all, givens seem to represent participants' unyielding perceptions
of an urgency, that urgency may be said to be rigidly structured and
the potential for change through rhetoric will have to be judged very
limited. Sometimes the givens afford only two realistic choices—to
decide whether or not the company has broken a law; to vote either
for tax reform or against it; to go to war or surrender. The givens in
the Tower confirmation proceedings became highly structured. They
ultimately provided only the choice of voting for or against confirmation. Further, they forecast that party pressures would cause senators,

with rare exceptions, to vote their party's line and that the more numerous Democrats would prevail in the committee and in the Senate.
When givens express relatively unfixed, unstable, or unsteady
patterns of influence, the participants' perceptions of that urgency
are less structured, and the possibilities for change are probably multiple. In the case of the Canadian hearings on drugs in sports, the
master patterns clearly indicated that the hearings would result in
some kind of legislation and regulations to curtail the use of
performance-enhancing drugs. But the givens were not so structured
as to indicate exactly how athletes, coaches, and the public would respond to remedial measures proposed.

If we can estimate the change(s) that *could* be made in an urgency
at the time of the communication or communications, we can say to
what degree a rhetor or groups of rhetors achieved all that was *possible*
in that situation. This is true whether one is observing a single rhetorical effort such as Calhoun's March 4 speech or a series of messages such as those of an advertising campaign—or some other type
of campaign. One can explore protracted arguments that occur in
evolving urgencies: those that mark the gradual breakdown of a marriage, those that characterized the "star wars" or stealth bomber controversies, or those that marked the controversies about *perestroika* in
Eastern European developments or about the best way for the world
community to respond to Iraq's invasion of Kuwait. Instead of exploring the urgency of the moment Calhoun addressed, we could
choose to explore the entire series of congressional debates on the
Compromise measures of 1850. If we studied any such series of rhetorical efforts, we would soon recognize that the givens identifying
the possibilities for modifying the urgencies changed by stages. And
as each change occurred, we would need to take a new sighting on the
givens that then defined the possibilities for modifying the urgency at
that stage.

Wise persuaders do not seek greater change in an urgency than
can be effected—unless, of course, they are compelled to do so by
their personal convictions, the nature of their spokesperson's role,
and so on. Nor do wise persuaders seek less change than the situation will allow. Successful persuasion is directed to the spectrum of

admissable change that can be made in an urgency. This point is so important that it bears emphasizing: [The only kind of persuasive effort that can succeed must be congruent with the collective influences reflected by the givens and by the potential for modification reflected by individual givens.]

We have seen how the givens derived from data about the Tower confirmation hearings explained the potentials for change before and after Senator Nunn's negative announcement. Following that announcement, the givens predicted a partisan vote and defeat of the nomination. In data I have reported concerning the sectional controversies of 1850, at least five givens are implicitly present, although I have not explicitly designated them in that way. My analyses suggest that there were five superordinate givens which, taken collectively, explain the potential for change in the exigential flow of which Calhoun made his speech a part.

The Givens

The first given was that an acute, uncompromisable conflict existed over the morality of slavery and the relation of slavery to national progress. This conflict exacerbated other differences between North and South.

The second given was that the North was determined that slavery should not expand in the territories and that the political strength of the South should be constrained. The South was equally determined to maintain her equal rights to the territories and all other manifestations of her equality.

The third given was that the necessity of establishing and maintaining territorial or state governments in lands acquired from Mexico and in the remaining unorganized lands of the Louisiana Purchase would produce a sectional collision. Organization would make it necessary to decide whether the territories should be free or slave areas.

The fourth given was that despite the points of conflict, there remained some degree of political stability deriving from the fact that both Northerners and Southerners accepted with some reservations that the party system and the normal political process protected their interests and gave expression to their individual and sectional griev-

ances. Traditionally the Democratic and Whig parties had permitted
the South tacitly to control national legislative responses to issues
concerning slavery.

The fifth given was that in consequence of sameness in political
institutions, social traditions, family ties, and so on, there was still a
strong love of the Union and a pervasive desire for peace in both sections of the country.

How the Givens Worked

From these givens, three still broader conclusions can be drawn
concerning the potential for modifying the urgency at the time of
Calhoun's speech.

First, the influences represented by the first three givens forecast that the ugly sectional confrontation over slavery in 1850 could
not be resolved by genuine compromise. Neither side would yield
concessions on the morality of slavery, relation of slavery to national
progress, expansion of slavery into the territories, political strength of
the South, or any other question seemingly linked with the equality
of the South. Among other things, this meant that any legislation emanating from Congress that violated any of these uncompromisable
positions would be rejected. Little or no change would be possible on
these matters.

Second, the forces represented by the fourth and fifth givens
forecast that any congressional attempt to evoke war-provoking measures would be incompatible with the potential for modification existing in the urgency in the spring of 1850.

Third, the contradictory nature of the two judgments above
shows that no real compromise was possible. Only an ambiguous
formulation that allowed representatives of both sections to sense
security and a possible victory could alter the stalemate in the Congress. It was the ambiguous nature of popular sovereignty that enabled its congressional adherents to modify the rhetorical urgency by
passing the series of "compromise" measures. One can predict, further, that as the struggle to control the territories intensified, the sectional positions reflected by the first and second givens would
become more rigid and the moderating influences implied by the

fourth and fifth givens would diminish. In the actual events, this is just what happened.

My case study illustrates what givens are and how they can be used. My five givens are basic conclusions inferred from study of the explicit/implicit patterns of influence discussed in the last two chapters. The nature of the modification that could be made in the provoking urgency of 1850 and during the next decade depended on the evolving influence represented by the collective givens.

How Givens Are Confirmed

A clinical psychologist is sitting in his office thinking about his approaching conference with the parents of an endangered family. Viewing this breakdown in family bonding as a configuration of forces, he quickly arrives at the key factors, or givens, in this provoking rhetorical urgency: the family's *economic* situation, in relation to the level of *stress* the individual family members have, in relation to career *goals* each parent has, in relation to the quality of *time* the family has together, in relation to the *desire* each person has to make the family work.

He reasons that the givens of economics, time, and career goals are inflexible. Both parents are committed to professional careers. Their jobs and transportation between office and home in the suburbs eat up more than eleven hours each weekday and part of the weekend. To pay for their expensive home and day care for the two children, the parents must maintain a high income. The enormous energy they devote to their work causes them to be tired at home and irritable toward each other and the children. Their high personal stress levels are shared by the children, who are experiencing minor emotional problems. The parents have a pretty good grasp of what causes their stress and seem willing to try ways to cope with it, like experimenting with the relaxation response technique. Fortunately, both parents and children value marriage and family and want to save them badly enough to seek professional help. The psychologist reasons that this family is endangered but that some improvement is possible because two of the givens identify conditions amenable to modification: the stress level can be lowered through therapy and ap-

plication, and the desire level can raised if the members are encouraged to value family more highly.

The psychologist is basically following the process I have been
describing for discovering and evaluating givens. Once a provocation
is identified, the next step is to understand how participants perceive
it. Usually, as in the trial of sports agents Bloom and Walters, we can
learn enough about perceptions by finding explicit situational patterns in the immediate circumstances of the communication(s).
Somewhat tougher urgencies, like John Tower's confirmation hearings or the hearings on drugs in Canadian sports, require us to search
out the historical development of an urgency in order to identify explicit historical patterns and, perhaps, the structuralization of major
groupings in order to locate explicit group patterns. Only in more difficult cases, as in the urgency of 1850, do we need to look for implicit
forces in society to discover *Zeitgeist* patterns or patterns of social
needs and pressures that affect perceptions of an urgency.

As we formulate the givens of an urgency, we need to concern
ourselves with whether these broad conclusions are fair, true to the
facts, and sufficiently inclusive to cover all of the major features of
the exigential flow. This we can do if we ask the following questions
as we try to discover the givens among our broader arrays of data.

1. Are all of the significant explicit/implicit influences reflected
in the givens as I have formulated them? In any configurational analysis of a provoking urgency, the ultimate generalizations offered as
describing an urgency's dimensions need to be at least implicitly inclusive of *all* significant explicit/implicit influences. I believe my analyses of the urgencies of the endangered family, John Tower's
confirmation hearing, and the sectional crisis of 1850 all meet this
test. None of the influences I uncovered vitiates my overall description of that urgency, and on review I do not see significant patterns of
influence that my givens fail to accommodate.

2. A corollary to the first question is: Does each given stipulate
a directly relevant dimension of the provoking urgency? If a proposed generalization lacks direct relevance to the urgency, that
"given" ought to be rejected as part of one's overall analysis. For example, during the first half of the nineteenth century a vigorous but

short-lived anti-Masonic movement developed. This was certainly a significant feature of the country's history, but it had little if anything to do with the slavery–antislavery crisis. It therefore cannot constitute a directly relevant dimension of the urgency concerning slavery. In this way the second test question reveals the relevance or irrelevance of a proposed given. All of the givens I have proposed clearly meet this test.

3. Is the idea represented by each proposed given related to, but distinct from, the ideas represented by the other givens? All givens need to be germane to the urgency under study, but it is uselessly repetitious and conceptually confusing to state them in ways that are ambiguous or allow them to overlap one another. Raising this third question about any set of givens simply exposes redundancies and confusions in analyses. The givens I have formulated meet this test.

4. Is each proposed given truly a *crucial* concept concerning the urgency? Once more, if someone proposed anti-Masonry or the "nativist" *Zeitgeist* that affected some parts of the country as givens concerning the slavery urgency, this test question would reveal that while both movements were historically significant, neither had much to do with the urgency concerning slavery. On the other hand, each of the givens I have proposed for the crisis of 1850 does express a crucial concept about that urgency. Still, if we were analyzing, say, the rhetorical urgency in American society concerning tolerance/intolerance, the existence of anti-Masonry and of nativism would be relevant and, indeed, *crucial* features of that urgency. So, too, would the fourth and fifth givens I have proposed for the urgency of 1850, for they too represent forces favorable to general tolerance, even as they bear on the slavery controversy.

The givens I offered for the urgencies represented by the endangered family, Tower's confirmation hearings, and the crisis of 1850 all meet each of the four tests I have proposed. Therefore, I am justified in believing that I have located the quintessential features for each of these urgencies. With givens formulated and tested for their appropriateness, it becomes possible to estimate the amount and kind of change that is possible in a rhetorical urgency. Since each urgency is unique in its receptivity to change, one can't presuppose givens.

They synthesize the explicit/implicit patterns; they can't be predicted before those patterns have been explored. The potentials for modification were very different in the urgency concerning John Tower's confirmation, in the urgency for help to an endangered family, and in the sectional crisis of 1850. In these and in all other rhetorical urgencies, the possibilities for change are specified by givens that can be validly supported at the time when particular communications take place.

Chapter Ten

The Potential
Influences of Communication
on a Provoking Urgency

Now that we have estimated the general potentialities for change in an urgency, we must ask: *How much and what kind of change could this rhetorical event potentially exert on the provoking urgency?* We are not asking here about a persuader's potential influence on other participants but about what the readers/listeners addressed could potentially do to change the urgency, under the circumstances. This question has enormous consequences for the remainder of our discussion of configurational rhetoric. For a rhetorical event to have the greatest possible influence on a provoking urgency, the attempted persuasion must be congruent with its potential for modifying the urgency. In the following chapter, I show that once we know the potential influence of our communication (or set of communications) on an urgency, we can judge the congruence of the communication(s) with these potentialities.

Influences of the Occasion

As I have said, the pressure that a particular audience can exert on a provoking urgency depends partly on the nature of the communicative occasion. This point especially concerns oral communication, which is always situational. Except for highly unusual circumstances (such as the Chinese practice of affixing important notices on designated walls or poster boards), we may read a written communication almost anywhere, in private or in public, on a commuter train, at a lunch counter, or at the kitchen table after the kids have been gotten off to bed. We may read only part of a message at a particular time, returning to the task until the reading is completed or ignoring the unread portions. For these reasons it is usually not useful to generalize about occasions for private reading.

When we think of rhetorical occasions for speech, we have to think about the environment, the physical and psychological circumstances in which communicators attempt to persuade audiences. Ordinarily a speaking occasion is a particularized extension of a provoking urgency. A face-to-face occasion draws speaker(s) and listeners together at a particular time and place. These afford the physical and psychological circumstances under which communication occurs. The same applies to a somewhat lesser extent to radio-television audiences that tune in to, say, an "electric church" service. As individuals or in small groups the audience members still respond to the urgency that provoked the communication, and during the presentation they listen, watch the television screen, and perhaps share reactions with their companions or even rehearse those reactions within their own minds.

One's conception of an occasion should not be restricted to the immediate environment in which the communication is presented. Sometimes a broader interpretation must be employed if one is to understand the physical and psychological circumstances. For example, to limit the concept of occasion for a presidential inaugural to the specific gathering of listeners and speakers on and about the steps of the Capitol would miss the accompanying tapestry that gives the inaugural its unique place in American culture. Much of the significance of that occasion comes from related ceremonies such as the formal breakfast and lunch for the presidential party, the swearing in of the Vice-President, the presidential caravan to the Capitol, the inaugural parade, and the inaugural balls—as well as from media coverage of the proceedings.

Consider also the occasion for a paper presented at a professional meeting. The occasion is a presentation within a larger occasion. The fact that the meeting is a professional one gives a special kind of ethos to every communication within it. Thus the "real" occasion is probably that a paper is given within a program of papers that is *one part* of a multiple-programmed conference built around certain professional goals, interests, and ideological concerns. The physical and psychological circumstances attending one individual program or one paper simply will not explain the conditions of communication for a single paper or even for a single program. The relevant boundaries of this occasion are in a sense coextensive with those of the entire professional meeting.

One could contrast this situation with the occasion of communicating at a rally. There the preparational-motivational activities that got the audience together would be part of the occasion. A famous recent example of this was the student demonstrations in China in May and June of 1989. The first Sino-Soviet summit in thirty years provided the excuse for students to vent long-standing frustrations. At times, during the fortnight that they occupied Tiananmen Square in the heart of Beijing, more than a million students and their supporters clogged the square. Their ostensible purpose was to honor visiting Mikhail Gorbachev for initiating widespread political reforms in the Soviet Union. Soon it became apparent that this throng was a planned peaceful demonstration calling for greater political and individual freedom in China. As hundreds of students went on hunger strikes, support for their cause mushroomed into a popular mass movement, producing, according to *Newsweek*, "a dazzling display of People Power." Putting their bodies in front of tanks and trucks at the outskirts of Beijing, workers and peasants immobilized army units ordered to enforce martial law. At a score of flash points throughout China similar demonstrations by students and their supporters took place. It would be a mistake to limit the occasions for the numerous speeches by student leaders and for the infrequent attempts at conciliation by government authorities to the immediate Beijing environment. Realistic boundaries of the occasions for these attempts at persuasion were coextensive with the convulsive protest itself, which for several weeks spread over the entire city of Beijing and its environs and touched more than thirty other Chinese cities. This is not to say, of course, that the boundaries of a speaking occasion were the same as those of the provoking urgency itself. The roots for the provocation lay deep within the Chinese psyche. Disaffection from Chinese society and the tradition of student protests and of substitution

of mass demonstrations for elections went back many years in the nation's past. Furthermore, in recent years China's major economic reforms had brought to public awareness official corruption and cronyism, great disparity of income, and disappointed expectations for the educated elite.

The Basic Nature of an Occasion

The reasons that bring persuaders and listeners together may constrain the pressure that an audience can exert on a provoking urgency. A meeting may come into existence in specific response to a provoking urgency: a forum addresses the problem of corruption in government; a public meeting of the town council and interested citizens considers the council's proposed change in garbage collection; a neighborhood meets to find ways to reduce the high incidence of local crime; a ceremony honoring those killed in the Vietnam war is televised. In cases like these, the meetings and their participants have been mobilized specifically to exert pressure on particular urgencies. On the other hand, a meeting may have somewhat less potential to change an urgency if it is simply a regularly scheduled meeting of some organization. Ordinarily such a meeting is neither mobilized nor energized to attack a particular urgency. Although exceptions exist, usually little concerted impetus to change things comes out of a mayor's weekly news conference, a monthly business meeting of a county trade association, a trisemester meeting of a university's faculty senate, or the broadcasting of the Columbia Broadcasting Company's evening news program.

Sometimes the sponsorship of an occasion influences communication's potential clout. One should be interested in questions like these: Who are the sponsors of the meeting? What is their relationship to the meeting? What benefits to themselves do they expect to get from their efforts? What is their status? How closely identified are they with the persuader(s) and persuadees? Does their identification help or impair the capacity of the rhetorical event to exert pressure on the flow of events?

The basic nature of the occasion for John C. Calhoun's March 4 speech enormously enhanced the capacity of his listeners to have impact on the provoking urgency. They were convened as the United States Senate, one of the two most important law-making bodies in the nation. The same listeners assembled under any other circumstances would have had far less capacity to effect movement or change in the urgency. Their authority was derived from the immediate sponsor of the occasion: the Senate. That is, their authority came from their membership in the convened Senate, which was charged with the responsibility of enacting legislation that theoretically would be binding on all actors in the urgency. As individual senators they could, of course, exert considerable influence on the flow of events, but their individual powers were much less than their collective authority to shape the laws of the land. In this case the Senate eventually had to legislate a response to the slavery-related issues posed by the acquisition of western land after the Mexican War. Ultimately, the sponsors of the occasion were the American people themselves— what they were, what they stood for, their national heritage, and their accumulated social, cultural, and ideological baggage. To mark the occasion for Calhoun's speech, then, one must take into account many situational factors beyond the isolated characteristics of the Senate chamber on March 4.

Circumstances of Time, Location, and Mood

Sometimes the date, place, and feeling of the occasion affect the capacities of those who respond. If someone writes an editorial, a quasi-official pronouncement, or a book about reducing nuclear threats, the power of the readers to exert pressure on the urgency would probably be increased under circumstances like these: if the message were published and read on, or about, the anniversary of dropping nuclear bombs on Japan; if the persuader were an international figure highly respected by both hawks and doves; if the anniversary and the impending publication of the message had been widely publicized around the world, producing a mood of anticipation; if prestigious political and moral leaders of nuclear nations were known to endorse the message and/or the persuader; and if the message were disseminated to a wide, international audience. What I have just said would also apply generally if the message were oral instead of written. In addition, the capacity of the listening audience to influence the urgency might be increased if the speech were delivered in either Hiroshima or Nagasaki on the anniversary of the dropping of the bomb on that city; if the immediate audience included major world figures; if the speech were broadcast over numerous radio and television stations in this country and abroad; and if the occasion for the speech had received much advance international attention. Comparable considerations apply to any effort to modify any urgency. The occasion for a classroom lecture is in part determined by the history of the course; the occasion for a sermon is frequently modified by the religious season. [Once again we see that occasions are very often considerably more complex than the *immediate* settings for discourses.]

To some extent the capabilities of the 1850 Congress may have been augmented by the timing and mood of the occasion for Calhoun's speech. His address was read at a time of national crisis. Both thoughtful citizens and the Congress were deeply distressed over the apparent threat to the Union and were convinced that, if the country were to be saved, Congress must come up with a suitable compromise. Too, some slight addition to the power of the rhetorical event may have been generated by the location of the speech—the old Senate chamber, rich in tradition and packed almost to suffocation with senators and invited guests.

The Agenda

Speeches and even written rhetoric rarely occur all by themselves. They are accompanied ordinarily by other presentations, ceremonies, events, musical selections, and the like. All items on the agenda contribute to, or detract from, the prestige of the occasion and thereby affect the influence that the rhetorical event can exert on an urgency. I have already suggested that the extensive pageantry accompanying the presidential inaugural address augments the potential influence of that occasion. In considering the agenda accompanying Calhoun's speech, I must consider the circumstances in Congress from the beginning of the congressional session early in December 1849 to the delivery of Calhoun's speech on March 4, 1850.

During this three-month period one of the most important and best publicized debates in our national history got under way. Many of the most respected political giants gave strident speeches in the Senate and House. The legislative agenda added to the potential power that senators had as convened senators to influence the urgency and as individual political leaders to mobilize public sentiment.

In contrast to the rather sweepingly inclusive occasion in Calhoun's Senate, let me cite a specific occasion that still has beyond-the-moment dimensions. Governor Clinton's failed speech at the 1988 Democratic National Convention, to which I have referred, was an example of the influence of *agenda* on rhetorical potential and of a communicator's failure to take it seriously. Clinton said afterward that he had thought his function was to "introduce" Michael Dukakis. If that really is what he thought, he failed to look carefully at the convention's agenda. All delegates knew they would nominate Dukakis an hour or so later. All were politicos who needed no further introduction to the man they had already effectively chosen as the Democratic nominee. The apex of the agenda was to do the nominating, not to meet some new figure. Clinton seems to have misread his place on the overall agenda; perhaps he thought too much of the TV audience. But even his "outside" audience knew that the next step of the agenda was the formal nomination. All kinds of announcements and published schedules had established that, so the TV audiences would be entirely willing to accept an "I give you a man who . . . " speech at this point in the convention. The agenda actually called for a pep talk for Dukakis, not for an introduction. That appears to have been clear to everyone except Clinton and his aides.

Influences of the Audience

The influence that particular readers/listeners exert on a state of affairs depends to a considerable extent on the nature of that audience itself. Perhaps the most useful way to consider the conditioning effects of an audience is to note its size and its special capacity to influence an urgency.

Size of the Audience

The size of the audience that reads or hears a communication may contribute to, or detract from, its potential influence on an urgency. For instance, the immensity of the audience that read and discussed Thomas Paine's *Common Sense* was a major reason for the publication's influence upon events. In 1775 the internal logic of events carried the Colonies into increasingly militant confrontations with England. The declaration of both houses of the British Parliament that Massachusetts was in rebellion was followed by battles at Lexington and Concord, the capture of Ticonderoga, the creation of the Continental Army, the appointment of George Washington as commander-in-chief, and an invasion of Canada. Men and events had determined that most Colonists agreed that Colonial assemblies alone should be the final judges concerning the amount of authority wielded by Britain in the affairs of the provinces. Although the die had been cast, much public opinion still hesitated on the threshold of asserting complete independence. No major public call for independence had been made. The Colonies had arrived at a juncture demanding symbolic modification. This need was satisfied in January 1776 by the publication of *Common Sense*. Summarizing the arguments of the radicals and energizing them with warrants drawn from venerated social philosophy, Paine's pamphlet seemed to crystallize opinion in favor of independence. Almost overnight, according to Carl J. Friedrich and Robert G. McCloskey, *Common Sense* produced "a wave of anti-monarchial feeling that was not to abate until the question of monarchy had become academic in America."[1] Within a few months almost everyone in the Colonies had read or had heard the postulates emotionalized by Paine. It was, among other things, the huge readership that gave *Common Sense* its power to modify the existing affairs in the interest of independence.

As another example, the unprecedented size of the audiences that attended George Whitefield's preaching in New England and the Middle Colonies during the Great Awakening, and the even larger auditories that heard him preach during the Methodist revival in England, were significant factors in quickening both evangelical movements. In the fifteen months (October 30, 1739, to January 24, 1740) that the English evangelist remained in America, he delivered over five hundred sermons, most of them in the large cities of Boston, New York, Philadelphia, and Charleston, or on tours between them. Innumerable references in newspapers, journals, letters, pamphlets, and in *Christian History* (*Christian History* was the first weekly religious magazine in America) mentioned audiences of many thousands. Apparently thousands of persons sometimes followed Whitefield from church to church to hear him preach, and over 23,000 persons attended his farewell sermon on the Boston Common. Even his enemies recognized that the very size of his congregations did much to stimulate pervasive religious turmoil.

During Whitefield's stay in America newspapers frequently devoted front pages to him, preachers eulogized him, and numerous pamphlets were published about him. Whitefield and his traveling companion, William Seward, were skilled propagandists. They sent to newspapers and to influential persons frequent letters containing accounts of the size and response of his audiences, as well as the locations and dates for the delivery of his forthcoming sermons. Also, people were kept constantly informed by special criers who rode along the proposed routes, announcing the time and place for his preaching. America had never witnessed itinerant preaching before; preaching to mass audiences on the commons and in the streets and fields on weekdays was excitingly different.

The fame of the evangelist caused villagers, farmers, and city dwellers "to come to preaching" with a holiday spirit. Merchants closed their stores, housewives left their chores, and farmers hurried in from the fields to attend his services. Although numerous other factors contributed to the extraordinary impact that Whitefield's audiences exerted upon the Awakening, his preaching could not have stirred to life the wildfire of revivalism if the size of his audiences had not been spectacularly huge.[2]

Because more than 200,000 persons massed in front of the Lincoln Memorial on August 28, 1963, and because millions more were gathered before radios or television sets to hear Martin Luther King, Jr., deliver his "I Have a Dream" speech, the audiences contributed to the pressure exerted by the rhetorical event on the civil rights urgency. If only a few hundred protesters had joined the March on Washington, the smallness of the auditory would have vitiated its impact; there would have been no dramatic thrust against racial injustice. Furthermore, since the delivery of the speech, millions of persons have read all or part of the speech or have watched televised recordings of it. This swelling of the audience has further increased the potential of that rhetorical event to influence the urgency of civil rights. More recent examples demonstrating that the large size of an audience may increase the capacity of a rhetorical event to influence its provoking urgency are provided by the massive antigovernment rallies in Seoul, South Korea, prior to the 1988 Olympics, the student demonstrations in China in 1989, and the prodemocratic demonstrations in Europe and the Soviet Union in 1989 and the early 1990s. These rallies were so incredibly large they captured world attention and, in turn, influenced governments' behaviors.

Often, of course, the size of an audience is not a major determinant of its capacity to affect an urgency. For instance, the limited size of John C. Calhoun's Senate audience did not add to, or detract from, the power of the speech to influence the sectional crisis.

Special Capabilities of Audiences to Influence Urgencies

Because of their natures, some audiences have a special intrinsic capacity to affect the state of affairs. Some have the recognized authority to legislate laws, evoke treaties, issue resolutions or proclamations, make agreements, or render judicial decisions that are binding on significant numbers of persons involved in an urgency. Examples of this point are endless. Stockholders, who are scattered throughout the country, may respond to the attempted persuasion of corporate officials by returning their mail-in ballots, registering their decisions on issues vital to the company. In response to lawyers' arguments the members of the United States Supreme Court can determine that a state law on abortion is or is not constitutional. A special committee of the House of Representatives has the authority to send a resolution to the full House to impeach the President; the House has the authority to impeach and the Senate to convict. The trustees for a "think tank" can set research and funding priorities for that institution. The legislative convention of the National Collegiate Athletic Association can set policies concerning academic qualifications for athletes at member schools. The power capabilities of all these audiences enable them to exert immediate, direct influence on urgencies.

The members of each of the above-mentioned audiences can also apply diffused, less immediate and less direct influence on events through their individual efforts over time. Thus, the delegates to the NCAA convention not only have the capability to enact policies determining academic qualifications for athletes at member schools but they also—as individuals—have power to influence others in special ways when they return home. They can influence other coaches and administrators, students, athletes, parents, government officials, fans, and the general public by means of speeches, letters, conferences, television appearances, and the like. All of these persuadees can in turn influence still other persons.

Some audiences have special capability to exert moral, political, or intellectual pressure on events because their individual members have impressive prestige, positions, socioeconomic status, and/or membership in important interest groups. The influence of such audiences depends upon the circumstances, but some suggestive generalizations can be made. Because they have high prestige and/or economic-social status, some readers/listeners are likely to be opinion leaders. Individually or as groups they can usually exert much more influence than can persons with low prestige or low economic-social status. An audience of presidents of major universities would ordinarily have far more potential to alter a relevant urgency than would an audience, say, of untenured faculty members or of students. I think of the National Conference of Catholic Bishops who held hearings and special discussions for nearly three years before issuing their prestigious *The Challenge of Peace*, the American Bar Association committee that collects testimony as a basis for rating nominees for judgeships, and the NCAA delegates who debate issues before taking their almost "legal" actions. All of these are audiences who exert much more influence than can persons of lower prestige. One reason the poor and the destitute are overlooked by the various levels of government is that traditionally they have not voted or otherwise influenced others in ways that apply crucial pressure on a significant urgency. In short, they have little, if any, public clout.

Persons who belong to relevant interest groups may have special capacities to influence members of their own groups and relatively less capability to influence members of other groups. Thus, given a reading/listening audience of blacks, Hispanics, and Wasps, one would ordinarily expect that blacks would influence chiefly other blacks, Hispanics other Hispanics, and Wasps other Wasps. Like most other generalizations about human behavior, however, these are only relatively true. One must study the particular circumstances in order to judge the potential influence of an event or audience on rhetorical urgencies.

Governor Clinton's nominating speech also fits what I'm saying here. He was addressing two audiences; one could serve his goals and the other could not. The delegates could influence both the ongoing rhetorical event and the urgency Clinton was addressing. The delegates could and did create noise, draw their fingers across their throats, and otherwise react unfavorably to the speech, thus influencing the rhetorical event. In the short run at least, the "outside" listeners' and viewers' perceptions of his rhetoric could have nothing to do with the outcome of the convention.

Influences over Time

So far, I have chiefly considered single communications, occurring at particular points in the flow of events. This may give the illusion of freezing the dynamics of configurations. This is not at all the case, of course. All elements in a rhetorical configuration constantly engage in configured interplay. This fact becomes even more important when we consider multiple communications, like the running debate in the early 1990s over whether drug war tactics were eroding constitutional rights in the United States or whether the Baltic States should receive their independence from the Soviet Union and, if so, when it should occur and what form it should take. In any set of communications extending over time, the givens of a provoking urgency constantly tend to soften or harden, old ones may disappear, and new ones may come into play. Such changes alter the nature and amount of modification possible in the urgency. Likewise, change inevitably occurs in the occasions for the communications and in the audiences who participate in the communications. The potentialities for communications to influence urgencies necessarily change in accord with the situational changes I have been talking about. Consider how the potentialities for communication to modify the Baltic situation altered after the Communist party of Lithuania broke with Moscow in 1989, after Lithuania declared its independence on March 11, 1990, and after Mikhail Gorbachev's ultimatum on Good Friday, 1990, demanding that Lithuanians rescind measures they had taken after declaring independence. The constant change in what was rhetorically possible in this matter was of practical concern to President George Bush, for example, who had to react publicly to changing conditions in the Baltic States while responding to those in this country who wished to influence his stand on the matter and while maintaining positive relations with the Soviets.

The consequences of any rhetorical event depend on how well the design and execution of the event match both (1) the *potential* for modifying the provoking urgency and (2) the *capacities* of those addressed to change the flow of events under the circumstances of the occasion. I have stressed in this chapter that one's answer to what sort of match occurred can be affected by the occasion for the communication, the size of the audience, the audience's own agenda, the audience's power to act, and the capacities of segments of the audience to influence special interest groups. Any or all of these factors may affect how much and what kind of change a communication could exert on its provoking urgency. Accordingly, an observer or critic wanting to understand a rhetorical event fully will need to consider which, if any, of these factors operated significantly in that case. When we are concerned with multiple communications over a period of time, what is communicatively possible changes from one rhetorical event to the next, as the configuration of relevant forces changes. We see once more why examining only the text or the immediate circumstances of presentation can yield only a partial view of a rhetorical event's potential for significance. As I have insisted throughout, no rhetoric is fully intelligible apart from its context.

Only after the numerous contextual influences on a communication's potential have been canvassed does it become plausible to try to estimate the "real" force of that communication. I turn now to how this may be done.

Chapter Eleven

Congruence of Communication with Its Potential for Influencing a Provoking Urgency

This book is based on the premise that the ultimate objective of all persuasion is to encourage changes in readers/listeners—changes that will in turn lead them to exert some desired pressure on a provoking state of affairs. Therefore, to judge the ultimate success of persuasion, one asks: *How congruent were the basic thrusts or theses of the communication(s) with the amount and kind of modification that such a communication could make in the urgency?* How we answer that question tells us how wisely persuaders used the available means of influencing the flow of events. To answer it, we must compare or match what we know of the rhetoric's basic thrusts against what we know of the potential for changing the urgency and the capacity of readers/listeners to influence the urgency under the circumstances of the situation. A central reason for inquiring into the congruencies of communications with their *potentialities* for influencing an urgency is to establish a basis for comparative evaluations of communications' actual satisfactions with the persuadees' readinesses to respond and to influence the urgency in question.

Congruence of Basic Thrusts with the Conditioning Influences of Audiences and Occasions

We need to match the basic thrusts (as we understand them) with what we judge to have been the potential influence the readers/listeners could have had on the urgency. Generally speaking, the more congruity we find between these two judgments, the wiser the persuaders' choices of rhetorical options will prove to have been, and

the better the communication(s) will have functioned to alter events.
I illustrate the structure of the matching process below

The Matching Process

Form a judgment   Form a judgment of the   Derive a judgment
of what the   influences of the   of the congruity
basic thrusts of the   occasion, given its   between your
communications   general nature,   previous two
were.   time,   conclusions.
                       location,
                       mood,
                       agenda;
                       then, form a judgment
                       of the influences of
                       the audience, given its
                       size, and
                       special capacities
                       to influence the
                       urgency.

If I apply this matching procedure to Calhoun's speech of
March 4, it becomes apparent that Calhoun's *explicit* thrusts did not
correspond to the influences of the occasion and the audience. The
convened Senate could address only three of Calhoun's explicit demands. If they chose, they could initiate a constitutional amendment
protecting slavery—but the House and the people of the North would
reject it; they could enact legislation conceding to the South equal
rights in the territories—but the House and the President would not
concur with them; and they could deny California admission as a
state. Beyond that they could not go. As the Senate of the United
States, they could not authorize secession if they admitted California,
and that was a most important thrust of Calhoun's speech. Matching
basic thrusts with what the occasion and audience *could* do about the
slavery urgency makes it clear that Calhoun's speech failed to suit the
potentialities of the immediate circumstances. On that basis we must
say the speech had little persuasive merit.

Rhetors do, however, imply desires as well as state them explicitly. From the character of the situation and Calhoun's personal na-

ture, I feel justified in speculating that he possibly had an *implicit* intent in presenting this speech. He may have wished to leave a persuasive call to the South. He may have felt that later conditions would create a configuration of forces favorable to that call, issued on March 4. If I look to postcommunication events, it is plain that this is exactly what happened. Later, the Southerners called Calhoun a prophet—one who should have been listened to and followed back in 1850. This post hoc view of Calhoun's rhetoric tells me that his speech matched well the *delayed* conditions and, in this speculative sense, had high rhetorical merit.

This kind of matching process gives us, in effect, two judgments of Calhoun's rhetorical merit. For the moment of its presentation, his speech was not wisely devised, but for another set of circumstances which might (and in fact did) develop, the basic thrusts of the speech were entirely capable of moving Southern respondents to effect a major change in the slavery urgency. Southerners were then conditioned by another set of events to accept his ultimate call—for secession if they were denied his other demands.

For another example of how this matching process works, let's return to the urgency of the endangered family I introduced earlier. The husband has just returned to the office after responding to an emergency call from the day care center. His little boy had hit his sister with a toy truck and opened a small but nasty cut on her forehead. The wife was out of town on a business trip. So he had to cancel several appointments to get the little girl and take her to the family doctor. The people at day care provided a suitable place for the little girl to rest, but they refused to keep the brother, who had become "unmanageable." The husband has brought the child back to the office, where the boy is driving a secretary and receptionist wild. Within a few minutes the husband is to meet with several important clients in a conference room down the hall. It is critical to his career that he sell them on his proposal, but somehow in the confusion he has misplaced a crucial data sheet. At this point the husband's mother unexpectedly calls his office to tell him what he should do about the general family problem.

At first the husband listens absently to his mother while he searches for the data sheet among the papers on his desk. "Your family is in trouble," his mother says, "and you've got to wake up and make that wife of yours take a sabbatical from her job at least until the kids get in school." After a few moments, he responds, "I've got to go now, Mom. I'll work on it." As he gets ready to go to his meeting, he fusses to himself: "What a time to call! With all that's happened and what I have to do . . . "As he snaps his briefcase closed, he mutters: "Why did she tell me this? I can't control what my wife does. That's pretty darn obvious. If I tell her to take a sabbatical, she'll tell me to do the same and then she'll storm out of the house and out of the marriage."

Though the mother meant well and her idea may have been wise, her communication was destructive because it did not address the potentialities of the situation. It was terribly wrong for the occasion, and it was addressed to an audience, her son, who lacked the power to carry out her injunction.

Congruence of Basic Thrusts with Potentialities for Modifying Rhetorical Urgencies

Once we have estimated how well the basic thrusts of communications match the influence of the audiences and occasions, we need to match those judgments with our judgments of the potentialities for modifying the urgency. From this matching we can derive a judgment of the congruity of the communications with the communicative possibilities in their situations.

The Matching Process

Match the judgment of congruity between the basic thrusts of the communication and the potential influences of occasion and audience	with the judgment of the potentialities for modifying the urgency	to determine how well the rhetorical act met the communicative possibilities in the situation.

Reconsider the case of the endangered family. Suppose that about a week after the mother's call, the husband and wife meet for consultation with the advising psychologist. According to his reading

of the givens of the urgency, the psychologist believes that nothing
can be done about the amount of time the couple can devote to family
bonding, the career commitments of the couple, or their income
needs. Therefore, he concentrates on trying to influence the two givens that have some potential for positive change. He offers help in
relieving stress in the family, and, by encouraging the couple to value
family more, he helps them improve their desire to make the family
work. The basic thrust of the psychologist's communication based on
these topics would match well the potential for modifying the provoking urgency.

A famous historical example is Woodrow Wilson's "Peace Without Victory" message. Its basic thrust failed to correspond with either the capability of readers/listeners to influence the situation or
with the potential for modifying the urgency. On January 22, 1917,
as accumulating events were pushing World War I to its final convulsions and a victor's peace, President Wilson delivered his "Peace
Without Victory" address to the United States Senate. One of the basic thrusts of this speech was that the belligerents should forsake war
gains and join with him in negotiating a peace "among equals," based
on Christian love. Only such a peace could last, he claimed. However, he argued further that the belligerents must accept certain
conditions that could only be imposed if Germany were defeated
and broken.

Were Wilson's contradictory thrusts consistent with the capacity
of the rhetorical event to influence the provoking urgency? Obviously
his immediate audience, the members of the U.S. Senate, could not
directly carry out the President's instructions. Wilson's intended
reading audience—the leaders of the Allies and the Central Powers—
could not accept Wilson's leadership for the sort of peace he urged.
Nor had they the power to impose a "peace without victory" even if
they wished to do so. Neither could the limited number of civilians
and military personnel of the belligerents who might read reports of
the President's speech exert pressure on the urgency in the way he
demanded. Taken at its face value, then, Wilson's speech seemed to
ask all segments of his reading/listening audience to do what they
lacked the capability to do.

Did Wilson's basic thrusts match the potential for modification in the state of affairs that, after a generation of alleged injuries, recriminations, and suppressed vengeance, had for three years threatened to destroy European civilization? Millions of lives had been lost; billions of dollars of property had been destroyed; ghastly atrocities had been committed. All the efforts of the involved nations had been directed at destroying the enemy and making them pay for their aggressions. Both sides had felt confident of ultimate victory. Both had hated too much for the leaders or the people themselves to accept a treaty empty of material gains. Germany's leaders had made plain that they planned to exclude Wilson from the peace negotiations. On January 8 they had secretly determined to begin full-scale submarine operations against all shipping that aided the enemy. On the other side, the Allied leadership at the end of December had rejected a German offer of peace negotiations and, in a joint statement on January 10, they had stated that they intended to carry on the war until they destroyed Germany as a force in Europe and until the Central Powers agreed to pay crushing reparations.

Even if Wilson had not been regarded as a quasi-belligerent by both sides, his demand for "peace without victory" was clearly not congruent with the potentialities for modifying the urgency. Likewise, his request that the belligerents adopt conditions for peace that were totally unacceptable to the Central Powers was incompatible with both his first thrust and with existing reality. Even if Wilson intended to secure a delayed impact—to establish himself as the leader of a liberal peace movement and to encourage world opinion to favor a "just" peace—his basic thrusts were not congruent with the changes that could be made in the urgency. The perceptions and responses of the persons who comprised the urgency simply would not accept an idealistic peace, especially when he also talked of imposed conditions. In these respects, Wilson's speech was deficient in rhetorical merit.

The matching processes I have used in the examples above show that one *can* derive reasoned judgments about the persuasive merits of rhetorical communications. If one can boil down background data into clearly expressed and cogent judgments of the thrust or thrusts

of the communications one studies, and if one can similarly form co-
herent, overall judgments of the potential for modifying the urgency
or urgencies, one can logically infer a judgment of how well (congru-
ently) a body of attempted persuasion matched or fit the possibilities
in the situation.

I have illustrated what kind of counsel could and could not fit the
urgency of the endangered family. I showed how and why Wilson's
"Peace Without Victory" address could not be persuasive either in
the local situation he directly addressed or in the world situation he
undoubtedly hoped to influence. In the case of Calhoun, the same
processes of matching explicit and possibly implicit thrusts with the
possibilities of modifying the urgency *at the time of the speech* and then
matching Calhoun's possibly implicit thrust *against the situation we
know evolved a decade later* help us make sense of an otherwise confusing situation. While Calhoun made unpalatable rhetoric for his time,
he made rhetoric that could strongly influence the urgency that did
evolve in 1860 and 1861. In those times the speech seemed a cogent,
relevant call to the South. In other words, the matching processes allow an observer to see how well rhetoric fits existing conditions *and*
what kinds of conditions and views would have to exist to allow a
given body of rhetoric to alter the urgency addressed.

When one considers a set of persuasive efforts over time, one
must recognize that the potentialities of rhetorical acts constantly
change, commensurate with changes in the givens of the urgencies
and with changes in the audiences and the occasions for the communications. Situational potentialities can be viewed as a kind of "arch"
under which one compares the basic thrusts of multiple communications with the potentialities of those communications to alter the urgency. In Carroll C. Arnold's study of early constitutional debates in
Pennsylvania, he reported that what he learned about voters' readiness to take seriously the Frame of 1776 (the state constitution) told
him that (1) it would be tough but not totally impossible for the Federalists to make a moving case for change in the state constitution,
because (2) there were faults in the system that *could* have given some
intensity to the sense of urgency, but (3) the Federalists didn't use
these opportunities fully. Most of their arguments and strategies

weren't sufficiently congruent with the possibilities for motivating audiences to change the urgency, even a little bit. In the end it took the influences of dissatisfaction with the federal Constitution and federal promulgation of the doctrine of accommodation to create a potentiality for the broad changes that Federalists wanted and that Pennsylvanians could and would then be willing to act upon. But the urgency was never wholly without potentialities for change, nor was the populace ever totally without capacity and perhaps even willingness to act on some of those potentialities. Arnold kept that in the foreground in order to show that the persuasion for change never took fullest advantage of the opportunities that *were* there. Change agents demanded too much at once, too early, and they were sometimes suspect as agents, and so on. Arnold found he could sense these things only in light of what he had found as possibilities for change that resided in the constitutional situation as an urgency from 1776 to 1789–90.[1]

In sum, the greater the degree of congruence between the thrusts of communications and (1) the potentialities for modification that exist in the urgencies and (2) the capacity that rhetorical events have to modify the urgency, the better the messages are for promoting changes in desired directions and the greater are their rhetorical merits. However, from what I have said so far a reader could infer that "bare" ideas thrust forward in communication are automatically endorsed or rejected by audiences. But responding to persuasion is subtler and more complex than that. We shall consider next how audiences are actually influenced.

Chapter Twelve

The Persuasive Process

Both persuaders and readers/listeners agree in a tacit sort of way that the immediate end of communicating is to promote closure. Any persuader wants to cause readers/listeners to change the ways in which they view their worlds. Change, of course, is movement from an initial position to a new one. The initial position of the readers/listeners at the beginning of communication is how they perceive *the urgency, the persuader(s),* and *the remedial action proposed by the persuader(s).* Thus, a persuadee might view an urgency in this way: "I think that Japan's dumping micro chips and other computer components in this country is a very serious problem." He or she might perceive a persuader like this: "From what I have read and heard, the person who wrote this editorial is a free-trader who doesn't know what she's talking about." Finally a reader's/listener's initial reaction to a proposed remedy might be something like this: "I don't want the unfair trade practices of the Japanese to be excused by any free-trade prattle."

The movements or shifts of view persuadees can experience may involve movement from an old position to a new one, or they may be shifts to a more intense adherence to an old position. Both adhering to a new position and reaffirming an old one involve movement toward intellectual and/or attitudinal closure.

The immediate objective of any persuader is to promote closure of this kind; that is, to get as much movement in the desired direction as is possible under the constraining circumstances. Thus, to promote closure means to narrow the gap between the initial views of the readers/listeners and the views the persuader wants them to adopt. The term "narrow" is important here because a communicator can persuade without achieving or even trying to achieve total

207

intellectual-emotional agreement. A complete closure or identification with a persuader's views is often not possible. What I mean by "closure," therefore, is as much movement toward complete closure as conditions permit.

We miss the whole point of configurational rhetoric, however, if we don't also keep in mind the constraints of the urgency and the overarching potentialities of the communication to influence change in the urgency. To induce audiences to move toward agreement, or greater agreement, with the persuaders is the immediate goal of persuasion. But the reason this goal exists is that rhetorical possibilities and necessities in dealing with audiences are determined by what changes are communicatively possible in the urgency. The ultimate goal of persuasion is to effect desired changes in the urgency. I make this point as emphatically as I can in later discussion.

Closure Involves Activity

Some people wrongly think of persuasion as a one-directional flow. To them, communicating is like writing on a chalkboard: persuaders impose messages on passive audiences whose self-identity and responses are held in abeyance until the end of the communication. They think that when persuaders do a good job, they "imprint" some new understanding or, perhaps, some new judgment on the readers'/listeners' minds. This, however, is not at all how the relationships between persuaders and readers/listeners work.

First, persuaders do not unilaterally determine the standards for judgments. By and large, it is the readers/listeners, under the constraints of the situation, who determine what are, and are not, acceptable patterns of thought and behavior. If their attention is voluntary, readers and listeners accept attempts to influence them as legitimate. But except in the most unusual circumstances, they reserve the right to accept or reject either the persuader or the persuader's ideas, or both.

Second, persuaders do not "convince" readers/listeners. No one can convince someone else. All that persuaders can do is attempt to induce others *to convince themselves.* They do this by supplying information and imagery in the form of symbols. The readiness of readers/

listeners to respond largely determines what they can do and what they choose to do with these symbols. The way one learns is not completely understood, but it is clearly an active, creative process. The learner grows, changes, extends himself or herself. The process involves more than thinking. One's relevant memories, experiences, knowledge, beliefs, values, attitudes, feelings, goals, and desires are activated. Using this conscious and unconscious background knowledge, readers and listeners determine *for themselves* whether they will attend to what persuaders say and what changes, if any, they will make in the ways they think and feel.

Certain empiricists make precisely the point I have just made. After reviewing theories and empirical research on persuasion since World War II, Gerald Miller, Michael Burgoon, and Judee Burgoon concluded that a major reason empirical research on persuasion has produced so little genuine understanding is "conceptual": "We are suggesting . . . [a] conceptual outlook that views all parties to a persuasive transaction as *changeable* and *interactive* rather than conceiving of persuasion as a process whereby the persuader(s) *act* and the target(s) *react*." Miller and the Burgoons charge that the *act-react* image is largely responsible for the meager contributions that empirical research has made to theory of persuasion.[1]

Third, communication involves sharing risk. It is not only readers and listeners who may be changed by communication. Persuaders too incur risk. As a result of the ways others respond to their attempted communications, persuaders may become more or less confident about their ideas, experience higher or lower self and group status, or even find that their careers have been benefited or harmed. A case in point is that of Joseph R. Biden, senator from Delaware. In public appearances Biden exaggerated his academic accomplishments and borrowed passages of speeches from others without acknowledgment. When this was publicized, Senator Biden was forced out of the race for the 1988 presidential nomination by the Democratic Party. Another dramatic instance of what I'm saying was the failed nomination speech by Governor Clinton at the 1988 Democratic National Convention. Before his address Clinton had been highly regarded as a speaker and was much in demand. But following his poor performance at the Convention, his stock as a political orator temporarily nosedived.

Fourth, listeners and readers are always active participants with speakers and writers. A communicative relationship begins as soon as a reader or listener becomes aware that a message is being offered by some source. Rhetors supply verbal and nonverbal symbols. Readers and listeners receive and interpret those symbols in terms of their own experiences, beliefs, knowledge, interests, and needs. They think about what a speaker or writer is saying, and, as they listen and see, they also judge that persuader. Throughout communication persuaders act toward their listeners, and listeners/readers act toward the persuaders. Speakers can sometimes pick up clues to how listeners are responding and can modify their content and delivery accordingly. Changes or lack of changes in speakers' presentations will, in their turn, be received and interpreted by listeners whose behaviors may further reveal their interpretations. In short, in speaking situations personalized, cyclical relationships evolve over the time of the speaking–listening. When face-to-face communication is at its best, the continuous intercommunication amounts to a dialogue between speaker and listeners. This is true whether the speaking is from a platform, in a board room, or over the telephone. Invariably listeners actively and creatively participate in the development of communicative thought and feeling.

Where there is no face-to-face or voice-to-voice relationship, successful communication still entails a degree of dialogue between persuader and persuadees. A successful author, television advertiser, or radio/television evangelist tries to anticipate the sequential responses of those he or she addresses and tries to adjust what is said to those anticipated responses. And, of course, each reader or viewer maintains his or her private side of a dialogue, in the manner I have already described. Interrelationship may not be as personalized as in face-to-face communication, but it is seldom totally absent.

Closure and Identification

The concept of identification is basic to understanding the entire process of influencing others. In his *Rhetoric of Motives*, Kenneth

Burke suggests that "you persuade a man only insofar as you talk his language by speech, gesture, tonality, order, image, attitude, idea, *identifying* your ways with his." Burke's major contribution to communication theory lies (as he himself has said) in his insistence on identification as the sole avenue of persuasion. According to Burke, you can hope to "talk the language" of another only after you understand his conscious and, as far as possible, his unconscious motivations and needs. Only by clearly fusing "your ways with his" will you reach another person; when such identification fades, so will that person's willingness to move toward closure.[2]

It is a mistake to conceive that identification means complete union with what a persuader says. Complete identification in this sense is normally impossible. As Kenneth Burke repeatedly insisted, we are all always divided from one another to some degree. Identification is a matter of degree. If communication is successful, readers/listeners experience an amount of sameness or identification with the communicator. Some degree of sharing of ideas and/or feelings is sensed. Identifications in this sense can range from identifying only a small area of agreement to making an extensive acceptance of a communication as "my very own voice."

We shall be clearer about how persuasion works if we return to a notion I have discussed earlier: that people have and constantly make use of their belief systems. We all operate according to the knowledge, beliefs, values, and attitudes we carry about with us. This gives an observer means of estimating the persuasive possibilities of situations. As observers we can usually learn enough about the belief systems of people addressed to allow us to estimate, at least roughly, what they know, believe, and feel about a given urgency that provoked an attempt to persuade. If we learn that much, we can usually make out two further things: (1) how far the readers/listeners are able and willing to see common ground between their own patterns of thinking and what a persuader says, and (2) how much and what kind of movement they can and will make toward closure with communicators' basic positions. These are judgments of the degrees of identification that can occur in a rhetorical situation. Making such judgments requires us to explore the relevant elements of persuadees' belief systems. I turn now to how such judgments can be made systematically.

Knowledge. Neither persuaders nor critics can learn the full extent of knowledge that readers/listeners have on a topic. Persuaders and critics are concerned with knowledge only to the extent necessary to answer this question: Do readers/listeners know enough about the subject matter to be able to perceive analogous relationships between their own knowledge and what is being said? There is, of course, no basis for identification when persons do not grasp the meaning of what a persuader is saying.

Beliefs. As in the case of knowledge, one is not concerned with *all* of the beliefs that readers/listeners may have—not even with all of their beliefs about the topic and proofs offered by persuaders. One needs to know only enough about their *relevant* beliefs to estimate whether these beliefs are likely to facilitate or inhibit their perceiving analogies with themselves in the attempted persuasion.

A belief has been defined as "any simple proposition . . . capable of being preceded by the phrase 'I believe that. . . . ' " There are three types of beliefs: descriptive or existential (I believe that Alan Greenspan is chairman of the Federal Reserve Board); evaluative (I believe that Greenspan's refusal to lower interest rates will cause a recession); prescriptive/proscriptive or hortatory, judging some course of action or state of existence to be desirable or undesirable (I believe that it is desirable that interest rates should be lowered immediately). Each of these three types of belief has several distinguishable components. This is to say that persons having a belief "know" the belief is correct, can feel emotional in its support, and may be motivated to act when the belief is aroused or activated.[3] The role of these components in influencing how a person responds to attempted persuasion will become clear in the next few pages.

Values. To value anything is to prefer it over something else. Any preference is a temporarily settled response to options in the world, so it will influence the ways a person will respond to attempts at persuasion. The nature, relevance, and even the existence of values have been subjects of controversy for more than a half-century, at least since L. L. Thurstone's first efforts in 1927 to measure them.[4] There are scholars in various disciplines who not only reject B. F. Skinner's denial of values,[5] but who believe that values are instrumental in determining a person's response to attempted persuasion.[6]

One of these scholars, Milton Rokeach, offers several ideas about values that, while controversial, are useful to the study of why people respond the way they do to communication. Rokeach says that values are prescriptive/proscriptive or hortatory beliefs. They are "cognitive representations of underlying needs—whether social or antisocial, selfish or altruistic—after they have been transformed to also take into account institutional goals and demands. In this way, all of a person's values, unlike all of a person's needs, are capable of being openly admitted, advocated, and defended, to oneself and to others, in a socially sanctioned language."[7]

Rokeach suggests that, without consciously thinking about the matter, we intuitively organize our values into value *systems*. I need not pause to detail Rokeach's extended analysis of different kinds of values. The essential point is that values are, in this view, "complex precodings for behavioral choice"[8] and value systems are "organized sets of preferential standards."[9] With these two notions, we can proceed.

The power values and hierarchies of values have in guiding the ways we respond to persuasion comes from their general importance in our personal lives. At least some scholars think that values exert transcendent influence over our attitudes and behaviors. For example, if a persuader induces a person to value "an exciting life," this valuation may change a great many of that person's other predispositions and actions. He or she may now be prone to buy a Corvette convertible because of its sporty looks, great acceleration, and high top speed, whereas he or she might otherwise have been prone to focus on the merits of investing the money to ensure a certain amount of steady income or investment growth. In short, if a person is persuaded to change his or her mind about something *significant*, that individual's entire value system becomes involved. To increase someone's valuation of an exciting life exerts an effect on the person's other values. "A comfortable life" and "family security" are likely to be devalued as a result of any new commitment to excitement.

The firmness with which we hold priorities among values—have value *systems*—preserves attitudinal consistency and helps us retain our identities as unique personalities. Such firmness can contribute to resistance to some attempts at persuasion or it can render people eager to endorse (identify with) other attempts to persuade. This does not imply that value systems are necessarily stable. They change in response to new circumstances, persuasive appeals, and shifts in desires. That is the part of their character that makes it possible for us to be persuaded to change our values and views.

The task of persuaders is to discover the right combination of circumstances that will enable readers/listeners to perceive inviting analogies between what is said and urged and their own immediate systems of valuing. Hence, to learn something about prospective persuadees' knowledge and beliefs, we need to consider, among other things, what their value systems seem to be relative to the subject of persuasion, how firmly they hold those values, and what priorities they give to those values.

Attitudes. An observer of communication also needs to consider the attitudes expressed in communication and the attitudes held by people to whom persuasion is addressed. There has been much technical argument about the psychological nature and significance of the concept "attitudes," but if one is careful in defining and explaining the term, it can be helpful in estimating the ability and willingness of persons to respond to attempts at persuasion.

[I mean by attitude a learned, relatively enduring predisposition to respond favorably, unfavorably, or not at all to some object, situation, or concept.]So conceived, an attitude is an outgrowth of a person's system of values. As a predisposition it points our attention toward relatively stable readinesses to respond in predictable ways. Readers/listeners do have specific, relevant, and discoverable predispositions toward persuaders, toward topics and arguments, toward provoking rhetorical urgencies, and toward remedial actions that may be proposed by persuaders. It will help an advocate or an interested observer to consider—and compare—the predispositions that seem to govern the outlooks of prospective persuadees and that are reflected in communications directed toward them. To do this will contribute to anyone's capacity to estimate what will happen when persuasion and predispositions are brought together.[10]

Behaviors. All human intercourse involves close relationships between internal belief systems and the ways in which the parties act. Doubtless internalized "behaviors" take place as transitions between inner belief and overt actions, but we can observe only overt, externalized behaviors. We can and do infer from overt behaviors that people's beliefs, attitudes, and values are such and such, although we usually know such inferences are arguable. Nonetheless, observers of communicative relationships will need to base some of their interpretations on what the parties to the communication *do*. Some of those inferences will have strong reliability. For example, what listeners/readers have said and done prior to engaging in communication has been shown to tell a good deal about the ways they will think and feel concerning the content and methods of attempted persuasion. Also, what they do after experiencing communication can, at the very least, suggest what internal changes took place during communication. Much the same is true of persuaders. What they have said and done earlier, the ways they do and do not act during communication, and their subsequent behaviors are at least suggestive of their actual inner states and intentions. The nub of the matter is that although attitudinal inferences based on overt behaviors need to be treated as tentative, they remain legitimate and valuable means of estimating what potentials there are for communication-induced change and what happened during communication. Indeed, sometimes people's behaviors are almost the only data one has for thinking about potential and actual responses to communication. Modern marketing practices testify that this kind of analysis is at least somewhat predictive in practical terms.

You'll get a swarm of software advertisements in the mail because you bought a computer. The record of that transaction (behavior) will be purchased by people who have computer software to sell. If you contribute once to a political party, that action will be recorded and circulated among various divisions of that party, and they will then try to persuade you to contribute to them also. Employers want to know students' grades, college activities, and affiliations as indications of whether these people are likely to be genuinely interested in and competent for the sorts of employment the employers have to offer. These predictive judgments based on observable behaviors are by no means sure, but salespeople are confident that behaviors predict interests, attitudes, and values enough of the time to make them worth using in business. In interpreting rhetoric, comparable predictions need to be made as one estimates the potentialities for change in rhetorical urgencies. One's inferences are most useful if they can be confirmed by additional reasoning and evidence.

How Closure Is Achieved in Persuasion

Persuading is stretching or extending persuadees' belief systems, and it takes place essentially through the action called identification. This means that to begin persuading, an advocate must meet readers and listeners where they are at the outset of a communication. He or she must provide them with language and ideas that will enable them to perceive analogies between what is being said and some aspect of their own relevant knowledge, beliefs, values, attitudes, and behaviors. Without some initial identification, persuasion cannot begin. To promote further movement toward closure, the persuader must enable his or her readers/listeners to enlarge and reinforce the initial beachheads of identification and to perceive fresh areas of identification. The persuadees must continue to recognize analogies between themselves and what is being said as communication develops.

Areas of identification are established and/or enlarged when rhetorical satisfactions supplied by a persuader match the rhetorical constraints imposed by the ability and willingness of readers/listeners to respond. In other words, success in persuasion depends on the use of strategies that induce others to continue to perceive analogies between themselves and developing arguments.

Although disagreement exists among contemporary students of persuasion, there is considerable acceptance that "a necessary prerequisite to cognitive change is the presence of some state of imbalance within the system."[11] In other words, persuasion involves addressing an existing imbalance or creating some sense of imbalance within the readers/listeners. This implies two things. First, unless persons are already bothered by some contradiction, inconsistency, or incongruity within their belief systems, it is necessary to induce them to experience bothersome dissonance. Second, it is then necessary to induce them to move toward a new balance that is not bothersome to them. This two-stage action is required to encourage uncommitted or negatively committed persons to move toward acceptance of new belief and also to encourage persons who are positively committed to move toward greater acceptance, stronger belief, or more intense feelings of justification. In the latter case, if persons fear—or are caused to fear—that they do not believe or feel as strongly as they should, a sufficient imbalance exists to prepare them for reinforcing persuasion and greater commitment. Thus, "disciples" attend church or synagogue to get their faith uplifted and refreshed.

Resistance to persuasion follows a similar pattern. When it is cognitively possibly for them to do so, persons who are induced to experience bothersome dissonance will ordinarily revert to some already familiar state of acceptable balance. The reasons that prompt them to resist bothersome imbalances are brought into play as they automatically seek to reject the ideas or courses of action proposed by a persuader. If they succeed in persuading themselves that their former structures of belief are satisfactory, they restore the psychological comfort of the old balance. That is, they conclude that the way they already think or feel or act has substantially withstood the disparate information presented by advocates. They conclude that it is OK for them to be the way they were before the attempted persuasion. They feel adequately at peace with themselves.

Upon experiencing bothersome dissonances, people may be so successful in constructing logical, emotional, and social refutations that they not only come to reject the dissonance but grow even more convinced that they were right all along. When this happens, they move farther away from the persuader's point, adopting as their new balance a changed, more extreme version of their old position.

Sometimes, however, when persons are induced to experience bothersome dissonance, they recognize that, for one reason or another, they have been changed. They may perceive that they cannot return to the psychological comfort of their old position. In such a case a persuader has convinced them that a position they formerly held violates one of their "high" values, or will result in some loss, or is simply insufficient to meet an urgency. They then have several choices, short of fully accepting the solutions offered by the persuader. They may be unable to accept everything endorsed by the persuader and so pick and choose among options the persuasion seems to allow. This is illustrated by a relatively new phrase that has cropped up in discussions of Roman Catholicism. It is "cafeteria Catholics," a phrase recognizing that some followers of the Church choose some of its teachings but reject others. Similarly, persuadees may sense that they cannot accept the position offered by a persuader but can find an accommodating balance somewhere between their prior positions and the persuader's position. Thus, an opponent of abortion might respond to prochoice rhetoric by actively supporting attempts to place unwanted infants in adoptive homes.

From a persuader's point of view, the ideal outcome of persuasion is that people become bothered by dissonance and are led to alleviate the dissonance by endorsing the persuader's plan of action. This would mean that on this particular matter they substitute a new and psychologically acceptable balance for the old one that has become bothersome. It does not mean that related aspects of their belief systems remain the way they were before persuasion. Because the elements of a belief system are functionally interrelated, a specific change in one belief may require some adjustment in associated beliefs, values, attitudes, and/or behaviors. Thus, significant changes can be psychologically "expensive." When people adopt new ways of thinking or acting in order to alleviate dissonance, they pay a price. Consciously and subconsciously they must bring other aspects of their belief systems into harmony with this change. Only then will the belief system itself yield a desired state of acceptable balance. For instance, through the writings of A. G. Matt, Jr., editor of *The Wanderer*, a Catholic weekly, some Christian readers may come to believe, or to believe more strongly, that "Pope John Paul II is the successor of St. Peter. Therefore, he speaks with the authority of Christ." In that event, they need either to accommodate their thinking and behaviors on various social and theological matters to pronouncements by the pontiff or to find psychologically acceptable rationalizations. If they do not, the discrepancy between their belief in the absolute authority of the pope and their other beliefs and actions will remain psychologically disturbing.

The point of view I have offered in this chapter can be summed up as follows. If a person is induced to move toward a new sense of balance and to do so by accepting some or all of what a persuader offers, there has been some degree of *identification*. That identification is made possible because the person perceived analogous relations between the persuader's message and aspects of his or her own belief system. Ongoing identification depends on the persuader's supplying a flow of ideas and imagery that matches the ability and willingness of readers/listeners to find personalized analogies in what is said. Put differently, successful identification (1) is perceiving analogies that (2) result from a proper fit between between rhetorical satisfactions supplied by a communicator and the rhetorical constraints influencing the persuadee's readiness to respond; (3) this "fit" induces persuadees to participate actively toward closure by experiencing some bothersome dissonance sufficient to move them toward some acceptable, new sense of balance that is consonant with a persuader's position(s). In successful persuasion the desired new balance is congruent with the potentialities for change in the urgency.

Chapter Thirteen

Assessment of Readinesses
of Readers/Listeners
to Be Influenced

Each reader/listener brings to a communication an initial readiness or resistance to being influenced by the attempted persuasion. That this readiness is part and parcel of the total configuration is obvious when we reflect that it influences *directly* the kind and amount of change a person sustains as a consequence of discourse, and that therefore it influences *derivatively* the nature of the force he or she will eventually exert on the provoking urgency. Although our immediate concern in this chapter and in the following one is the congruence of persuadees' readinesses with persuaders' proffered satisfactions, we should view this matching in relation to the possibilities of the rhetorical act to influence the urgency.

Before one can estimate the potentiality of people to be influenced, it is necessary to identify who they are. I have already discussed this point in general terms, but in this connection it is convenient to think of two basic types of audiences. Sometimes for a relatively small audience one can identify and secure the necessary data about most, or all, of the individuals involved. This would be true of a joint union–management committee that hears and judges employees' complaints, a panel that reviews applications for admission to the freshman class, a county zoning commission that listens to arguments concerning proposed exemptions to the building code, the First Continental Congress that rejected Joseph Galloway's Plan of Union, the House Judiciary Committee that held hearings and eventually recommended impeachment of President Nixon, or the senatorial audience that heard John C. Calhoun's speech on March 4,

1850. Often, however, the audience is too large for one to identify the persuadees in detail. Examples of this kind of audience include the stockholders of a corporation who read the proffered literature about a policy question before returning their proxies, the howling crowd of partisan Whigs in the great hall of Niblo's Saloon in New York who broke windows and furniture in their enthusiasm over Daniel Webster's demagogic defense of Whiggery, the audience of stalwart Republicans who assembled in blizzard weather at Stockton Hall, Leavenworth, Kansas, to hear Abraham Lincoln deliver a dress rehearsal of his Cooper Union address, and the mass of aroused blacks in Cambridge, Maryland, who, during the height of the civil rights movement, listened to Rap Brown's exhortation shortly before fires were started and other violence began.

Whichever type of audience is encountered, one needs to plan a research design that will produce an estimate of the potential responsiveness of the readers/listeners. There are several interrelated tasks to be carried out.

The General Belief Systems of the Readers/Listeners

The force that participants will exert on a flow of events is primarily the consequence of their being influenced by others. The amount and kind of change they sustain in any particular communication or series of communications depend basically on their relevant complex of knowledge-beliefs-values-attitudes-behaviors relating to the persuader(s) and what the persuader(s) says.

Analysis of general belief systems can be most precise when the identities of individual persuadees are known, the size of the audience is manageably small, and sufficient relevant data are readily available. An example of the usefulness of this kind of situation is afforded by Harold J. Spaeth's value judgment study in which he forecast rulings by the Supreme Court. Spaeth, a political scientist at Michigan State University, correctly predicted how the Court would vote on thirty-three of thirty-four cases during a two-term period. On two of the biggest of those decisions, he forecast not only the exact margin of the vote but also how each Justice would vote.

Spaeth based his study on the assumptions that people are creatures of habit and that by studying the past voting records of the Justices he could predict how they would vote in future decisions. Going
back as far as fifteen years in some cases, Spaeth rated each Justice as
"positive" or "negative" on some eighty different subthemes, such as
desegregation and sex discrimination. He refined these data by clus-
tering them into three "supercategories" and by assigning each Justice
a quantified rating for each supercategory. Two of his supercategories
were equality and freedom. The third was New Deal economics—a
category that represented government intervention in the economy.
Spaeth assumed that nearly all of the Court's decisions are determined by individual Justices' predispositions toward equality, freedom, and New Deal economics. On the whole, his analysis did give
him a sound basis for predicting the Justices' probable responses on
specific issues, although on some topics he had to make some "very
drastic inferential leaps."[1]

Professor Spaeth's work illustrates the value of analyzing belief
systems, but he had the advantage of dealing with a small number of
persons about whom much relevant background information was
available. One can sometimes get equally useful information by other,
less time-consuming means. For example, in studying John C. Calhoun's speech of March 4, a pilot study showed me that analyzing
the writings and speeches of selected Northern and Southern senators
enabled me to say with confidence that there were two groups of specially targeted potential senators who differed significantly in their
devotion to *equality* (for all persons), *freedom* (for all persons), *honor,
dignity, and virtue.*[2] Expanding my exploration to include all senators
seemed unlikely to tell me more about how and why senators responded to Calhoun as they did. My pilot study had focused on *key*
senators who seemed to represent the range of opinions of the total
body. Other evidence I had already collected confirmed that the evidence from my sample was probably correct. We can conclude,
then, that Professor Spaeth's type of analysis can be exceptionally
predictive with a small body of readers/listeners who can be studied
in detail. On the other hand, when one deals with large numbers of
persons, Spaeth's kind of analysis will be difficult to carry out, and

other methods such as careful sampling must be employed. In either case there are a number of commonsense considerations about the persuadees that can profitably be raised.

Broadly generalized data about opinions can be helpful in estimating the receptivity of potential persuadees. For many urgencies such insights can be gained from considering age, sex, education, income, occupations, and special-interest affiliations. If a rhetorical urgency is general and has developed during the latter two-thirds of this century, public opinion polls are likely to be available. They can help you sort out important differences in value systems among groups of people addressed. This is always true in modern election urgencies and generally true concerning international, national, and regional issues. For example, as this is being written, international polls are providing continuous evidence about the shifting values and judgments of American and West European citizens respecting the status and future of USA–USSR relations. However, one always has to be cautious about accepting what is statistically representative of a large body of people as also representative of specific groups within that collectivity. American citizens are almost unanimous about the importance of freedom of expression as a public value, but they qualify that value significantly on issues such as what is and is not obscene or inflammatory in a community, religion, or the nation.

One needs also to be careful not to project upon a group of potential persuadees values and interests that were or are significant in some *other* time or place. For example, in writing about the Reverend Solomon Stoddard's efforts to stir up revivals soon after he assumed the Northampton, Massachusetts, pulpit in 1669, some observers have treated the young people who crowded his meetinghouse as if they were prototypes of the casual, fun-loving, and often sexually liberated youths of the twentieth century. In fact, they were very different—in the ways they looked upon themselves, their parents, their religion, society, and their future roles in society. Years of patriarchal upbringing, the exceptional importance of church membership and salvation, constant discourse about the "lamentable decay of religion," the practices of living in the parental home or in another home as an apprentice, the fact that the customary age for marriage was 26 to 28 years for men and 24 to 26 for women, and repressive practices in child rearing were just some of the things that conditioned Stoddard's young auditors to be uniquely receptive to his sulfurous preaching.[3] To project on them the beliefs and attitudes of any other time—or even of most other regions in the Colonies—would badly distort understanding of the young people in Northampton in 1669. The problem here is not simply one of keeping one's mind within the time frame of the urgency, but, as contemporary anthropologists justly emphasize, there is the problem of getting inside an often alien culture and viewing urgencies, interests, and values as persons belonging to that culture or subculture would view them. One must focus on the relationships that persuadees have with the urgency being studied.

If we know the identities of the persuadees, standard research procedures will probably help us to determine the interest groups that they represent. For example, one can easily learn the group affiliations of each senator who attended Calhoun's March 4 speech. We can do the same for those who participated in Senator Tower's confirmation hearings for Secretary of Defense. Even for large audiences standard kinds of research will usually show us the interest groupings that are represented. For the large, general audience in the Canadian drugs in sports hearings, one can probably estimate roughly the number of persons who belonged to the interest groupings of athletes, coaches, sports officials and administrators, and the general-interest public.

In studying Calhoun's speech I found complete consistency between the views of the major political interest groups of 1850 and the ways individual senators perceived the slavery urgency, Calhoun as a credible persuader on the topic, and Calhoun's specific proposals and arguments. The votes on the various compromise bills introduced in the Senate were consistent with the political interest groups, with one exception: certain "Conscience Whigs" abstained from voting and thus permitted key compromises to pass. The urgency of 1850 and the political interest groups were so firmly structured that to know an interest group's nature and value system was to know its members' readiness to be persuaded in one direction or another.

Persuadees sometimes have significant, special relations to the occasions.
William Jennings Bryan's "Cross of Gold" speech was such a rhetorical event. So too were the senatorial debates on the Treaty of Paris of
1898. The debate of the House of Representatives in deciding the disputed presidential election of 1824–1825 was another such instance.
Consider the influences of the occasions in these cases.

The occasion for Bryan's speech is an example of how the physical and psychological circumstances of an immediate environment
may strongly and overtly condition the persuadees' readiness. The
boundaries for this occasion can be identified as encompassing the
political activities attending the Democratic National Convention in
Chicago, June 29–July 9, 1896. I suggest June 29 as the start—more
than a week before the Convention was officially scheduled to con-
vene—because it was on that date that the leaders of the Democratic
National Bimetallic Committee arrived in Chicago to plan strategies
for taking over the Convention from the pro–gold standard conservatives. From my perspective, the occasion ended with the close of
Bryan's speech. The subsequent events at the Convention, including
Bryan's selection as the Democratic presidential candidate on July 10,
were part of the postspeech exigential flow.

"Silver Republicans," who also arrived early, set about immediately to impress on the Democratic delegates that they should nominate as their presidential candidate Colorado Senator Henry M.
Teller. With a small group of silver zealots he had bolted the Republican Party during its national nominating convention in St. Louis a
few weeks earlier. Before the Convention opened Populist leaders had
also arrived, as had a host of radical reformers—prohibitionists,
single-taxers, Socialists, woman suffragists, and the like. They would
do what they could to radicalize the Convention in support of their
causes. Of great significance were caucuses of pro-silver delegates under the auspices of the Democratic National Bimetallic Committee.
These began on June 30. At those meetings strategies were devised to
wrest operating control of the Convention from the Democratic National Committee.

When the Convention formally convened on Tuesday, July 7,
the free-silver majority, after rancorous debate, reversed the National

Committee's selection of Senator David B. Hill of New York as the temporary chairman. Silverite Senator John W. Daniel of Virginia was appointed. Bryan had declined to be considered for this post because he thought it would give him too much prominence too soon in the Convention, thereby hurting his bid as a dark-horse candidate for the presidential nomination. In his keynote address Daniel found that his voice was not strong enough to reach all of the delegates and that his dry style of speaking could not hold the attention of those delegates who could hear him. A dark-horse candidate for the nomination himself, Daniel muffed his chance to impress the delegates.

Following Daniel's address, the Convention adjourned to permit the various committees (now stacked with pro-silver delegates) to determine the nature of the party platform, the seating of contested delegations (several states had sent both pro-silver and pro-gold delegations), and the like. Because of the ineptitude of the largely inexperienced committee members, the delegates had to sit through the second day of the Convention awaiting the reports of the committees and listening to a seemingly endless stream of uninspiring pro-silver orators. By the evening session on Wednesday, the credentials committee had given the silver faction a two-thirds majority, the number needed to nominate a presidential candidate. This meant that the silver faction had completely routed the conservatives.

The next morning, Thursday, some twenty thousand delegates and supporters packed the great hall of the Coliseum to hear a formal debate on the financial plank of the platform committee. Senator James K. Jones of Arkansas, who might have been expected to manage the silver side of the debate, asked Bryan to take charge of the silver argument. Thus, another competitor for the nomination failed to take advantage of his chance to capture the attention of the delegates.

Senator Benjamin "Pitchfork" Tillman of South Carolina had indicated to Jones that he was interested in participating in the debate in defense of silver, and Bryan did not attempt to secure other speakers. If they were to do well in their speeches, others would detract attention from Bryan, who hoped to use his debate speech as a catapult to the nomination. As Bryan anticipated, Tillman launched into a long, vituperative harangue that based the cause of silver on narrow sectional interests, a stance that demeaned the merits of free-silver coinage and offended the patriotism of all delegates. So another prominent Democrat had had his chance to impress the convention and had failed to do so.

The conservative side of the debate was presented by Senators Hill and William Vilas of Wisconsin and former governor William Russell of Massachusetts. All three advanced the conventional gold-standard arguments, but Hill's speech was dull, Vilas had serious trouble with his hoarse voice, and Russell had a physical impairment that prevented his being heard beyond the first few rows. Understandably, the silver delegates grew increasingly restless and frustrated. They had had little to cheer about since their victory over the conservatives at the first session on Tuesday. By the time Bryan began to speak they desperately wanted their views articulated and their "sacred" cause recognized for its patriotic and humanitarian qualities. They trusted Bryan as a young, vigorous, striking, eloquent spokesman who understood their needs, their cause, and their "salvation."[4]

In sum, Bryan's speech came at just the right moment to satisfy the needs engendered by other features of the occasion. The great hall, the raised platform, the huge audience demanded an imposing presence, a heroic figure. As Bryan bounded to the speaker's stand, saluting the crowd with outstretched arms, wave after wave of cheers and applause swept over the delegates. Soon his great voice filled the arena, telling the delegates what they wanted to hear, with the rhythm, homey images, and allusions that converted abstract concepts into understandable realities of right and wrong, virtue and sin. "I would be presumptuous, indeed, to present myself against the distinguished gentlemen to whom you have listened if this were a mere measuring of abilities; but this is not a contest between persons," he began. "The humblest citizen in all the land, when clad in the armor of a righteous cause, is stronger than all the hosts of error. I come to speak to you in defense of a cause as holy as the cause of liberty—the cause of humanity."[5]

Few audiences have been so mesmerized by a speaker as were the delegates at the Coliseum. A major reason they responded as they did was that they had been strongly predisposed to do so by the developing events of the occasion. It cannot be known how much Bryan's speech contributed to his nomination as the Democratic standard bearer on the following day. We can probably assume, however, that the speech alone did not win him the nomination but that he would not have won the nomination without his having given the speech.

In the case of William Jennings Bryan's "Cross of Gold" speech the occasion exerted tremendous direct influence on the responses of the listeners. At other times the occasion for a communication may influence the readiness of persuadees to respond to communication in decisive yet largely hidden ways. Such "covert" situations are extremely difficult to detect, but, since they do occasionally exist, one should at least be alert to their possible presence. Here are a couple of examples.

In his study of the Senate debates on the Treaty of Paris of 1898, L. Raymond Camp found no evidence that the speeches caused any changes in the responses of senators concerning ratification. On February 5, the day before the vote was taken, the Republican leadership believed that three votes were "doubtful." All three of these senators voted *for* ratification on February 6. Camp could not determine the reason one of them voted affirmatively, but he did discover that covert influences determined how the other two senators voted. Their votes supplied the one-vote margin by which the treaty was ratified. In examining the John L. McLaurin Collection in the Library of Congress, Camp found that on the morning of the vote Senator McLaurin decided to vote *against* ratification. Then, just before the executive session got under way, Senator James Jones, chairman of the Democratic Executive Committee, threatened McLaurin with expulsion from the party if he voted *for* the treaty. McLaurin became so incensed that he voted "aye." The third doubtful Senator, Samuel McEnery, turned to his friend McLaurin to learn how he had voted; then he changed his own vote from "pass" to "aye." The shift was caused by the negative reaction of two senators to coercion from their own party.[6]

Another example of covert influence of an occasion involved General Stephen Van Rensselaer. The presidential election of 1824 had been declared void because no candidate had received a majority of the electoral votes. On February 9, 1825, the members of the House of Representatives met to choose one of the three leading candidates: John Quincy Adams, Andrew Jackson, and William H. Crawford. The balloting by states soon disclosed that Adams had the support of twelve states, Jackson seven and Crawford four. New York was divided, with seventeen congressmen for Adams, sixteen opposed, and one—Van Rensselaer—undecided. Van Rensselaer was originally a Crawford supporter, but Crawford had recently been incapacitated by a stroke. Van Rensselaer had been privately warned by Henry Clay and Daniel Webster, just prior to the balloting, that his vote against Adams would result in another voided election. As the agitated Van Rensselaer waited in his seat for the ballot box to reach him, he bent his head asking silently for divine guidance. Opening his eyes, he saw "a ticket bearing the name of John Quincy Adams" on the floor at his feet. Taking this as God's answer to his prayer, he voted for Adams. Thus the disputed election of 1824 was resolved by the margin of New York's vote, which was decided by "hidden" influences in the occasion.[7]

The last two cases illustrate why we cannot safely assume that all outcomes of rhetorical events result from the *rhetoric* involved. Other forces in the occasion may have had more crucial influence. Despite the obviousness of this, observers too often leap to unexamined conclusions that because there *was* rhetoric, *it* must have been the full and sufficient cause of the outcomes of those events. One needs at least to be alert to other possible influences deriving from the occasion.

For Calhoun's speech of March 4 features of the occasion that influenced the outcome were historic, extensive, and psychological, as the brief review below shows. In this case background *and* immediate circumstances had special influences on the intensity of feeling and the expectancies with which the audience greeted the speech.

I think this occasion began with the convening of Congress on December 3, 1849. So understood, the occasion consisted of the activities in both branches of Congress and of outside pressures insofar as they bore on slavery/territorial questions. Intrigues, party strategies, rumors of bribery and collusion, and a general sense of crisis influenced members of Congress, including the senators. Much relevant political maneuvering took place in coffee shops, boarding houses, and hotels in Washington, and there was continuous interaction between Washington and the rest of the nation. The major reason for conceiving of the occasion as beginning with the opening of the thirty-first session of Congress is that congressional fireworks having to do with the slavery urgency began immediately, and all helped to shape the receptivity of senators and others who on March 4 would hear Calhoun's speech. The end of the occasion for Calhoun's speech came with his final words; however, if we want to understand the full configuration of the slavery/territorial urgency we must also consider what followed this event, in the Congress and outside—the postspeech urgency.

The total occasion, with all of its subtle nuances and suggestiveness, led those who listened to do so with tense curiosity and expectancy. How would the terminally ill Southern "ultra," who had a reputation for abrasiveness, respond to Henry Clay's "patchwork compromise" and to the crisis state of the slavery urgency? Nothing that is known suggests that the occasion made senators more or less favorably responsive to Calhoun, but numerous features of the occasion certainly contributed to their tensions and expectations.

Parliamentary difficulties caused by pro- and antislavery sentiments contributed to the aura of dissonance in both houses of Congress. The Senate was paralyzed for three weeks while Southerners and Northerners squabbled over organizing the House of Representatives. It took 63 ballots to elect a speaker of the House, 3 ballots to choose a chaplain, 20 to choose a clerk, 8 to choose a sergeant at arms, and after 14 ballots the House still had not chosen a doorkeeper. Once the House was organized, President Taylor's first annual message (December 24, 1849) further intensified tensions. Taylor repeated the fact that California had adopted a constitution that barred slavery and would soon apply for statehood. He then urged prompt action on California's application and on the application that was expected soon from New Mexico. Taylor closed by promising to resist with all of his constitutional power any attempt at disunion. This message, of course, made slavery-related issues more pressing, so, with Daniel Webster's tacit support, Henry Clay responded by offering eight separate but related proposals, which he defended in debate on February 5 and 6.

Clay's proposals were not new. Most had been offered earlier. What was new was that as a series of measures they seemed to offer a compromise between Taylor's plans to exclude slavery from the territories and Calhoun's insistence on Southerners' rights to take slaves into the territories. Also behind the scenes, Stephen A. Douglas and some legislative colleagues produced another set of compromise bills which were similar to Clay's. They would admit California as a free state, organize New Mexico and Utah as territories under "popular sovereignty," and retain slavery in the District of Columbia.

The moves by Clay and Douglas and certain other negotiations suggested that there were ways of at least easing tension in Congress, but President Taylor's additional public statements against disunion and threats that he allegedly made constituted counteractions. A correspondent to the New York *Herald* may well have been right when he reported on March 2 that "the danger is more deep than apparent." In these circumstances, rumors spread that Calhoun intended to reply to Clay's defense of his compromise proposals. It was true. Calhoun dictated his speech, and his fellow senator from South Carolina, Butler, scheduled it for one o'clock in the afternoon of March 4. As they had been when Clay had spoken, the Senate chamber and the galleries were crowded by late morning. The visibly ailing Calhoun was helped into the Senate and sank into his seat a little after noon. Finally he rose and thanked the Senate for reserving time for his speech and handed the text to Senator James Mason of Virginia, who read it to the audience. The tensions I have described were in no way diminished and the expectancies that something very important was about to happen were surely heightened by the drama of this moment.

In each of the three cases I have just cited, both the overall occasion and circumstances surrounding the immediate presentation of rhetoric significantly influenced the attitudes and expectancies of the audiences. Intraparty conflicts and other factors set up a special kind of urgency that Bryan was equipped to exploit. Nonrhetorical events accounted for the positions taken by two of the crucial voters in the debates over the Treaty of Paris and over the election of a President in 1825. The long-standing slavery/territorial urgency was intensified by a series of political events following the convening of Congress, and the actions of the ailing Calhoun rendered the moment when his speech was delivered specially dramatic.

Latitudes of Readiness to Be Influenced

I have so far discussed audiences' readiness to be influenced as though they either were or were not accepting. A qualification needs to be inserted. Listeners/readers can be predisposed strongly/moderately, positively/negatively, or they can be essentially indifferent to an urgency, an occasion, and/or a communicator. I call the degrees of readiness their "latitude of readiness to be influenced." The diagram below (Figure 1) provides a way of visualizing an audience's latitude of willingness to identify with a communicator, his or her notion of a provoking urgency, and his or her proposed remedial actions. The two sides of the diagram are mirror opposites. Persons in an audience are visualized as *extremely* ready to identify or to reject identification with what is said, or they are seen somewhere between these extremes—that is, they could be *definitely* or *moderately* ready to identify or to reject identification, or could be essentially unpredisposed either to identify or to reject identification.

The more sympathetic readers/listeners are to communicators and their messages—that is, the more ready they are to identify—the easier it is for them to be persuaded by what is said and done. Generally speaking, those who are very receptive to a set of ideas may be almost completely uncritical of communicators' uses of images, myths, and contentions if those reinforce the listeners'/readers' belief systems. Audiences who are slightly less receptive are eager to identify, but may be more analytical than extremely favorable persons. Those who are only moderately receptive may be ready to identify, but they are not strongly predisposed to perceive analogical relationships. In these situations, then, a successful persuader is actually telling sympathetic readers/listeners what they want to hear, what

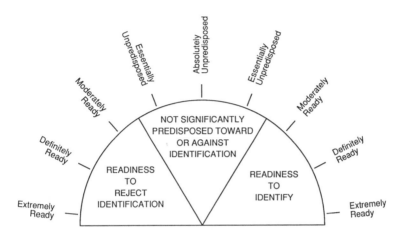

Figure 1. Latitudes of Audiences' Readiness to Identify.

corresponds to relevant elements in their belief systems, and what they can readily accept as correct perceptions of reality. By enabling favorably disposed readers/listeners to justify their existing beliefs-values-attitudes-behaviors, a persuader encourages them to acquire a more ardent conviction—and, it is hoped, a willingness to act in a desired way on the urgency.

Sometimes the bulk of an audience or important segments of it are not predisposed to identify or to reject identification with a persuader and/or a message. Readers/listeners may be uncommitted because they lack information or interest, or because they simply have not yet made up their minds. To persuade such persons to act on an urgency in a desired manner, persuaders must enable them to experience a sense of bothersome imbalance, or dissatisfaction, with their state of indecision, doubt, or neutrality. Then, persuasion must move them to accept a new balance closer to the persuaders' position. This movement is not easy to effect, but it is much less difficult than is persuasion of hostile persons.

There are also degrees of readiness to reject identification and they affect what rhetorical attempts are wise and feasible. A persuader is in serious difficulty when most or important segments of an audience reject identification with him or her and/or with the basic thrust of a message. If an urgency is truly significant for readers and listeners, it is almost impossible to convert them if they are initially hostile. They are intellectually and emotionally predisposed against finding analogous relationships between their own beliefs, values, and attitudes and those that negatively perceived persuaders offer. In such cases the best strategy is usually for a persuader to ask for only small changes in views at any given time. "Total" identification is seldom possible, and it is almost certainly impossible with those who reject identification and do so strongly. Figure 1 illustrates that such readers/listeners would have to move from their definitely hostile position to a moderately hostile position to a relatively uncommitted position, and finally to a position sufficiently favorable to motivate them to try to influence the urgency in the desired direction. If their negative predisposition is firm, that amount of shifting is very unlikely to occur as the result of any one exposure to persuasion. Wise persuaders will usually attempt to secure small degrees of favorable identification, and they will hope to build on those small but favorable dispositions later. This is why strategic campaigns of persuasion are built.

Hostile persuadees *can* sometimes be converted to a communicator's position by an orchestrated campaign of persuasion. For example, after the Democratic Convention of 1988, presidential candidate Michael Dukakis raced to a large early lead in the national polls. Following the Republican Convention, George Bush, stung by attacks on his manhood and competence, embarked on a negative campaign to exploit "hot button" issues. He successfully destroyed the "wimp factor" by looking and sounding presidential and by labeling the Massachusetts governor a big-government, tax-raising, card-carrying ACLU liberal who was weak on patriotism, soft on crime, and ignorant on national defense. The "new" Bush seemed to represent values, stability, and security strongly endorsed by most voters. Dukakis countered too late and too ineffectively. His once commanding lead in the polls evaporated into defeat in the national election, particularly in the electoral college. One should note, however, that it required a *campaign* to produce this reversal.

In rare circumstances a single attempt at persuasion can be enough to win over people who are negatively predisposed to a moderate degree. When Illinois Senator Stephen A. Douglas returned to Chicago to explain why he had engineered the Compromise of 1850 through Congress, his major opportunity to confront his opposition occurred at a mass meeting that had been called to ratify resolutions denouncing the Compromise and branding its supporters "Benedict Arnolds." In his speech Douglas was able to link his position to important and strongly held beliefs and values of his listeners: the revered Constitution should be honored; Americans should have the right and freedom to determine their futures through the ballot box; the Union must be preserved. He argued that the Constitution required the return of fugitive slaves, defended the concept and application of popular sovereignty, and claimed that the Compromise was necessary to preserve the Union. Immediately after Douglas's speech, the meeting endorsed his counter resolutions. The next day the City Council, which had sponsored the critical resolutions, reversed its earlier position. During the following weeks Douglas repeated his arguments in speeches throughout the state. So influential was he that the Illinois legislature commended his position on the Compromise and rescinded its previous directives that the state's representatives and senators in Washington vote for the Wilmot Proviso. In this situation Douglas's rhetoric had the capacity to succeed because, although the opposition was widespread and vocal, the relevant values and attitudes had not yet firmed into unyielding emotional sets.

Far more commonly, persuaders are unable to convert hostile readers and listeners. For instance, even though much of Bush's support in 1988 was "soft," once persons decided they could not identify with Dukakis as President and/or with his proposed policies, the Massachusetts governor found it impossible to win back sufficient numbers of them. Failure also attended Douglas's persuasive efforts when he addressed a second mass meeting in Chicago four years after his earlier success. This time he sought to explain why he had maneuvered through Congress a bill organizing the territories of Kansas and Nebraska and opening them to slavery. Since 1850 much had happened to cause Chicagoans to close their minds to the Senator's position. Most had become convinced that the Northern white man's self-interest, the interests of the region, the interests of the nation, and the interests of humanity all demanded unyielding opposition to slavery. The passage of the Kansas-Nebraska bill had stirred northern Illinois, and much of the rest of the North, to violent abuse of the "Little Giant." Douglas admitted that he could travel from Boston to Chicago by the light of his burning effigies. Under the virulent denunciation of press and pulpit, the situation in Chicago grew so ugly that a riot seemed likely on the day set for the meeting at which he would appear. During the afternoon flags were lowered to half-mast. At dusk church bells began a continuous clanging that persisted until time for Douglas's speech. Well before Douglas's appearance the square was packed and the crowd extended to nearby roofs and windows. For several hours Douglas attempted to reason with the hooting, jeering crowd. Finally, defeated, he stormed from the platform. The reason Douglas failed to convert the crowd was not that he had lost his oratorical ability; it was that the task of persuasion was too great on this occasion. The listeners were so intensely ready to reject identification with him and his position that he could not make any headway with them.

In sum, persuaders change readers and listeners in order to change urgencies. Each reader/listener brings to a communication an initial readiness or resistance to being influenced by the attempted persuasion. Because this readiness influences the changes a person sustains as a consequence of communication, it influences the way he or she eventually acts on the urgency. In estimating the readinesses of readers/listeners to be influenced by communications, it is helpful to assess their general belief systems and to visualize their latitudes of willingness to identify with their communicators, the communicators' notion of the provoking urgencies, and their proposed remedial actions. In the next chapter I take up ways to judge how well a communicator selects rhetorical options to match these readinesses to respond and to influence urgencies.

Congruence of Rhetorical Satisfactions with Readers'/Listeners' Readinesses to Be Influenced

In this chapter I wrap up the basic assessment of forces that give us the measure of what was, what was possible, and the wisdom of the rhetorical practitioners we choose to examine.

All persuaders necessarily use rhetorical strategies. Their strategies are designed to satisfy constraints—that is, to try to give readers/ listeners some degrees of satisfaction, thereby changing them in order to change provoking urgencies. Offering these presumed satisfactions is intrinsic to all human communication, hence to all rhetorical configurations. Even the wino protesting eviction from his cardboard home exercises these attempts at satisfying his audience—and hence influencing a provoking urgency—through rhetoric. He may not be aware of this, but his profane responses to a police officer and his appeals that he is doing no harm and has no other home are rhetorical strategies that seemingly give him some satisfaction and, in part, appeal to the officer to find satisfaction in trying to help the poor man.

In chapter 11 I pointed out that the basic thrusts of a communication must satisfy that communication's potential for influencing a provoking urgency. In the case of multiple communications over time, each of the rhetorical acts possesses distinctive potentialities for modifying the urgency, depending upon how the urgency itself has changed. Therefore, the basic thrusts of each communication must match the basic constraints on what was communicatively possible in modifying the urgency.

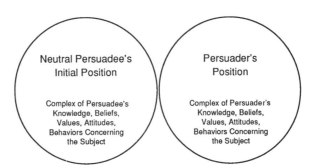

Figure 2. Position of a Persuader and Position of Neutral Readers/Listeners at the Beginning of Communication.

Integrating Familiar Concepts

In earlier chapters I discussed establishing and expanding areas of identification; managing imbalance; and exploiting the willingness and ability of readers/listeners to identify with a persuader's notion of a provoking urgency, with the persuader, and with the persuader's proposed remedial actions. These ideas are integrated in the following diagrams.

Figure 2 suggests in a general way a persuader's position and the position that *neutral* readers/listeners have at the beginning of a communication. Although the relevant belief system of the persuader interfaces with the belief systems of neutral readers/listeners, there may seem to be little overlapping—that is, few substantive agreements seem to exist concerning the persuader's point of view. In other words, neutral persons are uncommitted. They are not clearly predisposed either to identify or to reject identification with the message. However, numerous beliefs, values, attitudes, and behaviors *are* shared, although persuadees may not be aware of them or may not perceive that they are related to the topic. But if some overlappings did not exist, communication itself would be impossible. A persuader must successfully exploit these general overlappings to change a neutral person. A persuader must supply rhetorical satisfactions that can induce the persuadees themselves to create desired images. To do this, a persuader must somehow induce others to use their own

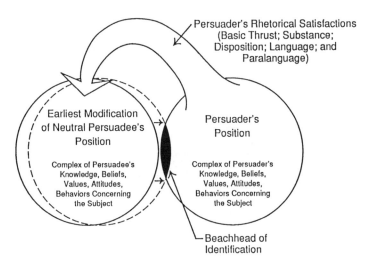

Figure 3. Beginnings of Persuasion. Earliest words in a communication should encourage at least a tentative identification between neutral readers/listeners and the persuader and the message.

knowledge, thoughts, and feelings as the basis for evolving the images he or she wants them to have. This is the "secret" of persuasion that I talked about in chapter 12.

Figure 3 represents the beginnings of persuasion for readers/listeners who are initially neutral. At this stage they perceive some agreement—that is, they recognize there are some substantive, relevant analogical relationships between what they like and accept and what the persuader is saying and doing.

Figure 4 portrays the continuation of persuasion for neutral readers/listeners. By means of the communicator's developing strategies, they are induced to perceive growing agreement with what is being said. It is this perceiving of areas of identification and the enlarging or expanding of these areas that constitute movement toward closure with the persuader's position.

Figures 5 and 6 represent the position of the persuader and the position of readers/listeners who are *favorably disposed* or *negatively disposed* at the beginning of communication. Those favorably disposed recognize that they already have substantial agreement with the

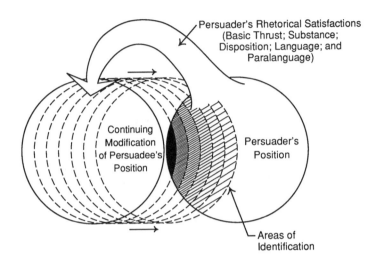

Figure 4. Continuation of Persuasion. By means of the persuader's rhetorical satisfactions, initially neutral readers/listeners are enabled to consolidate, expand, and coalesce areas of identification established earlier in the communication. Thereby, they move, or extend, themselves toward further agreement with the persuader.

persuader's notion of the provoking urgency, the persuader as a source of persuasion on the topic, and/or the persuader's recommended remedial action. By means of rhetorical satisfactions the persuader seeks to exploit "what is already there"—that is, these preexisting areas of identification. The persuader wants to induce favorably predisposed readers/listeners to extend and intensify what they already believe and feel, thereby moving further toward closure with the persuader's position.

In contradistinction to favorably disposed readers/listeners, persons who are initially hostile do not want to accept the persuader's views. They have a preestablished readiness to resist persuasion. Depending on the intensity of their beliefs, the degree to which they feel personally involved, the importance of the belief to their belief system, and so on, these persons will be inclined to reject identification with the persuader and/or the persuader's views. By means of selecting appropriate rhetorical satisfactions, the persuader hopes to induce them to discover that areas of agreement *do* exist between

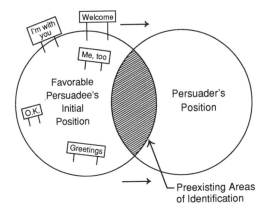

Figure 5. Position of Persuader and Position that Favorably Disposed Readers/Listeners Have at the Beginning of Communication. Such persuadees have already established significant areas of identification with the persuader and/or the persuader's views.

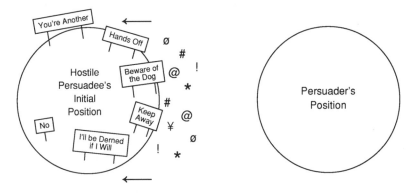

Figure 6. Position of Persuader and Position that Negatively Predisposed Readers/Listeners Have at the Beginning of Communication. These persuadees have a preset readiness to reject identification with the persuader and/or the persuader's views. At the outset there is *no* beachhead of identification.

some elements of their belief system and the persuader's cause. If this is accomplished, the persuader hopes to enable them to expand these nascent areas of agreement, thereby becoming less hostile and possibly even moving toward acceptance of his or her position.

As these diagrams suggest, success in persuasion hinges on the extent to which persuaders can establish and/or expand "beachheads of identification." Persuaders' strategies are the means by which this is undertaken—well or ill. The task of an observer or critic is to match the satisfactions persuaders offer strategically against the given set of readers'/listeners' readiness to be influenced. As the diagrams indicate, those readinesses may be very different from audience to audience and situation to situation. In what follows I shall explain and illustrate the several aspects of possible readiness that one needs to consider in matching strategies against the possibilities for perceivers to identify with persuaders.

Matching Rhetorical Satisfactions with Readers'/Listeners' Readiness to Be Influenced

In this section I am concerned with matching the readers'/listeners' readiness to be influenced with the persuader's or persuaders' use of rhetorical strategies. As I analyze them, there are five kinds of strategic satisfactions that need examination: basic thrusts, substance, disposition, language, and paralanguage.

The Basic Thrusts

I have called what a persuader indicates as his or her goal(s) in a message the basic thrust(s) of the communication. Sometimes the thrust is obvious, as it was in a 1988 "sound bite" that showed a middle-aged couple frozen in horror as Dukakis's tax-hike notices were thrust through their mail slot. The basic thrust was clear: Vote for George Bush—he won't raise your taxes and Dukakis would. Sometimes the basic thrust or thrusts of a message are multiple and even implicit, as I have illustrated in analyzing Calhoun's speech on March 4, 1850. In any case, a critic determines the basic thrust(s) of messages by looking at how the messages were constructed.

The distinction between a persuader's rhetorical intent and basic thrust is clear. In discourse persuaders translate their rhetorical intentions into the basic thrusts of what they say. Whereas rhetorical intent is what a persuader wants to accomplish, a basic thrust is part of what he or she actually does to accomplish it. Because of this relationship between thrust and intent, a basic thrust has a unique function. *It is both constraint and satisfaction.* It is a rhetorical constraint because it constrains what a persuader can, or should, choose as satisfactions. It is a rhetorical satisfaction because it is a strategy a persuader chooses in partial answer to impinging constraints, which include his or her own intent and relevant self-system, the audience, occasion, and provoking urgency. We have already seen how to match basic thrusts against the potentialities of communications to influence urgencies. I want now to look at how well basic thrusts satisfy the constraints of the persuaders' intentions and self-systems and the readinesses of the readers/listeners to be influenced.

The matching process, which is basic to configurational analysis, involves making informed judgments about two selected elements in the configuration and then estimating the amount of consonance or compatibility between them. The assumption is that, generally speaking, the greater the degree of congruity between the two elements, the wiser the persuader's choice of rhetorical strategies has been and the better the communication has functioned to modify events. In viewing basic thrusts as satisfactions, we ask first: *How well does the basic thrust(s) of a message match the persuader's intent and self-system?* Aspects of a persuader's self-system cause him or her to want certain things to happen in consequence of communicating. Therefore, the basic thrust of a message, in a sense, is an extension of a persuader's self-system, as well as of his or her rhetorical intent. There must be a close congruence between thrust and intent for a message to point in the right direction. Calhoun's speech illustrates this point, in a rather unusual way.

The Matching Process

Match the basic thrust(s) of the communication(s)	with the persuader's or persuaders' rhetorical intent and self-system	to determine the degree of congruity between the two.

Listeners in the old Senate chamber (and, later on, the readers of the message) understood that Calhoun proclaimed that the North must act positively on a series of ultimatums. They also understood that if Northern senators failed to capitulate to his demands but accepted California as a state, Calhoun wanted the South to secede. This *explicit* thrust may not have mirrored the South Carolinian's intent, however. In debate in the Senate, on the day following his speech, he disclaimed that he had had any wish to prescribe conditions for settlement. His intention had been, he said, to warn that "great discontent" existed in the South and that this discontent must be removed by permanent guarantees, because "as things now stand, the South could not remain with safety in the Union."

This thrust seems more flexible and conciliatory than the explicit thrust in the speech. Such a discrepancy between intent and performance is critically significant both to the wisdom with which a persuader selects rhetorical options and to the way rhetoric functions to modify the state of affairs. If Calhoun really meant simply to warn of "great discontent" and to complain that under the circumstances it was unsafe for the South to remain in the Union, he concocted an address that went well beyond that intention rhetorically. To proclaim secession as desirable and inevitable in the absence of conciliatory guarantees and to warn of "great discontent" strike me as more than academically different. This discrepancy tells me that Calhoun (1) missed his aim the first time around, (2) sought on March 5 to change people's impressions of the speech he had given, or (3) because of his illness, or some other reason, was confused in the debate on March 5.

I argued in chapter 5 that if Calhoun had any implicit persuasive intent in his speech it was to leave a persuasive call for the South—a call for which ensuing events were likely to create a configuration of forces that would render the call persuasive. I find this implicit thrust, or delayed call to history, reflected in the confrontational, absolutist tone that pervades the entire message, as well as in the negative character of his proposed remedial action. His demands could not be met by the North, even if Northern senators violated their consciences by enacting legislation, and he made no effort to develop his bare-bones plan of action. This implicit thrust matches the psychological and rhetorical profile of Calhoun that I developed in chapter 5: Calhoun was a doctrinaire given to pronouncing and prophesying.

Secondly, a critic asks: *As mediated by the persuader's intent and self-system, how well does the basic thrust of his or her message match the readiness of readers/listeners to be influenced?* This question does not focus exclusively on how pleasing the basic thrust is to the readers/listeners. Just gratifying existing beliefs and values can accomplish little more than reinforcement, altering the intensity with which views are held. Dedicatory and epideictic situations are among those that encourage this kind of rhetoric, but in very many persuasive situations reinforcement is insufficient to accomplish persuaders' intentions. If a persuader's intention is to alter the directions in which readers/listeners think and feel, simply to reinforce will do less than the intention requires. What we want to find out primarily by matching thrusts with audience responsiveness is the following: Considering the persuader's self-system, intent, personal urgencies, and so forth, how well does the basic thrust of the communication match the readiness of readers and listeners to perceive analogous relationships between the thrust and their belief systems? A subsidiary but crucial question is: Could the persuader have chosen a thrust that would have matched better the readiness of the audience and still remained consistent with his or her beliefs and values?

The Matching Process

Match the basic thrust(s) of the communication(s) as mediated by the persuader's or persuaders' rhetorical intent and self-system	with the readiness of readers/ listeners to be influenced	to determine the degree of congruity between the two.

An interesting case relative to this second question is provided by Calhoun's speech. There were, of course, numerous options that were theoretically available to Calhoun. A number would have been more acceptable to his senatorial audience than the explicit thrust he chose. But these would not have been consistent with the nature of the man or his beliefs. Who the man was, what he stood for, what his rhetorical experience dictated, what his imagined future commanded—all required that he pronounce judgment ex cathedra on the crisis. It is obvious that Calhoun's rhetorical intent and his explicit thrust did not match at all the readiness of his audience to be influenced. This rhetorical failure stemmed from faults in Calhoun's character and perspectives, as well as from the values of a society that had nurtured him and made him a respected, though not beloved, elder statesman. Calhoun could not have selected a different thrust and still have been the "Calhoun" he was during the last twenty years of his life.

More frequently one knows the general intentions and commitments of persuaders: to raise money, sell a product, secure votes, or otherwise influence public attitudes. There is still the basic question of how well the basic thrust matched the readiness of the readers/listeners. If we know a candidate wants to be elected, and he or she points to a problem without offering a solution of any sort, it is evident that the basic thrust does not match the readiness of normal audiences, who look for solutions when problems are raised. In the study I have already referred to, George Cheney shows that in their Peace Pastoral, the National Conference of Catholic Bishops tied their advocacy of arms control to the broader theme of the dignity of the individual and, in turn, to the Church's stand against abortion and for protection of all human life. In doing so, they preserved their churchly self-system, but they could not fully match their basic thrusts to the readiness of a wide range of secular audiences. A critic would need to take note of the fact that within the constraints of Catholic teaching, the bishops *could not* effectively address all their available audiences. Given their doctrinal constraints the bishops simply could not and would not want to fashion rhetorical satisfactions for all non-Catholics as well as Catholics.

Substance, Disposition, Language, and Paralanguage

In addition to basic thrust, several different rhetorical satisfactions are always offered in some form or another. It is enough for our purposes to identify the general nature of these resources. *Substance* is a synonym for "content." It refers to the essential matter, the gist, of what a persuader says and does. So conceived, substance consists of

the persuader's major contentions and their supporting materials—
that is, the ideas, evidence, references, appeals, and reasoning that
persuaders use in developing their basic contentions. *Disposition* refers
to the way a persuader puts together what he or she has to say. All
except the briefest communications involve an unfolding—a sequential disposing of the substance of the discourse. *Language* is self-
explanatory. Spoken and written words are the basic means by which
communicators represent their thought to others. *Paralanguage* includes all aspects of delivery or presentation that do not directly involve formal language usage. In addition to the complex formal
language systems that we all have, we necessarily use paralanguage in
any communicating that we do.

The sole concern of a configurational critic in matching substance, disposition, language, and paralanguage is the extent to
which the persuader's satisfactions seem to promote identification.
One discovers this by combing through the message for unusual
congruence or incongruence that satisfactions seem to have with
the audience's readiness to be influenced concerning (1) the persuader's notion of the provoking urgency, (2) the persuader as a
source of persuasion on the topic, and (3) the persuader's remedial
action.

The Persuader's Notion of the Provoking Urgency

Ordinarily, when proposing a new policy or course of action, a
persuader has this preliminary persuasive task: If addressing readers/
listeners who are neutral or hostile to the proposal, the persuader
tries to enable them to identify sufficiently with his or her notion of
the provoking urgency so that they first become dissatisfied (that is,
experience bothersome cognitive imbalance) with their existing notions and, second, move toward accepting the persuader's views about
the importance, nature, and cause(s) of the problem. Similarly, if addressing persons who already substantially agree with his or her conception of an urgency, the persuader tries first to induce them to
become dissatisfied with their present level of agreement (experience
bothersome imbalance) and then to strengthen their support (arrive
at a new balance).

Also, when arguing that a belief is true/false or good/bad, a persuader needs to ensure that readers and listeners substantially share his or her notion of the urgency. A claim that something is a fact or has a particular value is made simply because an existing urgency or set of circumstances has welcomed, or necessitated, the communication. A persuader is responding to a provoking state of affairs when asserting that the President's foreign policy is working, that animals have rights, or that the policies of the Environmental Protection Agency do not adequately protect the nation's natural resources. In making a claim of fact or value, the degree of explicitness with which a persuader spells out his or her notion of the urgency depends on the particular circumstances. Nevertheless, the ultimate purpose of such a communication cannot ordinarily be achieved unless the audience shares the persuader's view of the urgency.

The Matching Process

| Match the rhetorical satisfactions (substance, disposition, language, paralanguage) as mediated by the persuader's basic thrust, rhetorical intent, and self-system | with the readiness of readers/listeners to be influenced concerning the persuader's notion of provoking urgency | to determine the degree of congruity between the two. |

The degree of congruity between rhetorical satisfactions and audience readiness to be influenced suggests how persuasive this particular point was. It indicates the extent to which the rhetorical satisfactions should have enabled readers/listeners to perceive analogies between the persuader's notion of the provoking urgency and their own.

To illustrate how this process works, I return to Calhoun's speech. In an extended passage the South Carolinian detailed his notion of the sectional crisis, what had caused it, and what its consequences were and would be. The sectional confrontation, he declared, had reached the supremely critical stage, demanding a final choice. The South was helpless to defend her equality, rights, and honor within the Union because the North, through its aggressions, had transformed the national government, giving it absolute power to work its hostile will on the South. Unless appropriate action was taken, slavery agitation in the North would force the South to secede.

In a terse introduction Calhoun directed striking attention to the severity of the sectional crisis. He then began a long analysis of the urgency, which was the first of two main contentions in the body of the message. (The second contention would be his statement of remedy.) The great length of this passage, about six thousand words, clearly demonstrates that he assigned immense significance to the urgency. In developing the point Calhoun's satisfactions of substance, disposition, and language matched well the capacity of listeners and readers to understand and to follow what was being said. He structured his ideas neatly under "cause" and "importance" of the problem, supplied numerous internal summaries and transitions, and used clear explanations that were reinforced by restatement, statistical data, comparisons, and so on. Because Calhoun's language was exceptionally precise, listeners and readers should have been able to follow his thoughts easily, despite the tendency of his style to be essay-like, his sentences to be complex, and his thought units to be long and involved.

Thus, there is no doubt that Calhoun's analysis of the urgency fit the audience's requirements for understandability. However, Calhoun did not offer Northern senators the means to perceive significant analogies between their belief systems and his notion of the urgency. He began didactically by asserting that "the nation is in danger" because the North's many aggressions against the South had caused Southerners to "believe they cannot remain as things now are . . . in the Union." Continuing in a doctrinaire, lecturist manner, Calhoun made no apparent effort to win over Northerners. His strategies of substance, language, and paralanguage (remember that Senator James Mason, chief author of the new fugitive slave bill, read Calhoun's speech orally) were all abrasive to Northerners. Because the satisfactions he offered had little, if any, potential to encourage Northerners to perceive analogous relationships between his developing argument and their attitudes, values, beliefs, or self-conceptions, they would not have been encouraged to begin to experience a stage of bothersome cognitive imbalance and move toward a new balance.

Furthermore, even if Calhoun had converted Northerners to his notion of the urgency, this change in his listeners (except in one regard—discussed below) would not in itself have encouraged them to become more receptive to his proposed remedy. According to Calhoun, the North had deliberately permitted agitation for the purpose of ultimately freeing the slaves, launched aggressions against the South to weaken her position, altered the Constitution and the national government to benefit its own economic and political power, and had gained complete control of the government. These claims led Calhoun to the conclusion that the North had won the political contest with the South and could control the destiny of the South. While rejecting his claims that it had caused the crisis, the North (unlike the South) would not have been displeased that it had become the dominant section. In itself, this would not cause Northerners to placate the South, as Calhoun would demand.

The only aspect of Calhoun's analysis of the crisis that had potential to evoke identification by Northerners was his claim that continued slavery agitation would result in secession. The North highly valued the Union. If he had been able to prove that a "supremely critical" threat to the Union existed, Northerners might have become more responsive to the remedial actions he was to propose. But discussion of this alleged threat came late in the speech, after nearly five thousand words had encouraged the rejection of identification. Furthermore, he offered no evidence that dissolution was taking place, beyond citing that several Protestant churches had split. He merely asserted in less than one hundred words—without proof—that political cords had snapped. The only way that he could have shocked Northerners into a more receptive attitude toward his ultimatum would have been to convince them that the people of the South were united behind him in believing that under the existing circumstances the South was unable to defend her interests and honor within the Union. Without carrying this point, he could not begin to induce agreement.

Everything in my analysis of Calhoun's rhetorical satisfactions reinforces my belief that his intent was to proclaim his notion of the urgency, not to attempt to persuade Northerners to accept it. If he did try to convince them, his speaking had little persuasive merit.

Let us now look at how well Calhoun's rhetorical satisfactions matched the readiness of Southern senators to be influenced concerning his notions of the urgency. Except for a handful of supporters, Southern senators did not accept that the sectional confrontation had reached the "supremely critical" stage requiring a final showdown. They did not believe that the South had exhausted all resources within the existing system. Although most would have agreed that the North had transformed the nature of the federal government and had provoked the current state of affairs, they still retained hope that through the normal political process they could work out viable accommodations within the Union. Although they subscribed to the principle of secession, they were not yet ready to apply it. In short, because they did not share Calhoun's prescience, they were much more optimistic than he. To persuade these Southern senators, Calhoun somehow had to cause them to conclude with him that the cause of the South was hopeless under the existing system and also that the time to act was at hand.

The satisfactions Calhoun offered concerning the urgency were vastly more likely to encourage identification by Southerners than by Northerners, however. His disposition, substance, and language probably had good potentiality for Southerners to identify with his analysis of the *cause* of the situation. There was strong potential for Southerners to identify with his argument that the North had already secured a predominance in every department of government and that, if the North succeeded in excluding the South from the new territories, the next decade would see a drastic worsening of the sectional imbalance. Furthermore, most Southerners would probably accept his argument that the North created the sectional imbalance by three types of legislative acts. However, few Southerners would have accepted Calhoun's conclusion that the government of the United States had become "as absolute as that of the Autocrat of

Russia, and as despotic in its tendency as any absolute government that ever existed." Calhoun's discussion of the cause of the crisis may have encouraged the few initially favorable Southern senators to feel stronger agreement and most of the initially hostile Southern senators to experience some compatibility with what he was saying.

Calhoun's analysis of the *importance* of the problem was even more significant to persuading Southerners than his treatment of the causes. His attacks on the North for its hostility toward the South and "the social organizations of the South" and his tracing the history of antislavery agitation in the North probably had strong potential to encourage identification. However, most Southern senators who still endorsed political parties as the best means to solve sectional problems would have been disturbed by his attempt to blame the parties for the situation. The crucial part of his argument of importance was the attempt to show that slavery agitation would result in emancipation or disunion. His contention that antislavery sentiment had constantly grown stronger, while means to control it had weakened, should have induced strong fear responses from Southerners. But he offered limited evidence to support this claim or his claim that the Union was beginning to disintegrate.

My analysis shows that Calhoun did not offer hostile Southern senators sufficient means to identify with his position that a supreme crisis existed. Calhoun did not attempt to demonstrate that he spoke for a united South or that the survival of the South depended upon her people being unified. Although he was acutely aware of all these considerations, he chose not to deal with them in the speech. Therefore, whereas Calhoun's rhetorical satisfactions admirably served an intent to *proclaim* his view of the provoking urgency, they had limited potential to *persuade* most Southern senators.

The Persuader as a Source of Persuasion on the Topic

Although "who is doing the persuading" may be extraneous to the formally logical merits of communication, Aristotle wrote that "we might almost affirm that" the persuader's character, or ethos, "is the most potent of all the means to persuasion."[1] Aristotle's judgment of the importance of a persuader's credibility is supported by traditional, intuitive, and empirical evidence.[2] The believability of a persuader becomes especially important when he or she addresses significant urgencies—that is, when the stakes are high, the consequences great. In addition to its pervasive importance, a persuader's credibility may present specific rhetorical needs in a particular communication. For example, because of insufficient information, readers/listeners may not have formed clear impressions of a persuader prior to the communication; they do not know how much to trust that persuader's judgments or believe his or her testimony. In another situation readers/listeners may bring with them strong positive or negative biases about the persuader's character, experience, knowledge, intelligence, or judgment. In still different circumstances, readers/listeners may sense, or think they sense, that the persuader does, or does not, feel good will toward them. William Jennings Bryan's speech advocating free silver stampeded the 1896 Democratic National Convention and helped win him the party's nomination for President. The tumultuous success of his speech depended partly on the delegates' positive prior identification with him. Conversely, Vice-President Dan Quayle had a hard time overcoming the negative image he acquired during the 1988 campaign, and Calhoun's persuasive task was made more difficult in 1850 because he lacked credibility as a source of persuasion on his topic. Except for a few supporters, senators rejected identification with Calhoun's image as a doctrinaire radical who for twenty years had been pushing confrontations with the North.

To match a persuader's rhetorical strategies with the readiness of readers/listeners to be influenced concerning the persuader as a source of persuasion on the topic, one estimates how well the persuader's ongoing satisfactions matched the readers'/listeners' initial predispositions toward him or her and how well they subsequently led readers/listeners toward considering the persuader more believable—that is, how well they encouraged persuadees to have greater willingness to accept what was said *because* he or she was saying it. As one might expect in the case of Calhoun's speech, the South Carolinian made no attempt to persuade others to accept his credibility— he proclaimed his own ethos.

The Matching Process

Match the rhetorical satisfactions (substance, disposition, language, paralanguage) as mediated by the persuader's basic thrust, rhetorical intent, and self-system	with the readiness of readers/listeners to be influenced concerning the persuader as a source of persuasion on the topic	to determine the degree of congruity between the two.

Except for a few Southern followers, senators would view him negatively as a source of persuasion on this topic. Probably most senators esteemed him highly for his intelligence, devotion to public concerns, and for many of his qualities of character. However, most—even those senators from the Middle and Deep South—questioned Calhoun's motives, distrusted his radicalism, disliked his persistent aggressiveness, and were wearied by his repeated attempts to rally a united South behind his leadership and by his ever present sheaf of resolutions aimed at the North.

Calhoun pronounced his credibility with both bald and more subtle means. His first sentences claimed that his judgments and policies had been correct from the beginning of the sectional controversy and that the present crisis had developed because his advice was not followed. Midway through the speech he again claimed that he had invariably been right in the past and that the "present perilous condition" would not have developed if his advice had been followed. In both cases Calhoun's bald self-praise was more than personal vindication; it invited others to accept that he was worthy of belief in 1850 because his perceptions had been correct in the past. It is doubtful, however, that these pronouncements of ethos would have promoted identification on the part of those who disliked or distrusted him or who still placed their trust in the normal political process. Calhoun's third expressed use of personal proof constituted the close of the speech. Here he asserted that his purpose in the speech, as throughout the entire controversy, had been to save the Union, "if it could be done; and if it could not, to save the section where it has pleased Providence to cast my lot." His tone may have seemed uncompromising, detached, and even self-laudatory to hostile auditors. They would have found scant reason to identify with his final sentence: "Having faithfully done my duty to the best of my ability, both to the Union and my section, throughout this agitation, I shall have the consolation, let what will come, that I am free from all responsibility."

In addition to his explicit pronouncements of credibility, Calhoun made the speech a personal manifesto by frequently using the pronoun "I" and making assertions and interpretations whose persuasiveness depended on his personal credibility. These more subtle uses of ethos probably would not induce hostile listeners to think more highly of Calhoun as a source of persuasion and, consequently, would not in themselves encourage greater identification with his message.

In summary, Calhoun's rhetorical satisfactions did not match the way his listeners initially viewed his credibility as a source of persuasion on the topic and did not encourage them to think better of his credibility as the speech progressed. Conversely, his attempts at ethos probably encouraged Northern senators and, to a lesser extent, Southern senators to reject identification with his speech. Calhoun's few Southern supporters would identify with his pronouncements of credibility, naturally, but they were already conditioned to approve his message.

The same sort of analysis of other rhetoric needs to be made in order to reveal the congruency of persuaders' credibility as persuaders with readers'/listeners' dispositions. As I mentioned previously, in recent years the Mobil oil company has regularly published essays ("advertorials") on general subjects in their advertisements in major newspapers. Their obvious intention is to convince readers of the company's general good citizenship. The attempt is fitting because in the 1990s social responsibility of corporations is a widely discussed topic. To exactly what extent Mobil's strategies have raised the company's general ethos is not known, but, given the widespread readiness to consider corporate responsibility, the company's strategy is at least a sensible one for seeking to show that Mobil is more than a money maker and that it takes public responsibilities seriously.

Matching strategies with readinesses is universally important, if for no other reason than that the entire enterprise of "image making" is an enterprise in trying to fit persuaders' credibility to presumed expectations and demands of audiences.

The Persuader's Remedial Action

When several things are essential, it is a solecism to claim that one of them is "more essential" or "most essential." Nevertheless, I am tempted to argue that, although readers/listeners should come to share a persuader's concept of an urgency and to accept him or her as a credible source of persuasion on the topic, the "most crucial" aspect of persuasion is matching the rhetorical satisfactions that are offered with the readers'/listeners' readiness to be influenced *concerning the persuader's proposed solution.* The other aspects just mentioned serve a supportive function: they help condition readers/listeners to accept proposed remedies, which is ordinarily the real point of communication. In response to policy recommendations, persons will not act on an urgency in the way a persuader wants unless they substantially agree with the proposed remedial action. This is true even though they may accept both the persuader's notion of the urgency and his or her credibility on the topic. Similarly, in response to claims that something is a fact or has a particular value, readers/listeners must come to accept the persuader's remedy—that is, his or her position concerning the alleged fact or value. Otherwise, they will not exert a desired force on the exigential flow, even though they may substantially share the persuader's explicit or implicit concept of the urgency that provoked the communication and even though they may think highly of the persuader's credibility.

The Matching Process

Match the rhetorical satisfactions, (substance, disposition, language, paralanguage) as mediated by the persuader's basic thrust, rhetorical intent, and self-system	with the readiness of readers/listeners to be influenced concerning the persuader's notion for remedial action	to determine the degree of congruity between the two.

How this procedure works is illustrated by my application to
Calhoun's March 4 speech.

The disposition Calhoun used to present his proposed policy
had the same exceptional clarity and logical unfolding that characterized his analysis of the urgency. It represented well his intent to proclaim, but it did not match the listeners' readiness to be influenced.

After almost six thousand words documenting his notion that
the sectional confrontation had reached a "supremely critical" stage
demanding final resolution, Calhoun moved smoothly into his policy
recommendation. He began this argument with the transitional sentence: "Having now, Senators, explained what it is that endangers the
Union, and traced it to its cause, and explained its nature and character, the question again recurs—How can the Union be saved?" Before he gave his answer, however, Calhoun explained at length how he
thought the Union *cannot* be saved. After this, he stated his remedy
in about three hundred words. Finally, he charged that "the responsibility of saving the Union rests on the North, and not on the South"
and claimed that the time had come to determine whether the question could be settled.

Although this sequence of arguments facilitated the clear understanding that *proclaiming* required, Calhoun's explanation of "what
should be done" was much too terse to foster identification. If he had
hoped to persuade hostile listeners to accept his plan, he committed
a basic tactical error in devoting only two short paragraphs to its explanation whereas he gave almost four thousand words to the preliminary argument on "what cannot save the Union."

In developing "what cannot save the Union," Calhoun supplied
basic contentions and extensive supporting materials. Attentive listeners should have been able to understand easily *what* he believed
were unsatisfactory ways to relieve the crisis and *why* he thought they
were unsatisfactory. It is doubtful, however, that this attempt to eliminate counter ideas would have encouraged others to be more receptive to his own plan.

First, the Union could not be saved by eulogies. Usually "the
cry of Union" came from the assailants of the South, he said. These
eulogists did not sincerely love the Union nor the Constitution, and

their "profession of devotion" was a deception "intended to increase the vigor of their assaults and to weaken the force of our resistance." There was nothing here to encourage hostile Northern senators to accept his point. Also, Calhoun claimed that "the cry of the Union" by "those who are not our assailants" was not sincere and would fail to save the Union. They "pronounce eulogies upon the Union" with the apparent "intent of charging us with disunion, without uttering one word of denunciation against our assailants." This attack on "friendly" Northerners also did not contain a basis for identification.

Second, the Union could not be saved by invoking the name of George Washington. Calhoun scored "debater's points" by identifying Washington as "one of us—a slaveholder and a planter." Nevertheless, Northern listeners rejected his claim that Washington would sanction Southern secession. Critical Southern listeners probably accepted the abstraction that Washington's beliefs were consistent with the principle of secession, but they did not accept Calhoun's claim that Washington would endorse Southern secession under the immediate circumstances.

Third, the Union could not be saved by adopting Henry Clay's compromise proposals. This contention could not have had much positive impact because Calhoun failed to develop it. In fewer than one hundred words he explained that he would bypass Clay's plan because it had already been discussed. His failure to refute the Kentucky senator's proposals meant that he did not really contest the beliefs of many Northern Democrats, most Southern Whigs, and some Southern Democrats who were already looking to Clay's plan as a way out of the crisis. Calhoun's decision not to disprove this possible solution may have been useful for proclaiming but not for persuading.

Fourth, the Union could not be saved by accepting President Taylor's plan. The length of this statement, about 3,200 words, was more than twice as long as his refutation of the first three counter plans combined, and it was more than *ten times as long as the explanation he would make of his own remedial plan*. It is not clear why Calhoun gave almost one-third of the entire speech to attacking the administration's plan. Perhaps he wrongly identified Taylor's scheme as the major threat to his policy of ultimatum. Again, his statement matched well the needs of proclaiming, but his persuasive target—if he had one—seems uncertain. Northern Whigs would support the President's program, regardless of what Calhoun or any other senator said; many Northern Democrats and all senators from the Middle and Deep South would oppose it—without any encouragement from Calhoun. Much of his argument consisted of abstract reasoning: that Taylor's plan was unconstitutional and "contrary to the entire practice of the Government, from its commencement to the present time." Calhoun's mesh of constitutional abstractions did not give hostile Northerners the means to discover analogies between their belief systems and Calhoun's contention. Furthermore, few Southerners, even those who agreed California should not be admitted as a state, would have accepted his conditional syllogism: If California is admitted under the present circumstances, the South should secede.

After Calhoun's lengthy attempt to eliminate the ways that could not save the Union, he stated in a starkly terse passage what he thought the North must do to convince the South she could live with honor and safety within the Union. This statement served adequately the purpose of proclaiming, but it did not contain the basic contentions and supporting materials necessary for persuading. (1) He did not explain the nature of the demands he was proposing. (2) He did not attempt to prove that his ultimatum had the support of anyone besides himself. He did not offer evidence that (3) his plan would solve the sectional problem or that (4) the North would not experience additional severe problems if it adopted his requirements. Moreover, (5) his only attempt to prove his proposals could be put into effect was to assert that the North could easily meet his ultimatum if it wanted to, without any sacrifice. In short, Calhoun's sketch of his solution almost totally lacked developing arguments and supporting evidence and reasoning.

The conclusions I have drawn about Calhoun's disposition and substance are generally applicable to his use of *language*. His long sentences, involved thought units, and the essay-like quality of the whole were vintage Calhoun. These features should not have interfered with the listeners' grasp of what he said, but they could not help to reinforce his ideas. On the other hand, the unusual clarity and vividness of his word choices contributed to the understandability and impressiveness of his argument and met the needs of both proclaiming and persuading. There remained, however, the difficulty that Calhoun's language was confrontational and absolutist, that his language, like his ultimatum, was abrasive and autocratic. This could not encourage Northern senators to identify with his ideas, and it may have had unfortunate influence on moderate Southerners who still sought a compromise solution.

It is reasonable to observe, however, that the subjectivity of Calhoun's language matched reasonably well the persuasive needs of a "delayed call to history." His absolutism epitomized an insolvable cleavage between North and South and stressed the futility of attempted accommodations. In the general situation of 1860 and after, this absolutism would appear prophetic.

Calhoun's proposals for remedial action did not suit the configuration of forces of 1850. If we were to examine the Exxon Company's public proposals for remedial action following the giant oil spill in Alaskan waters in 1989, we would find that the sufficiency of the proposed actions did not satisfy environmentalists and became the focus of continued debates and court battles between the Alaskan government and the company. As this is written, there has yet to be a national consensus on the merits or demerits of Exxon's remedial actions. In a different set of circumstances, when Franklin D. Roosevelt gave his declaration of war speech in December of 1941, the previous day's attack on Pearl Harbor had so radically changed American readiness for action that even most former "America Firsters" were ready to accept the declaration of war as the only reasonable remedial action. The majority of the Senate of 1850 was, in fact, ready to accept something like Clay's compromise actions but not Calhoun's radical proposals for action. The general point is that rhetoric normally deals with perceived problems, and the issue of what to do arises automatically as soon as a problem is recognized. Therefore, it is essential for an observer to ferret out how much and what kinds of actions listeners/readers are ready to look on with favor—in whatever time period one is studying.

The principles I have been discussing apply both to individual communications and to multiple communications. As I have pointed out, in his study of the early Pennsylvania constitutional debates, Carroll Arnold found that the situational potentialities were a kind of "arch" under which he inspected the readinesses of persuadees and the satisfactions offered by proponents of change during the fourteen years between 1776 and 1790. The same idea holds true for any other set of persuasive efforts over time. In the case of the Baltic self-government agitations of the 1990s, the overarching potentialities for change in the urgency constrained the basic thrusts of all successful rhetoric on the topic, even including the public utterances of President Bush. Therefore, the ultimate constraint of what change and how much change particular communications can make in an urgency constantly alters as the urgency itself changes and as audiences/occasions of communications change. What was communicatively possible in each case underscores our analysis of how persuaders' rhetorical strategies match the readinesses of audiences to accept the basic thrusts of persuasion and to exert pressure on an urgency.

Integrating Rhetorical Assessments

Our last step is to exploit the individual assessments we have made, blending them into a unified rhetorical judgment. This process is basically a matter of summing up. My study of Calhoun's speech illustrates how this is done.

If Calhoun's intent was to *proclaim*, as I believe was the case, his choice of rhetorical satisfactions deserves high commendation. What he said matched extremely well the rhetorical needs that proclaiming ex cathedra imposed.

On the other hand, to the extent that his intent was to *persuade* his listening and reading audiences to accept the explicit thrust of his speech now, his selection of basic thrusts, disposition, substance, language, and paralanguage had scant persuasive merit. The rhetorical satisfactions he offered gave the immediate audiences so little inducement to identify with what he was saying that he seemed insensitive to the needs of persuading. That is why he seems to have been

issuing a personal manifesto, or position statement. He did not provide hostile Northern senators and the Northern public with the rhetorical means even to begin to change their minds about him as a
source of persuasion (his claims of ethos were abrasively sanctimo-
nious) or about his claims that a supremely critical sectional crisis existed and that extraordinary social, political, and constitutional
reforms must be adopted to save the Union. They would not have
identified with him well enough even to start to experience bothersome cognitive imbalance, much less to move toward accepting a new
balance by adopting his position. Neither did Calhoun offer rhetorical satisfactions that would induce the critical Southern senators and
the Southern public to accept his basic thrust.

As a conventional attempt at persuasion, Calhoun's speech can
be dismissed as a nonevent. When viewed as a position statement, it
assumes an almost unique position in world literature. Under this
view, it is an austere, arrogant model of *proclaiming*. A lamentation
about what is and is to be. A lonesome hound baying protests to the
moon.

The rhetorical satisfactions offered by any communication have
little significance unless they match some readers'/listeners' readiness
to be influenced by those satisfactions. To return to the instance of
Governor Clinton's introduction of Michael Dukakis at the 1988
Democratic National Convention, Clinton's problem was not that he
offered inappropriate rhetorical satisfactions for *an* audience; the
problem was that his immediate audience, in the moments he spoke,
was not ready for introductory satisfactions but for praise-giving and
enthusiasm-rousing satisfactions. The National Conference of Catholic Bishops was qualified to offer moral counsel and satisfactions to
those inclined toward their views on nuclear arms, but as clerics they
could not offer doubters, antagonists, or pragmatically minded other
persons politically practical satisfactions by means of arguments and
appeals concerning overall foreign policy. Those audiences simply
did not see the provoking urgency in the same moral terms as the
bishops.

In all cases, the degree of congruence between rhetors' proffered
satisfactions and the readinesses of audiences must be located by look-

ing at the basic thrusts of the communications, at the degrees to which conceptions of provoking urgencies were shared, at the status or ethos of the communicator(s), and at the situational acceptability of remedial actions proposed. When these factors have been taken into account, one can arrive at an informed judgment of how persuasive the rhetoric probably was to the persuadees. In other words, one can give a reasoned judgment about how well the rhetoric functioned within the configuration of forces of which it was a part. We cannot "measure" the potentialities of rhetoric in this way, but we can *estimate* how wise the communicators' choices were and why what was done worked (in whole or in part) or did not work. We can also explain why this degree of achievement came into being. Background knowledge needed for such assessments includes estimates of the intentions of the persuaders, knowledge of the perceived natures of the provoking urgencies, interpretations of the readinesses of particular readers/listeners to be influenced, and analysis of the satisfactions offered by the would-be persuaders. When rhetoric proves highly successful in practical terms, it will be so because of a tight congruence among all of these elements of rhetorical communication. Most communications are, of course, less than totally successful. That is why it is especially important to find out the *degrees* of their fitness for the circumstances—discovering where there was strong congruence and where congruence was less strong. Put in language I used early in this book, critical inquiry should aim at discovering the degrees to which congruence provided by symbolic inducement contributed to identification between rhetors and persuadees *within the configuration of interrelated forces* that were already at work and that were rhetorically introduced.

Secondary Assessments
of Rhetoric

Chapter Fifteen

Supplementing
Basic Assessments

Not well developed

We have seen that to evaluate rhetoric one judges how well persuaders selected rhetorical options to answer or satisfy the various constraints on themselves and on their communications. But to understand fully what was, what was possible, and what was the consequent wisdom of the persuaders, one should reinforce or modify these basic judgments by making certain supplementing assessments. One should estimate the congruity between rhetorical satisfactions in the communications and subsequent changes in the exigential flows. Also, one should ask whether other options realistically available to persuaders might have served their rhetorical purposes better than those chosen.

Congruence of Rhetorical Satisfactions with Changes
in the Exigential Flow

In order to understand fully the relationships between rhetorical satisfactions offered and subsequent changes in exigential flows, one needs to ask several questions I have not yet raised in discussing critical procedures. One needs to ask at least these questions: Given a persuader's intent and internalized input, how congruent with immediate and later changes in the urgency were the satisfactions offered? With changes in the readers/listeners? With the evolving status of the persuader? Then one needs to ask whether answers to these questions call for modifying the basic assessments already made. If not, the basic assessments are reinforced.

Sometimes, but by no means always, consequences occur and can be judged almost simultaneously with communications. Then one can judge what happened to the exigential flow without pondering

long-range consequences. Oratory at street rallies and many advertisements for special sales fall roughly into this category. A more
complex example is illustrated by Martin Marprelate's attack on the
sixteenth-century English episcopate. Among the numerous protests
that Puritans made against the established church during Queen
Elizabeth's reign was the secret printing over a period of months of a
series of seven tracts. Beginning late in 1587 one or more Puritans using the pseudonym Martin Marprelate issued pamphlets ridiculing
the bishops. A critic can dissect and categorize the ribald humor and
the scurrilous ridicule found in the tracts. A critic can ascertain that
the literary form was innovative and that the purpose of Martin was
unique: to destroy the traditional veneration of the bishops by means
of humor. A critic can even estimate the potential for change in the
provoking urgency. On the basis of this analysis, a critic could tentatively conclude that Martin selected rhetorical options wisely. This
conclusion, though thoroughly reasonable, needs to be confirmed or
amended by knowledge of the consequences of the communications.
Historian J. B. Black says that the pamphlets immediately "swept
away in a tide of unrestrained jocularity all the traditional reverence
for the episcopate."[1] Although configurational critics do not speak in
terms of the linear causation claimed by Black, a configurational
study of the immediate sequential flow confirms that the rhetorical
strategies in the pamphlets matched the changes that occurred. What
the author(s) wanted to have happen to the readers and to the provoking urgency seems to have happened. This judgment of congruency between the rhetorical satisfactions offered and the immediate
exigential flow provides all the information necessary to reinforce the
view that Martin's rhetoric merits praise as persuasion.

In general, however, instant criticism of speeches, editorials,
proclamations, or campaigns is unsatisfactory because there hasn't
been time for much to happen after the rhetorical events. One can't
measure the rhetoric against the consequences because the consequences haven't happened yet. Rhetorical configurations are not
complete until the relevant significances in their exigential flows have
had a chance to unfold. In what follows I will consider and illustrate

assessments that need modifications in consequence of changes in urgencies, in readers/listeners, and/or in the status of persuaders.

Changes in the Urgency

The first step in studying the relation of communications to their sequent urgencies is to fix cutoff points for the urgencies. Sometimes the practical consequences of a rhetorical event seem virtually endless. When President Nixon resigned his office in 1974, his son-in-law David Eisenhower thought that Watergate would "look pretty small" in fifteen years. But when that time came, few disagreed that the consequences of Watergate would continue for decades to come.

Sometimes the long-term unraveling of an urgency does more than flesh out the consequences of rhetoric, as in the case of Watergate. It may yield the real significance of the piece(s). For instance, one gets a badly distorted understanding of *The Federalist* as a piece of political rhetoric if one considers only its immediate setting. The "Federalist Papers" were, after all, only part of numerous efforts to influence the ratification of the United States Constitution. *The Federalist* appealed chiefly to a particular leadership class already largely convinced, and the papers apparently exerted little influence on ratification. They failed to win over the people of New York, the audience that the authors of the essays especially hoped to influence. Although New York permitted universal adult male suffrage, the vote was overwhelmingly against the position represented in *The Federalist*, with forty-six anti-Federalists and only nineteen Federalists being elected to the state ratification convention. The full significance of *The Federalist* does not derive from its impress on New York voters in the winter of 1788, however. Even today *The Federalist* influences political thinking, supplying insights to lawyers, historians, judges, politicians, and political scientists. According to Jacob Cooke, "The United States has produced three historic documents of major importance: the Declaration of Independence, the Constitution, and *The Federalist*."[2] According to Clinton Rossiter, "*The Federalist* is the most important work in political science that has ever been written, or is likely ever to be written, in the United States. It is, indeed, the one

product of the American mind that is rightly counted among the classics of political theory."[3] The urgency which the authors of *The Federalist* sought to modify did not terminate upon its publication or
upon New York's ratification of the Constitution; the essays are in fact
timeless, and the relation of *The Federalist* to the continuing postcommunication stage of its urgency should be recognized in any evaluation of this collection of essays.

Likewise, a true assessment of the Gettysburg Address cannot
be achieved by measuring Lincoln's skill in meeting the constraints of
the immediate situation at the Gettysburg battlefield. The true great-
ness of that communication does not lie in its impact on the throng
gathered upon the rolling hillsides at Gettysburg. The crowd became
restless as Edward Everett's featured address stretched some two
hours. After a dirge was played, Lincoln read his brief remarks. Unfortunately the audience did not settle down before his speech was
over. According to contemporary reports, only a few persons heard
the President and even fewer thought the speech outstanding. To assess the Gettysburg Address as a piece of rhetoric one must consider
its relationship to the postcommunication stage of its urgency. Although the sustained thrusting power of the Gettysburg Address derives partly from the hallowed circumstances of dedicating a vast
cemetery for the war dead, it is also indebted to the desperate trauma
of the Civil War that was to stretch on for almost two more years and
to the later martyrdom of the President. The ultimate significance of
Lincoln's speech exists in its continuing capacity to assuage universally experienced exigencies of mind and spirit that involve people's
relationship to each other and to their governments.

Few rhetorical events, of course, possess the climactic consequence of Watergate, or the prophetic wisdom of *The Federalist*, or the
ennobling sentiments of the Gettysburg Address. A limited examination of the sequent flows following most communications is sufficient to supplement basic assessments. At this writing the presidents
of the universities comprising the Big Ten have met officially as the
Council of Ten. After discussing their earlier unofficial decision to
invite the Pennsylvania State University to join their conference, and
after reviewing the opinions of athletic directors, coaches, and faculty

representatives of their various institutions, the presidents by a majority vote officially welcomed Penn State. One cannot understand the true significance of this action without considering what consequences were likely to flow from the presidents' deliberations, but neither could anyone in 1991 know with certainty what those consequences would be. A serious rhetorical critic would need to estimate those consequences and—with some arbitrariness—decide when, in the future, reasonable judgments about the event can be made with some finality. The benefits anticipated from the union will depend on such sticky problems as athletic scheduling, revenue sharing, and feasible integrations of various kinds of academic programs. In some sports the Big Ten conference may have to abandon its round-robin system, perhaps splitting the conference into two divisions; which, in turn, would argue for adding a twelfth member to the conference.

Joining the Big Ten conference also means complicated problems for Penn State. Penn State has no history of sharing academic planning with other universities, but departments and colleges of Big Ten universities do frequently plan in concert with one another. In athletics the men's basketball program at Penn State does not match similar programs at, say, Indiana University or the University of Michigan. So far, basketball has generally drawn sparse crowds at Penn State, partly because the university has only a small, antiquated arena. All such conditions mean the discussions and agreements by the presidents of the schools will have ramifications extending well into the future. For example, certain exchange agreements exist among Big Ten academic departments, schools, and colleges. Further, the Pennsylvania State University is a state related university with its own board of trustees. It is responsible to no state board of regents, nor is it owned by the state as are the other Big Ten schools except Northwestern University. Will these differences lead to changes in policies and decision making at Penn State? One must wait some time to find out.

Obviously Penn State's joining the Big Ten has consequences that will unravel endlessly. Nevertheless, we can forecast a practical cutoff for the sequent stage of the urgency. It appears now that, partly because the Big Ten schools will be slow to share their present football and basketball TV revenues with Penn State, the Lions won't participate fully in those sports until 1992 and 1993. So far, there are no strong signs that academic integration will present critical problems. Therefore, we can conclude that a *full* configurational analysis of the Council of Ten's decision and rhetoric requires a sequent stage of something more than five years. Once the football and basketball teams are integrated into Big Ten schedules, a year or two should be sufficient to tell how well the merger has worked athletically and what the ripple consequences have been for other conferences and schools. Therefore, it is reasonable to predict that somewhat less than a decade—perhaps five or six years—of watching the sequent flow unravel is sufficient to confirm or modify basic assessments of the presidents' rhetoric in the Council of Ten. Of course, critics are already assessing the rhetorical choices of the presidents and their staffs. But because such analyses are not yet grounded in the reality of what actually ensued, they are not configurationally complete.

In the case of John C. Calhoun's March 4 speech, the sectional urgency of 1850 concerned not only the prickly problems of managing the existence of slavery in the United States but also the underlying and predisposing issues of the status of slavery in the nation and the preservation of the Union. A practical cutoff for the sequent stage of this urgency is the advent of the Civil War, which ended such questions. Unlike the Gettysburg Address there is no practical reason to link this rhetorical event to timeless themes like race relations, social justice, or human perfectibility.

After determining a cutoff for the sequent stage, one needs to plan how to treat that stage to supplement basic rhetorical assessments already made. Generally speaking, there are two ways to accomplish this. The first is simply to match the rhetorical satisfactions used against the ensuing flow of events. This is what I did when I criticized the Martin Marprelate attack on the episcopate and, in an earlier chapter, when I criticized Woodrow Wilson's "Peace Without Victory" speech. For the next few years this procedure will inform criticism of rhetoric used by the presidents of the Big Ten in admitting Penn State to their conference. The following analysis of Lincoln's First Inaugural illustrates how this matching process works.

In an earlier chapter I explained that, although critics differ in their interpretations of Lincoln's intentions in his First Inaugural, all agree that he wanted to keep things cool for the time being. Assuming this general purpose, we can easily match the satisfactions Lincoln offered with what actually happened in the months following his in-auguration. To keep things cool, Lincoln was compelled in the ad-dress to maintain two incompatible policies. I follow here David M. Potter's analysis in his *Lincoln and His Party in the Secession Crisis*.[4] Lin-coln had to uphold federal authority, but he also had to avoid any confrontation that would deepen existing antagonisms and weaken Southern Unionism. "In strict logic this was impossible, for the very process of enforcing the Federal functions was certain to produce the sort of clash which had to be avoided."

To accommodate these two needs, Lincoln pursued three strat-egies. First, he sought to reassure the South concerning "the good will, conciliatory purposes, and Constitutional scruples of the new administration." In the very beginning of his address, Lincoln gave explicit reassurances to the South, and he returned to this theme later in the speech, expressing his willingness to accept the proposed Thir-teenth Amendment guaranteeing slavery in the states and to respect the constitutional directives pertaining to the return of fugitive slaves.

Second, with Southern fears thus assuaged, Lincoln sought to strengthen the hands of Southern Unionists. Denying the right to se-cede, he defended Unionism on the basis of pragmatism and ideal-ism, and he vigorously affirmed the national authority: "The Constitution itself expressly enjoins upon me, that the laws of the Union be faithfully executed in all the States. . . . I trust this will not be regarded as a menace, but only as the declared purpose of the Union that it *will* constitutionally defend, and maintain itself. . . . The power confided to me, will be used to hold, occupy, and possess the property, and places belonging to the government, and to collect the duties and imposts."

Third, with the fears of the South theoretically allayed and with the symbolic supremacy of the Union forcibly asserted, Lincoln was ready for his key strategy: the "thinly veiled intimations that he would temporarily suspend the operation of the authority which he had so firmly asserted." In 1861 there were only four ways in which the federal government directly impinged on individual citizens or upon state authorities: federal law, the mails, customs, and forts and arsenals. If activities in these areas were suspended wherever necessary, "the question of Federal authority would become an abstraction" and the sectional crisis "might continue indefinitely without leading to actual conflict." According to Professor Potter, at the time of his inauguration, or soon afterward, Lincoln planned to suspend the operation of each of these four types of federal authority.

In the Inaugural, the function on which Lincoln placed greatest stress was the enforcement of the laws. Yet in conjunction with his insistence that he would enforce the laws vigorously and constitutionally, he added the disclaimer that "where hostility to the United States, in any interior locality, shall be so great and so universal, as to prevent competent resident citizens from holding the Federal offices, there will be no attempt to force obnoxious strangers among the people for that object. While the strict legal right may exist in the government to enforce the exercise of these offices, the attempt to do so would be so irritating, and so nearly impractical with all, that I deem it better to forego, for the time, the uses of such offices." "In other words," said Potter, "he would enforce the laws, unless such enforcement should be unwelcome."

In regard to delivery of the mails by postal officials, Lincoln by-passed the issue by saying that "the mails, unless repelled, will continue to be furnished in all parts of the Union."

The third exercise of federal authority, the collection of customs, posed more of a rhetorical and actual problem than the first two. If collection of duties were suspended in the South, much of the nation's importations would be diverted to Southern ports, thereby rewarding rebellion with economic prosperity and inhibiting the growth of Unionist sentiment in the South. When Lincoln asserted, "The power confided to me will be used . . . to collect the duties and imposts," he seemed to be endorsing the application of this authority. Nevertheless, in actual practice Lincoln did not attempt to enforce the collection of duties in the South, and when the war came he was in the process of evolving a strategy by which duties could be secure but which would not necessitate "specific Southern submission."

In regard to the fourth exercise of federal authority, the maintenance of forts and arsenals, Lincoln's alteration in his speech text seems to document his peaceful intent. In the initial draft he had written: "All the power at my disposal will be used to reclaim the public property and places which have fallen; to hold, occupy and possess these, and all other property and places belonging to the government. . . . " At the suggestion of Orville H. Browning, the final text omitted any threat to "reclaim the public property." Thus, the inauguration audience heard Lincoln merely promise to "hold, occupy and possess the property and places belonging to the government." This meant that the symbolic maintenance of federal authority was limited to the retention of the only Southern fortresses still remaining in Union hands: the offshore fortifications of Sumter, near Charleston, and Pickens, near Pensacola. According to the knowledge Lincoln had on March 4, both of these forts could be held indefinitely without need for federal supportive action.

The rhetorical satisfactions Lincoln offered were designed to provide a tranquilized period of "masterly inactivity." His hope was that forbearance of threat or coercion by the federal government would give (or would seem to give) Unionist sentiment in the South an unharried opportunity to develop. Unprovoked and unchallenged, the people of the South would be encouraged to believe that their interests could be protected best within the Union. "It was a superb pattern for reconstruction," according to Potter, "one which seemed to eliminate every possibility of a clash. The rival sections were segregated by a sanitary cordon of neutral states which would prevent the possibility of any border incident causing an outbreak. Behind this barrier, the operation of Federal forces would be, in effect, suspended so far as seemed necessary to give Unionism full and free scope. With every point of contact carefully muffled, friction might be avoided indefinitely." And of greatest significance, "meanwhile the abdication of Federal authority would be concealed and Union sentiment would be rallied by the firm language of the President, and by the retention of Fort Sumter, which had come to have enormous emotional significance as a symbol of the national authority."

A look at the postcommunication stage of the urgency reveals that one of Lincoln's basic strategies was incompatible with what happened. Because of this incompatibility, his rhetoric failed in its purpose to keep things cool for the time being. Keeping things cool depended on holding, occupying, and possessing at least one of the two Southern federal garrisons still in Union hands. On March 5, Lincoln learned that his strategy had been based on faulty intelligence. Unexpectedly, word came from Major Robert Anderson, commander of the federal forces in Fort Sumter, that the fort would run out of supplies within a few weeks. The contradictions of Lincoln's strategic needs had come home to an early roost. He would have to choose almost immediately between sacrificing that symbol of nationalism or abandoning his plan of "masterly inactivity." With his cabinet almost uniformly favoring evacuation and with the public accepting evacuation as almost inevitable, Lincoln seriously considered abandoning Fort Sumter. Before the inauguration he had placed such reliance on the triumph of Southern Unionism that he had offered to withdraw from Fort Sumter if the Unionists would adjourn the Virginia state convention sitting at Richmond. Some evidence indicates that, after he received Major Anderson's message, he repeated the offer. Also, he ordered the preparation of a supply expedition for Sumter, which was to be sent upon order. He was still prepared to abandon the fort, however, if symbolic federal authority could be maintained through the reinforcement of Fort Pickens. As he later stated in his message to Congress of July 4, 1861, "This last would be a clear indication of *policy*, and would better enable the country to accept the evacuation of Fort Sumter as a military *necessity*."[5] Troops had previously been sent to Pensacola Harbor by President Buchanan. Under a truce arranged by Buchanan, they had not been thrown into the fort but had been held on board ship. Lincoln considered that the reinforcement of Pickens could easily be accomplished. Accordingly, on March 11 he ordered the War Department to move the troops into the fort. Lincoln's directive was sent by sea and, because of the slow transit, a response was not received from Pensacola Harbor until

April 6. "On that day," Potter related, "the news of an ironic failure arrived. The orders of the War Department had been delivered, but Captain [Henry A.] Adams, commanding the ship on which the troops were waiting, was not subject to Army orders. He was still under Navy Department instructions to respect Buchanan's truce. Consequently, he had refused, without further orders, to render the aid essential for throwing the troops into Fort Pickens." The reinforcements, "therefore, were still on board ship, and would necessarily be there when Anderson's supplies were exhausted. This meant plainly that Lincoln could not display at Pickens that 'clear indication of policy' which would 'better enable the country to accept the evacuation of Fort Sumter as a military necessity.' " Consequently, on that same day Lincoln informed the governor of South Carolina that provisions were being sent to Fort Sumter. Through inefficient handling of Lincoln's order and an arbitrary "following the book" response of a naval captain, Lincoln's plan of masterly inactivity had failed.

It is plain that Lincoln's strategy concerning federal forts and arsenals was incongruent with what happened. The incongruity reinforces reservations a critic should have had in making basic assessments of Lincoln's rhetoric in the First Inaugural. If we operated completely within the parameters of Lincoln's purpose to keep things cool for the time being and his assessment of the situation, we would conclude that his selection of rhetorical options was magnificently conceived. Nevertheless, our basic assessment should have recognized that Lincoln's rhetoric was badly flawed because he did not see the provoking urgency clearly. Historians tell us that Lincoln badly misunderstood the potential for change in the rhetorical urgency, as well as the readiness of his readers/listeners to be influenced, particularly the people of the South. Along with other Republicans during the election of 1860 and until after the Inaugural, Lincoln "grossly underestimated the extent of the crisis, and, perhaps, totally misconceived its nature." He erred in considering the crisis "self-liquidating" and misunderstood both the quality and responsiveness of Southern Unionism.[6] Furthermore, although it is debatable whether Lincoln should have known that Sumter would run out of supplies before long or whether he should have made certain that his message to Captain Adams was sent in appropriate form, it seems clear that Lincoln's plan to keep things cool for the time being was very likely doomed to failure. The incongruity between the satisfactions he offered and actual features of the sequent urgency reinforces a basic assessment of his rhetoric: (1) Lincoln seriously underestimated the seriousness of the secession threat; (2) unless it was accompanied by significant changes in the policy of the North and/or the South, rhetoric could not forestall armed hostilities; (3) Lincoln's rhetoric could—and did—arrange circumstances so that when war came the South would appear the aggressor; (4) despite Lincoln's misperceptions of the situation, his rhetorical strategies responded about as well to the impinging constraints as rhetoric could.

Sometimes matching rhetorical satisfactions against the unraveling course of events needs to be supplemented by exploiting the *givens*. In that event, one determines, first, what changes occurred in the givens. Which givens grew more dominant? Less dominant? Which givens, if any, gave way to new ones? What was the role of the new givens? Then, keeping in mind the persuader's rhetorical intent and internalized input, one estimates the degree of congruency between the rhetorical satisfactions offered and the perceived changes in the givens. To show how this works, I return to Calhoun's March 4 speech.

During the decade of the 1850s the first two givens of the sectional crisis remained inflexible and became even more absolute, emotionalizing, and dominant. By 1861 the "uncompromisable" conflict over the morality of slavery and the relation of slavery to national progress had polarized the nation. Northerners became more set in their perceptions that slavery should not expand and that the political strength of the South should be constrained. Conversely, Southerners were equally determined to defend their rights and honor.

Perceptions concerning the third given also intensified. The perceived necessity of establishing and maintaining territorial or state governments in lands acquired from Mexico and in the remaining unorganized lands of the Louisiana Purchase provoked increasingly serious sectional collisions. Both North and South determined to win Kansas—to freedom or to slavery. Disorder in Kansas developed into open warfare. Charles Sumner's inflammatory speech "The Crime Against Kansas" in the Senate was followed by Sumner's being caned at his desk in the Senate chamber. The question of establishing and maintaining territorial or state governments in federal lands lost its practical relevance in 1858 when the people of Kansas rejected statehood under a proposed constitution permitting property in slaves. Slavery was legal in Kansas under the recent Dred Scott decision, but it became virtually nonexistent because of Free Soilers' domination. Nevertheless, antislavery forces, having thus lost "bleeding Kansas" as an issue, focused on an alleged Democratic plot to force slavery on the nation. Ever since Democrats pushed the Kansas–Nebraska Bill through Congress in 1854, radical elements in the North claimed that the slave power had entered upon a program of aggression. This idea gained widespread credence when Lincoln endorsed it in his "House Divided" speech. Although there were no actual territories under contention at this time, the questions of popular sovereignty, territorial governance, and Southern aggression dominated the Lincoln–Douglas debates, Lincoln's Cooper Union speech, and the election of 1860.

Thanks to the unceasing pressure exerted by perceptions of the third given, perceptions of the first two givens intensified during the decade. At the same time perceptions represented by the fourth and fifth givens gradually lost their hold on American minds. Although both North and South in 1850 had some reservations about the political system, both sections accepted that the party system and the normal political process protected their interests and gave expression to individual and sectional grievances. One of the first major indications that a breakdown of the party system was near was the refusal of Northern Whigs and some Democrats to adhere to the tradition of deferring to the South on all matters relating to slavery. By 1854 the Whig Party had become so fractured over the slavery issue that it disappeared and was replaced by the sectional, antislavery Republican Party. For a while the Democratic Party was the only national party, but it became increasingly dominated by Southern interests. In the trauma of the 1860 election, the Democrats split into regular Democrats and Southern Democrats; and former members of the Whig and American parties established the Constitutional Union Party. The Republican candidate, Abraham Lincoln, did not receive a single Southern electoral vote and got less than 40 percent of the popular vote, virtually the same share that Herbert Hoover received in 1932. Even in the states that fought for the Union, Lincoln was outvoted by 100,000 votes. What this meant to Southerners was that most Americans did not approve of slavery's exclusion at the cost of secession and that the political party system and the normal political process did not protect their interests. The fourth given no longer existed.

Although not moribund, perceptions of the fifth given drastically changed from 1850 when they had favored some sort of compromise. The North and South developed unrealistic stereotypes of each other. Perceptions of sameness in political institutions, social traditions, family ties, and so on that had long bonded Americans into a nation were substantially replaced by perceptions in both North and South that the other section represented an alien and hostile culture.

All of this means that without the moderating influence of the fourth and fifth givens, and without the intervention of some new given or givens, armed hostilities became inevitable.

I have argued that in addressing Northern or Southern senators in his speech of March 4 Calhoun had little, if any, persuasive intent, in the conventional sense. If he consciously sought to convert others, he used rhetoric badly. However, I have also suggested that he may have had an implicit persuasive intention: to leave a persuasive call for the South. If his purpose was to serve as prophet, his rhetoric certainly accomplished that, as shown by the congruity between the rhetorical satisfactions he offered and the changes in the givens of the urgency. What he thought would happen did happen. If the South had heeded his advice in 1850, she might well have established her independence. The fact that the South waited ten years to act diminished her chances for success, but it made Calhoun's rhetoric prophetic.

Calhoun's March 4 speech illustrates the point that the ultimate configurational test is how well rhetorical strategies match changes in givens. One should not conclude, however, that only great speeches or treatises are suitable for such analysis. In an earlier chapter I discussed the situation of an endangered family. A clinical psychologist determined that perceptions of five factors or givens had produced a crisis in a family's bonding. By a series of counseling sessions, he attempted to alleviate the crisis. Here we note that if the psychologist followed up the case, he would match the rhetorical strategies he used against the changes that occurred in the givens. He had accepted that he could do nothing about three of the givens (both parents were committed to professional careers; their work and transportation left them little time for family needs; their life style and day-care expenses required that the parents maintain a high income). Instead, he tried to influence the other two givens: he attempted to help the parents and two children reduce their levels of stress and to value their family more. In reviewing what had happened to the family following the therapy sessions, he noted that the first three givens remained unchanged, but the family members were able to handle their tensions somewhat better and they were more strongly committed to make things work out. On this basis, he could conclude that, although the family was still endangered, his strategies had functioned about as well as immediate and unfolding circumstances had permitted.

Changes in Readers/Listeners

In small urgencies, such as that of the endangered family or a committee trying to prepare a report for some other body, the readers/listeners may themselves be the provoking and subsequent urgency. When this is true, as soon as we determine the changes that have occurred in the audience, we have also determined the nature of the sequent flow.

On the other hand, in more complex urgencies like the crisis of 1850, the immediate participants may be but small elements of the total exigential flow. Then, identification and interpretation of changes in the readers/listeners will give only an incomplete understanding of the rhetoric's context and actual or probable consequences. This is true even when critics can apply testing devices before, during, and after a rhetorical event. To a degree they can

measure changes in the persuadees, but testing devices cannot estimate the consequences of those changes. On occasion critics of recent
communications can identify the readers/listeners involved and elicit
from them their recollections of how they were changed during and
after communication. But, once again, the consequences of those
changes have to be found beyond the event and its immediate aftermath. In most situations, particularly when the communication being studied occurred in a fairly distant past, a critic must explore a
wide variety of sources to discover changes in listeners/readers and
the consequences thereof. Such sources usually include voting
records, newspaper accounts, and testimonies found in diaries, journals, letters, and the like. Though fragmentary and subjective, such
data sometimes yield valuable insights even though they rarely provide definitive answers to critics' questions.

For example, from the period immediately after Calhoun's
speech of March 4 one finds very few statements of approbation from
Southern radical senators and even fewer from moderate senators of
North or South. One can discover enough negative testimony, however, to suggest that Calhoun may have lost support among some followers who thought he had gone too far. This conforms pretty much
to one's expectations, inasmuch as we know that even moderate
Southern senators were predisposed to reject his attempt to force the
issue into an ultimate crisis. When one examines changes in Calhoun's readers/listeners over the longer term, however, one finds considerably more evidence available. One can document how each
senator voted on all of the compromise-related measures during the
spring, summer, and early fall of 1850, and one can follow the political activities of most of these senators during part or all of the decade
before the Civil War. Such investigations demonstrate that Calhoun's
denunciations of accommodation were substantially congruent with
the senators' voting record on the compromise bills. Although both
sides were willing to accept ambiguities masking sectional differences, neither Northerners nor Southerners would yield on the uncompromisable moral issue of slavery. As a rule, Northern senators
refused to vote for measures directly supporting slavery and Southern
senators for measures restricting slavery. Calhoun's message, there-

fore, had a much higher degree of congruity with the underlying pre-dispositions of Southern senators than my analysis of immediate changes in the audience seemed to indicate. Thus, a modest modification may be needed in my basic assessment that Calhoun's rhetoric did not meet identification needs of Southerners.

Furthermore, by 1860 the implicit thrust of Calhoun's speech and his rhetorical methods were essentially consonant with the perceptions of most Southern senators who had heard his speech in 1850 as well as with the perceptions of Southerners who had read his speech or had heard about it. Thus, analysis of changes in the audience over ten years reinforces my previous assessment of Calhoun's rhetoric as being prophetic.

Whether urgencies are large or small, subsequent changes in readers and listeners are important elements in the configuration of interrelated forces. Information about such changes help ground rhetorical judgments in the reality of what happened, and, thereby, it often reinforces or modifies basic assessments.

Changes in the Status of the Persuader

The last means of exploiting the sequent stages of exigential flows is to match rhetorical satisfactions offered against changes in the status of the persuaders. For instance, the professional reputations of the presidents of the Big Ten were put on the line following their decision to admit Penn State to the conference. It was widely rumored that the way the presidents conducted the matter represented an attempt to reduce the power of coaches and athletic directors over Big Ten athletics. Without consulting coaches or directors, they issued what seemed an informal invitation to Penn State in December, 1989. When confronted by heated protests, the presidents seemed to waffle on the invitation, but they made the invitation official at a meeting the next June. It is a feature of the Big Ten organization that the presidents of the universities—not the regents or trustees, the faculties, or directors of segments of the universities—are the final arbiters in policy decisions. The presidents thus had full authority to disregard doubts from other quarters, but this means their reputations will be the more affected by future results of their decision to expand the conference. Their reputations will be enhanced if Penn State fulfills its membership obligations well, if athletic scheduling and academic collaboration work out with acceptably few glitches, if revenues are maintained or increased, and if academic cooperation proves visibly constructive. This is the way matching the decision and rhetorical choices of the presidents against resulting changes can yield significant judgments as to how wisely they acted and used rhetoric on this occasion.

An example of how rhetorical choices can damage the subsequent personal and professional status of persuaders is Cotton Mather's apologia *The Wonders of the Invisible World*. In it he tried to legitimize the Salem court in Massachusetts Bay, which in 1692 tried and had executed a score of persons charged with witchcraft. Several girls in the area had suffered violent seizures marked by convulsions and sometimes unconsciousness. These attacks were widely assumed to be caused by demonic possession. During their seizures the girls claimed that specters, or the shapes of certain persons, had come to them, demanding they enter into a compact with the devil. When they refused, the specters beat and kicked them and threw them about, causing their contortions. News of the incursion of the witches soon convulsed New England society. Many accused persons were arrested, and the governor appointed a special court to try them on charges of witchcraft. By the time a score of convicted witches were executed and the jails were overflowing with accused witches, some of them from the most prominent families, an increasing number of leading citizens became alarmed. They feared that the indiscriminate accusations of the girls and the primary use of spectral evidence might have convicted some innocent persons among the guilty. Following considerable public turmoil over the correct way to prosecute the alleged witches, the governor called a halt to the trials and in May 1683 issued a general pardon. In his *Wonders*, Mather attempted to exonerate the court, to justify execution of the witches. In his argument he misread the true nature of his rhetorical-moral problems. From the options available to him, he selected some of the wrong ones, and he applied them in the wrong way to the rhetorical exigency. Instead of proscribing the court's admission of spectral evidence, as both he and his father, Increase Mather, knew he should have done, he responded to class and clerical loyalty. In a jeremiad of sin and affliction he attempted to justify the multiple killings by claiming that a crisis of sin had beset the land and that the social covenant between God and New England had compelled the civil magistrates to root out and repress all sin, especially witches, who were advance agents in the devil's final convulsive assault upon the chosen people.

Perry Miller has claimed that "by gathering the folds" of the national covenant around the court, Mather "fatally soiled it. The consequences were not to be fully realized for several years, but the damage was done." In assessing the long-range effect of Mather's misjudgment, Miller went so far as to say that "the onus of error lay heavy upon the land; realization of it slowly but irresistibly ate into the New England conscience. For a long time dismay did not translate itself into a disbelief in witchcraft or into anticlericalism, but it rapidly became an unassuageable grief. . . . Out of sorrow and chagrin, out of dread, was born a new love for the land which had been desecrated, but somehow also consecrated, by the blood of innocents."[7] Although some historians find Miller's assessments too sweepingly grim, it is clear that by his rhetorical choices Mather helped undermine the entire Puritan establishment, rendered Puritan pretentions ridiculous to succeeding generations, and reduced his personal stature in his time and through history.

In the case of Calhoun, we have already seen that his personal status may have suffered somewhat immediately after his March 4 speech but that a decade after his death he was considered the patron saint of secession by those whom he respected most and wanted most to protect. His choices of strategies were not well suited to persuading his reading/listening audience in 1850, but they were admirably suited to the configuration of forces in 1860–1861.

What happens during the sequent stage of exigential flows is important to a configured understanding of communication. The degree of congruence between rhetorical satisfactions offered and subsequent changes in urgencies, readers/listeners, and status of persuaders informs us about the consequences of rhetoric. It enables us to reinforce or modify basic assessments of rhetoric we have previously made, and it completes the dynamic Gestalt of configurational inter-relatedness.

What Might Have Been: Rhetorical Strategies Used versus Those Not Chosen

There are always more than one or two ways of trying to persuade in a given set of circumstances. A function of any critic should be to consider the wisdom of persuaders' choices from among their viable options. The object is not simply to discover better strategies than were used; rather, it is to determine whether, under all the circumstances, the persuaders could have made better choices. One asks such questions as the following: Is it reasonable to expect that a different rhetorical intention might have been adopted in this case? Was there a viable basic thrust that would have matched better the readiness of persuadees to be influenced and consequently would have done more to lead them to influence the urgency? Could changes in the rhetorical satisfactions of substance, disposition, language, and paralanguage have better induced persuasive identification? What changes, if any, would have had greater congruence with what happened subsequently—to the urgency, to the readers/listeners, to the status of the persuaders? When one has answered such questions, one acquires grounds on which to reinforce or modify earlier basic assessments.

It was philosophically possible, of course, for Calhoun to have chosen a rhetorical intent for his March 4 speech that would have had greater congruity with the potentialities in the situation. Theoretically the crusty old slaveholder could have reversed his customary hard-line attack upon the North and sought compromise, or even the abolition of slavery. But I have explained why any rhetorical purposes other than the ones he chose would have been unrealistically alien to his self-system. Should Calhoun have selected a different basic thrust to carry out his intent? Calhoun pronounced what he thought were minimum requirements to ensure the security of slavery and the Union. He was not interested in compromise. In his view the South had nothing to compromise. Delay in gaining absolute guarantees would gravely hurt the South. His basic thrust was vintage Calhoun. He wouldn't have been Calhoun if he had done differently.

Could Calhoun have improved the capacity of his substance, disposition, language, and paralanguage to promote identification and reinforcement? There is no doubt that his satisfactions could have been better chosen for this purpose. But, based on what I know about his self-system, his previous rhetorical practices, and his despair over the crisis, I don't believe that this was something that he could have done. From a practical standpoint, I think it unlikely that Calhoun would depart from his habitual stance of proclaiming what he thought must be done to save the South and the Union.

If I am correct in saying that Calhoun could not change his "rhetorical spots" and still be Calhoun, does this make his rhetoric any wiser? If his purpose in his March 4 speech was to persuade, he was pigheaded in attempting to coerce instead of trying to win over the opposition; he was a nonpersuasive speaker who used his satisfactions unpersuasively. If his intention was to pronounce or proclaim, what he said in the speech matched that intent, but one would criticize this intent as being unwise. If we speculate that Calhoun may have had a desire to prophesy, to issue a call to history, his speech matched this purpose well, but under the circumstances such a purpose was puerile. In sum, an examination of unchosen strategies reinforces the basic assessment that Calhoun did not use rhetoric wisely.

Although our basic assessments of Calhoun's rhetoric are unchanged, we find a very different situation if we return to Cotton Mather's *The Wonders of the Invisible World*. If Cotton Mather was sincere in believing in witches and in claiming that the incursion of the witches was God's way of punishing Massachusetts for its sins, he was dishonest to his beliefs in defending the Salem court's use of spectral evidence. In this respect at least, one can argue that Cotton Mather reasonably could have chosen different rhetorical strategies that would have served his cause better.

At this point we can only speculate, as some critics are doing, that the presidents of the Big Ten might have used different strategies in admitting Penn State. Would the presidents have been wiser to decide that there was no provoking urgency that required an expansion of the Big Ten? Although they had no formal obligation to do so, should they have consulted others before extending their informal invitation to Penn State? Should they have chosen not to go ahead with the formal invitation when their initial invitation encountered opposition? Should they have decided against placing a moratorium on further expansion of the conference for four years? Could the presidents have handled better the interpersonal and the public relations aspects of the merger? Should they have made clearer to the public that their action had wider, nonathletic involvements? The basic assessment of the presidents' rhetoric needs to be reinforced or modified according to the extent that there were choices realistically available to them that would have served their purposes better.

By examining the congruence of rhetorical satisfactions with subsequent changes in the exigential flow and by speculating on whether the persuaders could have made better rhetorical choices, we complete the configurational examination of rhetoric. By using these supplementing means to reinforce or modify basic assessments, we gain the fullest possible understanding of what was, what was possible, and what was the consequent wisdom of the persuaders.

Notes

Chapter One

1. Karlyn Kohrs Campbell, *Critiques of Contemporary Rhetoric* (Belmont, CA, 1972), 33.
2. Richard M. Weaver, *The Ethics of Rhetoric* (Chicago, 1953), 83.
3. Herbert W. Simons and Aram A. Aghazarian, eds., *Form, Genre, and the Study of Political Discourse* (Columbia, SC, 1986), 301.

Chapter Two

1. Paul Meadows, "The Dialectic of the Situation: Some Notes on Situational Psychology," *Philosophy and Phenomenological Research* 5 (1944–45): 354–64.
2. Lloyd F. Bitzer, "The Rhetorical Situation," *Philosophy and Rhetoric* (Jan. 1968): 1–14, and "Functional Communication: A Situational Perspective," in *Rhetoric in Transition: Studies in the Nature and Uses of Rhetoric*, ed. Eugene E. White (University Park, PA, 1980), 21–38.
3. Richard M. Weaver, *Visions of Order: The Cultural Crisis of Our Time* (Baton Rouge, 1964).
4. Kenneth Burke, *Language as Symbolic Action* (Berkeley, CA, 1968), 164.
5. Richard M. Weaver, *The Ethics of Rhetoric* (Chicago, 1953) and *Visions of Order; Language Is Sermonic: Richard Weaver on the Nature of Rhetoric*, ed. Richard L. Johannesen, Rennard Strickland, and Ralph T. Eubanks (Baton Rouge, 1970).
6. Karl R. Wallace, "Rhetoric and Advising," *The Southern Speech Journal* (Summer 1964): 279–87.
7. Wallace, "The Substance of Rhetoric: Good Reasons," *The Quarterly Journal of Speech* (Oct. 1963): 239–49.
8. Kenneth Burke, *A Rhetoric of Motives* (New York, 1955), 55–56.
9. I think that my subsequent development of the rhetorical urgency of 1850 supports this point of view against the traditional emphasis reiterated by Kenneth M. Stampp that "1857 was probably the year when the North and South reached the political point of no return," (Stampp, *America in 1857: A Nation on the Brink* [New York, 1990], viii).

289

Chapter Three

1. I posit that a distinction exists between perceiving and symbolizing—perception and thought may precede symbolic expression and action—and that commitment, value, and interest are separable from symbolization. The historical study I propose does not strive after "objective anthropomorphism," nor does it seek the kind of "symbolic reconstruction" that transcends the data. The end of such study is not principally intellectual or cultural history. Although the approach I advance could yield characterizations of the symbolic significance of eras, the level of historical analysis and interpretation that I argue for here is more objective and less era-aimed. Therefore my argument differs from that of Ernst Cassirer and Susanne Langer. For similarities that may exist between my notion of history and the thinking of Cassirer, a distinguished philosopher of culture, and of Wilhelm Wundt and Franz Brentano, precursors of modern psychology, the reader is directed to these works: Cassirer, *An Essay on Man* (New Haven, 1944), "Fundamental Forms and Tendencies of Historical Knowledge," in *The Problem of Knowledge* (New Haven, 1950), 217–325, and *The Logic of the Humanities* (New Haven, 1961); Wundt, *Elements of Folk Psychology*, rev. ed. (London, 1921); Brentano, *Psychology from an Empirical Standpoint*, ed. Oskar Kraus, English ed., ed. Linda L. McAlister (1874; New York, 1973); Gary Cronkhite, "Perception and Meaning," in *Handbook of Rhetorical and Communication Theory*, ed. Carroll C. Arnold and John Waite Bowers (Boston, 1984), 51–229.

2. David Krech and Richard S. Crutchfield, *Theory and Problems of Social Psychology* (New York, 1948), 94.

3. I am following here conventional thinking concerning balance, consonance, and stabilization. For a somewhat different orientation, see James J. Gibson, *The Senses Considered as Perceptual Systems* (Boston, 1966). Gibson emphasizes that perception is the pickup of information over time, so that what the organism extracts from the ever-changing ambient array are invariants that are ecologically relevant. He argues that perception so defined does not involve memory or inference, or the "piecing together" of meanings from fragmentary snippets of information. But his point is similar to mine in that he makes perception a historical process that is meaningful only over time.

4. It is the past that largely determines the present *and* the future, not the opposite. Among the helpful and interesting comments that cognitive psychologist Walter B. Weimer, Pennsylvania State University, made to me after reading an early version of this chapter was that "behaviorism *may* have arisen from the misunderstanding of this simple point."

5. For neurophysiological support of the position that the nervous system is an instrument of historical classification, see Friedrich August von

Hayek, *The Sensory Order: An Inquiry into the Foundations of Theoretical Psychology* (1952; rpt. Chicago, 1976); Ronald Weiss, "The Problem of Psychological Organization: A Bioperational Approach to Brain Function" (Ph.D. Diss., Pennsylvania State University, 1977).

6. See *Selected Writings of Edward Sapir in Language, Culture, and Personality*, ed. David G. Mandelbaum (Berkeley, 1949); John B. Carroll, ed., *Language, Thought, and Reality: Selected Writings of Benjamin Lee Whorf* (1956; rpt. Cambridge, MA, 1967), 213.

7. "All thought models reality, not just 'scientific thought,'" (Walter B. Weimer, "The Psychology of Inference and Expectation: Some Preliminary Remarks," in *Induction, Probability, and Confirmation*, Minnesota Studies in the Philosophy of Science 6, ed. Grover Maxwell and Robert M. Anderson, Jr. [Minneapolis, 1975], esp. 484–85). As Weimer points out, his view that "there may be no satisfactory demarcation of science from its rivals on *methodological grounds*" is shared by Thomas S. Kuhn in his "Postscript—1969," in *The Structure of Scientific Revolutions*, 2nd ed. (Chicago, 1970), 174–210, and in his "Reflections on My Critics," in *Criticism and the Growth of Knowledge*, ed. Imre Lakatos and Alan Musgrave (Cambridge, 1970), 231–78.

8. What I have said so far is that we perceive and we order in all experiencing and that perception/ordering is *ongoing*. There is no such thing as a static or fixed perception. These are central doctrines of Gestalt psychology as represented by Kurt Koffka, Wilhelm Wundt, and Franz Brentano. Much of what they believed remains valid, especially the postulate that the "reality" of any event lies in the past, present, and future historical development—or the dynamic Gestalt—of which the event is an integral part. See Koffka, *Principles of Gestalt Psychology* (New York, 1935); Wundt, *Elements of Folk Psychology*; and Brentano, *Psychology from an Empirical Standpoint*.

9. This tension-evoking juncture is not necessarily "an imperfection, . . . a defect, an obstacle, something to be corrected," as Lloyd F. Bitzer asserts (Bitzer, "Functional Communication: A Situational Perspective," in *Rhetoric in Transition: Studies in the Nature and Uses of Rhetoric*, ed. Eugene E. White [University Park, PA, 1980], 26). On the contrary, the juncture may even represent a joyous state of affairs. For instance, a fraternal organization holds a dinner to celebrate the final payment of the mortgage on its lodge; a sports hero returns home to be feted at civic gatherings; a newly elected candidate entertains his campaign workers at a barbecue.

10. The alleged misadventures of the Reagan administration during this period included a "wobbly initial response" to the Soviet arrest of American journalist Nicholas Daniloff and the later "exchange" of Daniloff for a Soviet spy already in U.S. custody; an attempt to spread erroneous

information about U.S. intentions, in order to disturb the Libyan government; President Reagan's "fumbling" at the summit meeting at Reykjavik, leading to Chief of Staff Donald Regan's boast that he had had to lead a shovel brigade to clean up after the President's parade; the attempt to clandestinely supply Contra forces in Nicaragua by planes stationed in El Salvador, resulting in the shooting down of a supply plane over Nicaragua, the capture of Eugene Hasenfus, and the death of two other Americans.

Chapter Four

1. Bower Aly, *The Rhetoric of Alexander Hamilton* (New York, 1941), 196; Clarence Streit, *Freedom and Union* (July–August, 1957): 1.
2. Jackson Turner Main, *The Antifederalists: Critics of the Constitution, 1781–1788* (Chapel Hill, 1961), esp. 238; Linda G. De Pauw, *The Eleventh Pillar* (Ithaca, 1966), esp. 253; Clinton Rossiter, *1787 The Grand Convention* (New York, 1966), 293–94.
3. Robin Brooks, "Alexander Hamilton, Melancton Smith, and the Ratification of the Constitution in New York," *The William and Mary Quarterly*, Third Series (July 1967): 339–58.
4. Hiller B. Zobel and L. Kinvin Wroth, *Legal Papers of John Adams* (New York, 1968), 3 vols.; Zobel, *The Boston Massacre* (New York, 1970).
5. Peter Shaw, *The Character of John Adams* (Chapel Hill, 1976), 78.
6. Kenneth M. Stampp, *And the War Came: The North and the Secession Crisis, 1860–1861* (Baton Rouge, 1950), 280–86; Charles W. Ramsdell, "Lincoln and Fort Sumter," *Journal of Southern History* (Aug. 1937): 259–88.
7. Richard N. Current, *The Lincoln Nobody Knows* (New York, 1958), chs. 4, 5.
8. Roy P. Basler, ed., *The Collected Works of Abraham Lincoln* (New Brunswick, NJ, 1953), 4: 421–41. David M. Potter discusses Lincoln's intentions in his First Inaugural Address in *Lincoln and His Party in the Secession Crisis* (New Haven, 1962), xi–xxxii, 315–75.
9. Most historians seem content with this interpretation. See, e.g., James M. McPherson, *Battle Cry of Freedom: The Civil War Era* (New York, 1988), 264.

Chapter Five

1. James David Barber, *The Presidential Character: Predicting Performance in the White House* (Englewood Cliffs, NJ, 1972), v–vi.
2. David Abrahamsen, *Nixon vs. Nixon: An Emotional Tragedy* (New York, 1977). In contrast, Stephen E. Ambrose does not draw psychoanalytic

conclusions from Nixon's childhood in his standard biography: *Nixon: The Education of a Politician, 1913–1962* (New York, 1987).

3. George Cheney, *Rhetoric in an Organizational Society: Managing Multiple Identities* (Columbia, SC, 1991).

4. See William J. Cooper, Jr., *The South and the Politics of Slavery, 1828–1856* (Baton Rouge, 1978).

5. J. Franklin Jameson, ed., *Correspondence of John C. Calhoun*, Vol. 2, The Fourth Annual Report of the Historical Manuscripts Commission of the American Historical Association (Washington, 1900), 783.

6. Ibid., 776, 779, 781.

7. James M. McPherson, *Battle Cry of Freedom: The Civil War Era* (New York, 1988), 69, 71, 73. According to Richard N. Current, the business community in Boston and New York had swung to compromise (*Daniel Webster and the Rise of National Conservatism* [Boston, 1955], 159, 160, 192). Don E. Fehrenbacher has pointed out, however, that "a sizeable part of the electorate in South Carolina, Georgia, Alabama, and Mississippi continued to lean toward disunion even after the Compromise had been passed" (*The South and Three Sectional Crises* [Baton Rouge, 1980], 44, 75). Also see Cooper, *The South and the Politics of Slavery*, ch. 8.

8. Eugene E. White, "Solomon Stoddard's Theories of Persuasion," *Speech Monographs* (Nov. 1962): 235–59 and "Cotton Mather's *Manuductio Ad Ministerium*," *The Quarterly Journal of Speech* (Oct. 1963): 308–19.

9. See Thomas W. Benson, "Implicit Communication Theory in Campaign Coverage," in *Television Coverage of the 1980 Presidential Campaign*, ed. William Adams (Norwood, NJ, 1983), 101–14.

10. Charleston *Mercury*, Apr. 5, 1850.

11. *Correspondence of John C. Calhoun*, 780–81.

12. Ibid., 782–83.

13. Charles M. Wiltse, *John C. Calhoun, Sectionalist: 1840–1850* (New York, 1951), 459.

14. Gerald M. Capers, *John C. Calhoun, Opportunist: A Re-appraisal* (Gainesville, FL, 1960), 251; Wiltse, *John C. Calhoun, Sectionalist: 1840–1850*, 466–67.

15. New York *Herald*, May 3, 1850.

16. Maurice G. Baxter, *One and Inseparable: Daniel Webster and the Union* (Cambridge, MA, 1984), 412. Together with Merrill D. Peterson in *The Great Triumvirate: Webster, Clay, and Calhoun* (New York, 1987), John Niven, in *John C. Calhoun and the Price of Union* (Baton Rouge, 1988), Irving H. Bartlett in *Daniel Webster* (New York, 1978), and Robert F. Dalzell, Jr., in *Daniel Webster and the Trial of American Nationalism, 1843–1852* (Boston, 1973), Baxter fails specifically to mention the alleged meeting between Webster and Calhoun on March 5; none suggests that a secret

agreement existed between the two men. Besides Baxter, only Peterson of the historians mentioned above specifically mentions the March 2 meeting, and he devotes only one short sentence to it.

17. Photostat, Henry W. Conner Papers, Library of Congress.

18. *Correspondence of John C. Calhoun*, 784.

19. New York *Herald*, Mar. 6 and 7, 1850. Similar reports appeared in other newspapers, such as the Charleston *Courier*, Mar. 8, 1850; Charleston *Mercury*, Mar. 9, 1850; Philadelphia *Public Ledger*, Mar. 6, 1850; and Richmond *Inquirer*, Mar. 8, 1850. Also see Henry S. Foote, *War of the Rebellion; or, Scylla and Charbydis* (New York, 1866), 140–43.

20. Charleston *Mercury*, Apr. 5, 1850.

21. Photostat, Henry W. Conner Papers, Library of Congress.

22. Virginia Mason, ed., *Public Life and Diplomatic Correspondence of James M. Mason* (Roanoke, VA, 1903), 72, 73.

23. An editorial in the New York *Herald*, Jan. 14, 1859, states that, although "he entertained little hope," Calhoun sought to "obtain justice in the Union . . . on terms that he believed to be just and reasonable . . . before any steps were taken to dissolve it." It seems clear that the method Calhoun used to "obtain justice" was to declare "truth" rather than to attempt to win over the opposition through identification—or, that is, to create as much congruence as possible between what he had to say and the constraints within which his listeners/readers would make their decisions.

Chapter Six

1. Lloyd F. Bitzer's position is that rhetoric is a response to some problem that needs correcting ("The Rhetorical Situation," *Philosophy and Rhetoric* [Jan. 1968]: 1–14 and "Functional Communication: A Situational Perspective," in *Rhetoric in Transition: Studies in the Nature and Uses of Rhetoric*, ed. Eugene E. White [University Park, PA, 1980], 21–38).

2. David Brion Davis, *The Problem of Slavery in Western Culture* (Ithaca, 1966), *The Problem of Slavery in the Age of Revolution, 1770–1823* (Ithaca, 1975), and *Slavery and Human Progress* (New York, 1984).

3. David L. Swanson, "Political Information, Influence, and Judgment in the 1972 Presidential Campaign," *Quarterly Journal of Speech* (Apr. 1973): 130–42.

Chapter Seven

1. See, e.g., *The Wall and the Garden*, ed. A. W. Plumstead, (Minneapolis, 1968).

2. Ronald H. Carpenter and Robert V. Seltzer, "Situational Style and the Rotunda Eulogies," *Central States Speech Journal* (Spring 1971): 11–15.

3. Michael F. Holt, *The Political Crisis of the 1850s* (New York, 1978).

4. Douglas P. Starr, "Secession Speeches of Four Deep South Governors Who Would Rather Fight than Switch," *Southern Speech Communication Journal* (Winter 1972): 131–41.

5. Robert W. Norton, "The Rhetorical Situation Is the Message: Muskie's Election Eve Television Broadcast," *Central States Speech Journal* (Fall 1971): 171–78.

6. According to David Brion Davis, "It was only in the eighteenth and nineteenth centuries that views of slavery as a retrograde institution began to gain far-reaching acceptance" (*Slavery and Human Progress* [New York, 1984], esp. xiii–xix). Davis also insists that historians like Winthrop D. Jordan fundamentally err in claiming that the ideology of the American Revolution "presented a direct challenge to Negro slavery." Such historians, Davis believes, "confuse liberal principles with antislavery commitments." See Davis, *The Problem of Slavery in the Age of Revolution 1770–1823* (Ithaca, 1975), 48, 255, 256, 274, 286, 287, 295, 312, 317, 552; Winthrop D. Jordan, *White Over Black: American Attitudes Toward the Negro, 1550–1812* (1968; New York, 1977), ch. 7. See also Donald L. Robinson, *Slavery in the Structure of American Politics, 1765–1820* (New York, 1971); Edmund S. Morgan, "Slavery and Freedom: The American Paradox," *The Journal of American History* (June 1972): 5–29; Eric Foner and Olivia Mahoney, *A House Divided: America in the Age of Lincoln* (New York, 1990), ch. 1.

7. Don E. Fehrenbacher, *The South and Three Sectional Crises* (Baton Rouge, 1980), 23.

8. Glover Moore, *The Missouri Controversy, 1819–1821* (Lexington, KY, 1953), 342; David Brion Davis, *The Problem of Slavery in the Age of Revolution*, esp. 11.

9. William W. Freehling, *Prelude to Civil War: The Nullification Controversy in South Carolina, 1816–1836* (New York, 1966) and *The Road to Disunion: Sessionists at Bay, 1776–1854* (New York, 1990), 211–86.

10. Samuel Flagg Bemis, *John Quincy Adams and the Union* (New York, 1956), 326–51, 420–22, 424–39, 446–48.

11. David M. Potter, *The Impending Crisis, 1848–1861* (New York, 1976), 37–41, 49, 454–55; Potter's book is the best single source for the sectional controversy leading to the Civil War. See also Fehrenbacher, *The South and Three Sectional Crises*, 26–27.

12. See Don E. Fehrenbacher, *The Dred Scott Case: Its Significance in American Law and Politics* (New York, 1978); G. Edward White, *The American Judicial Tradition* (New York, 1976), 64–83.

13. Potter, *The Impending Crisis*, 116–17. William J. Cooper points out that "Southerners equated their right to carry slavery into the territories with the existence of slavery itself" (*The South and the Politics of Slavery, 1828–1856* [Baton Rouge, 1978], 64–65 and ch. 7). See also Chaplain W. Morrison, *Democratic Politics and Sectionalism: The Wilmot Proviso Controversy* (Chapel Hill, 1967); Eric Foner, "The Wilmot Proviso Revisited," *Journal of American History* (Sept. 1969): 262–79; Michael F. Holt, *The Political Crisis of the 1850s*.

14. The best account of the congressional effort to resolve the sectional conflict in 1850 is Holman Hamilton, *Prologue to Conflict: The Crisis and Compromise of 1850* (Lexington, KY, 1964).

15. See, e.g., Lloyd F. Bitzer, "Rhetoric and Public Knowledge," in *Rhetoric, Philosophy, and Literature: An Exploration*, ed. Don M. Burks (West Lafayette, IN, 1978), 67–95; and Gerard A. Hauser, "Administrative Rhetoric and Public Opinion: Discussing the Iranian Hostages in the Public Sphere," in *American Rhetoric: Context and Criticism*, ed. Thomas W. Benson (Carbondale, IL, 1989), 323–83.

16. Cooper says that "even the orthodox Calhounites thought in terms of an ultimatum not secession" (*The South and the Politics of Slavery*, esp. ch. 8); Fehrenbacher, *The South and Three Sectional Crises*, 44. See also Potter, *The Impending Crisis*, ch. 3, 4, 5; Carl N. Degler, *The Other South: Southern Dissenters in the Nineteenth Century* (New York, 1974); Daniel Walker Howe, *The Political Culture of the American Whigs* (Chicago, 1979); David Donald, *Charles Sumner and the Coming of the Civil War* (New York, 1960), 130–204; Kinley J. Brauer, *Cotton Versus Conscience: Massachusetts Whig Politics and Southwestern Expansion, 1843–1848* (Lexington, KY, 1967); Joel H. Silbey, *The Shrine of Party: Congressional Voting Behavior, 1841–1852* (Pittsburgh, 1967); Thomas B. Alexander, *Sectional Stress and Party Strength: A Study of Roll-Call Voting Patterns in the United States House of Representatives, 1836–1860* (Nashville, 1967).

17. Joseph G. Raybach, *Free Soil: The Election of 1848* (Lexington, KY, 1970), esp. ch. 17; also Robert W. Johannsen, *Stephen A. Douglas* (New York, 1973), 206–82.

Chapter Eight

1. The historical literature concerning the various topics covered in Chapter 8 are voluminous. To avoid overburdening the reader with historical citations I have in general clustered references at the end of the section to which they pertain and have included only those that I have referred to directly and/or those that represent especially valuable supplementing sources for the interested reader. George E. Mowry, *The Era of Theodore Roosevelt and the Birth of Modern America 1900–1912* (New York, 1958), 36–37.

2. David M. Potter, *The Impending Crisis, 1848–1861* (New York, 1976), 40. Eric Foner and Olivia Mahoney, *A House Divided: America in the Age of Lincoln* (New York, 1990), 40–41; Ronald G. Walters, *American Reformers 1815–1860* (New York, 1978).

3. Potter, *The Impending Crisis*, esp. 36–37; C. Vann Woodward, *The Burden of Southern History* (New York, 1960) and *American Counterpoint: Slavery and Racism in the North–South Dialogue* (Boston, 1971), 140–62; George M. Fredrickson, *The Black Image in the White Mind: The Debate on Afro-American Character and Destiny, 1817–1914* (New York, 1971); Winthrop D. Jordan, *White Over Black: American Attitudes Toward the Negro, 1550–1812* (New York, 1968).

4. Potter, *The Impending Crisis*, ch. 1 and *The South and the Sectional Conflict* (Baton Rouge, 1968), ch. 3; Karl W. Deutsch, *Nationalism and Social Communication: An Inquiry into the Foundations of Nationality*, 2nd ed. (New York, 1953); Avery O. Craven, *The Growth of Southern Nationalism, 1848–1861* (Baton Rouge, 1953); Hans Kohn, *The Idea of Nationalism* (New York, 1944) and *American Nationalism* (New York, 1957); Louis L. Snyder, *The Meaning of Nationalism* (New Brunswick, NJ, 1954); Paul C. Nagel, *One Nation Indivisible: The Union in American Thought, 1776–1861* (New York, 1961); Emory M. Thomas, *The Confederate Nation 1861–1865* (New York, 1979), 17–119.

5. See, e.g., Roy F. Nichols, *The Stakes of Power, 1845–1877* (New York, 1961), vi.

6. Avery O. Craven, *Civil War in the Making, 1815–1860* (Baton Rouge, 1968), 77.

7. Carl F. Kaestle, *Pillars of the Republic: Common Schools and American Society, 1780–1860* (New York, 1983).

8. Despite similarities between North and South, Potter believed that folk culture is a "possible key to Southernism": *The Impending Crisis*, 12, and "The Enigma of the South," in his *The South and the Sectional Conflict*, 3–16. In his pioneer work, *Plain Folk of the Old South* (Baton Rouge, 1949), Frank L. Owsley claimed that "appearance, the indefinable qualities of personality, and . . . manners and customs" distinguished Southerners "from the inhabitants of the other sections of the United States, and in this way strengthened their sense of kinship." Because of their sense of kinship, both the plain people and the Southern aristocracy "were folkish in their manners and customs . . . to a degree second only to the Highland Scots of an earlier time." In his *Cracker Culture: Celtic Ways in the Old South* (Tuscaloosa, 1988), Grady McWhiney goes beyond Owsley in pushing "the Celtic interpretation of Southern history." With Perry D. Jamieson, McWhiney even claims that a major reason the South lost the Civil War was that her Celtic-inspired culture "rejected careful calculation and patience" in military planning. (*Attack and Die: Civil War*

Military Tactics and the Southern Heritage [University, AL, 1982]). See also William J. Cooper, Jr., *The South and the Politics of Slavery, 1828–1856* (Baton Rouge, 1978), esp. 69–74; Thomas, *The Confederate Nation, 1861–1865*, 9–10.

9. Potter, *The Impending Crisis*, 11; Thomas, *The Confederate Nation*, 5–9; Eugene D. Genovese, *Roll, Jordan, Roll: The World the Slaves Made* (New York, 1974) and *The World the Slaveholders Made* (New York, 1969); James Oakes, *The Ruling Race: A History of American Slaveholders* (New York, 1982); John W. Blassingame, *The Slave Community: Plantation Life in the Antebellum South*, rev. ed. (New York, 1979); Kenneth M. Stampp, *The Peculiar Institution: Slavery in the Ante-bellum South* (New York, 1956); Staughton Lynd, *Class Conflict, Slavery, and the United States Constitution* (Indianapolis, 1967).

10. Clement Eaton, *The Mind of the Old South*, rev. ed. (Baton Rouge, 1967), 200–223; Genovese, *Roll, Jordan, Roll*.

11. For representative sources see Sean Wilentz, *Chants Democratic: New York City and the Rise of the American Working Class, 1789–1850* (New York, 1984); Jonathan Prude, *The Coming of Industrial Order: Town and Factory Life in Rural Massachusetts, 1810–1860* (New York, 1983); Catherine Clinton, *The Plantation Mistress: Woman's World in the Old South* (New York, 1982).

12. Holman Hamilton, *Prologue to Conflict: The Crisis and Compromise of 1850* (Lexington, KY, 1964), esp. 5; Eric Foner, *Free Soil, Free Labor, Free Men: The Ideology of the Republican Party Before the Civil War* (New York, 1970), 41; Thomas, *The Confederate Nation 1861–1865*, ch. 1; Eugene D. Genovese, *The Political Economy of Slavery: Studies in the Economy and Society of the Slave South*, 2nd ed. (Middletown, CT, 1989); Paul Wallace Gates, *The Farmers' Age: Agriculture 1815–1860* (New York, 1960); Thomas C. Cochran, *Frontiers of Change: Early Industrialism in America* (New York, 1981); Gavin Wright, *The Political Economy of the Cotton South* (New York, 1978); Robert W. Fogel and Stanley L. Engerman, *Time on the Cross: The Economics of American Negro Slavery* (Boston, 1974); Oakes, *The Ruling Race*, esp. 39.

13. Gordon Leff, *History and Social Theory* (Garden City, NY, 1971), 141.

14. Milton Rokeach, *Beliefs, Attitudes, and Values: A Theory of Organization and Change* (San Francisco, 1976), 123–24.

15. Eric Foner, *Free Soil, Free Labor, Free Men: The Ideology of the Republican Party Before the Civil War*, 4–5 and *Politics and Ideology in the Age of the Civil War* (New York, 1980).

16. Eugene E. White, *Puritan Rhetoric: The Issue of Emotion in Religion* (Carbondale, IL, 1972), 3–64.

17. Clinton Rossiter, *The Political Thought of the American Revolution* (New York, 1963), 215–28.

18. Nichols, *The Stakes of Power*, esp. vi and *The Disruption of American Democracy* (1948, New York, 1962); Thomas, *The Confederate Nation*, esp. 4; Potter, *The South and the Sectional Conflict*, ch. 3; Foner, *Politics and Ideology in the Age of the Civil War*, esp. 34–53, and *Free Soil, Free Labor, Free Men*; Craven, *The Growth of Southern Nationalism*; Cooper, *The South and the Politics of Slavery*, 63–65; Carl N. Degler, *The Other South: Southern Dissenters in the Nineteenth Century* (New York, 1974), esp. 1–123.

19. Ralph David Abernathy, *And the Walls Came Tumbling Down: An Autobiography* (New York, 1989).

Chapter Nine

1. Franklin L. Baumer, *Modern European Thought* (New York, 1977), 20.
2. David A. Stockman, *The Triumph of Politics* (New York, 1986).

Chapter Ten

1. Carl J. Friedrich and Robert G. McCloskey, *From the Declaration of Independence to the Constitution* (Indianapolis, 1954), xxxv. Also see Thomas Wendel, ed., *Thomas Paine's Common Sense: The Call to Independence* (Woodbury, NY, 1975).
2. Eugene E. White, "George Whitefield," in *American Orators Before 1900*, ed. Bernard K. Duffy and Halford R. Ryan (New York, 1987), 427–36.

Chapter Eleven

1. Carroll C. Arnold, "Early Constitutional Rhetoric in Pennsylvania," in *American Rhetoric: Context and Criticism*, ed. Thomas W. Benson (Carbondale, IL, 1989), 131–200.

Chapter Twelve

1. Gerald R. Miller, Michael Burgoon, and Judee K. Burgoon, "The Functions of Human Communication in Changing Attitudes and Gaining Compliance," in *Handbook of Rhetorical and Communication Theory*, ed. Carroll C. Arnold and John Waite Bowers (Boston, 1984), 456.
2. Kenneth Burke, *A Rhetoric of Motives* (New York, 1955), 19–31, 35–37, 45–46, 55–59.
3. Milton Rokeach, *The Nature of Human Values* (New York, 1973), 6–7 and *Beliefs, Attitudes, and Values* (San Francisco, 1976), 113.
4. See, e.g., L. L. Thurstone and E. J. Chave, *The Measurement of Attitude* (Chicago, 1929).
5. B. F. Skinner, *Beyond Freedom and Dignity* (New York, 1972), 101–26.

6. See Douglas Ehninger and Gerard A. Hauser, "Communication of Values," 720–45, and Roderick P. Hart, "The Functions of Human Communication in the Maintenance of Public Values," 749–81, in *Handbook of Rhetorical and Communication Theory*, ed. Arnold and Bowers.

7. Milton Rokeach, "From Individual to Institutional Values: With Special Reference to the Values of Science," in *Understanding Human Values*, ed. Rokeach (New York, 1979), 48.

8. Robin M. Williams, Jr., "Change and Stability in Values and Value Systems: A Sociological Perspective," in *Understanding Human Values*, ed. Rokeach, 21.

9. Rokeach, *The Nature of Human Values*, 5, 11–25.

10. Miller, Burgoon, and Burgoon, "The Functions of Human Communication in Changing Attitudes and Gaining Compliance," 406–09.

11. Rokeach, *The Nature of Human Values*, 217.

Chapter Thirteen

1. New York *Times*, July 28, 1974.

2. These values were subjectively determined, based on extensive study of the crisis of 1850.

3. See, e.g., Emory Elliott, *Power and the Pulpit in Puritan New England* (Princeton, 1975), esp. 30–31.

4. Stanley L. Jones, *The Presidential Election of 1896* (Madison, WI, 1964), 212–43; Louis W. Koenig, *Bryan* (New York, 1971), 155–208.

5. Robert T. Oliver and Eugene E. White, eds., *Selected Speeches from American History* (Boston, 1966), 209.

6. L. Raymond Camp, "The Senate Debates on the Treaty of Paris of 1898" (Ph.D. Diss., Pennsylvania State University, 1969), 213–16.

7. Glyndon G. Van Deusen, *The Life of Henry Clay* (Boston, 1937), 191.

Chapter Fourteen

1. Lane Cooper, *The Rhetoric of Aristotle* (New York, 1932), 9.

2. See, e.g., Carroll C. Arnold and Kenneth D. Frandsen, "Conceptions of Rhetoric and Communication," 10, 14–15, 18–19, and Gerald R. Miller, Michael Burgoon, and Judee K. Burgoon, "The Functions of Human Communication in Changing Attitudes and Gaining Compliance," 401, in *Handbook of Rhetorical and Communication Theory*, ed. Carroll C. Arnold and John Waite Bowers, (Boston, 1984).

Chapter Fifteen

1. J. B. Black, *The Reign of Elizabeth, 1558–1603* (Oxford, 1959), 201–02.

2. Jacob E. Cooke, *The Federalist* (Middletown, CT, 1961), ix.
3. Clinton Rossiter, *The Federalist Papers* (New York, 1961), vii.
4. David M. Potter, *Lincoln and His Party in the Secession Crisis* (New Haven, 1962), 315–75. Also, Roy P. Basler, ed., *The Collected Works of Abraham Lincoln* (New Brunswick, NJ, 1953), 4: 254, 262–71.
5. Basler, *The Collected Works of Abraham Lincoln*, 4: 424.
6. Potter, *Lincoln and His Party in the Secession Crisis*, 9–19, 315–18, and *The Impending Crisis, 1848–1861* (New York, 1976), 432–33, 526, 560; Basler, *The Collected Works of Lincoln*, 4: 204, 211, 215–16; 238, 240; James M. McPherson, *Battle Cry of Freedom: The Civil War Era* (New York, 1988), 230–31, 239; Allan Nevins, *The Emergence of Lincoln* (New York, 1950), 2: 305–09, 355–57; Benjamin P. Thomas, *Abraham Lincoln* (New York, 1952), 240.
7. Perry Miller, *The New England Mind: From Colony to Province* (Cambridge, MA, 1953), 204, 208. See also Robert Middlekauff, *The Mathers: Three Generations of Puritan Intellectuals, 1596–1728* (New York, 1971), 159–61; John Putnam Demos, *Entertaining Satan: Witchcraft and the Culture of Early New England* (New York, 1982).

Index

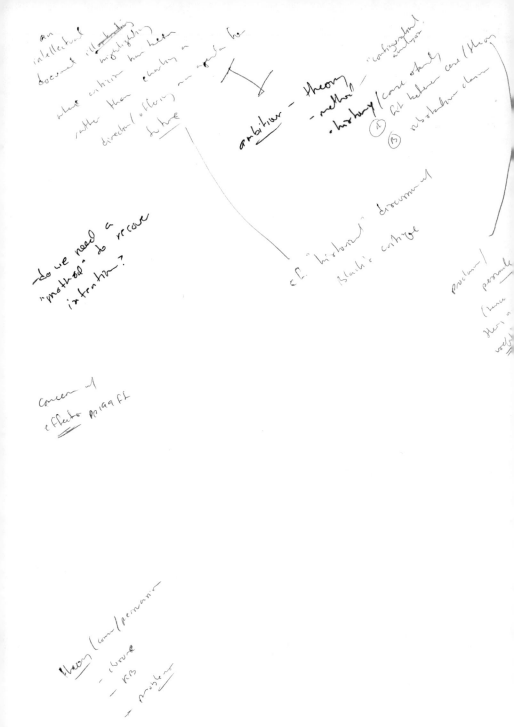